# New Approaches in Flaubert Studies

Front Cover:
Gustave Flaubert in middle age
*a photograh from life by Nadar*

# NEW APPROACHES IN FLAUBERT STUDIES

Edited by
Tony Williams
and
Mary Orr

Studies in French Literature
Volume 34

The Edwin Mellen Press
Lewiston•Queenston•Lampeter

**Library of Congress Cataloging-in-Publication Data**

New approaches in Flaubert studies / edited by Tony Williams and Mary Orr.
    p. cm. -- (Studies in French literature ; v. 34)
Includes bibliographical references.
ISBN 0-7734-8197-4
   1. Flaubert, Gustave, 1821-1880--Criticism and interpretation.
I. Williams, Tony.  II. Orr, Mary.  III. Series: Studies in French literature (Lewiston, N.Y.) ; v. 34.
PQ2249.N48   1999
843' 8--dc21
                                                          98-50516
                                                              CIP

---

This is volume 34 in the continuing series
Studies in French Literature
Volume 34  ISBN 0-7734-8197-4
SFL Series  ISBN 0-88946-572-X

---

A CIP catalog record for this book is available from the British Library.

Copyright  ©  1999   The Edwin Mellen Press

All rights reserved. For information contact

    The Edwin Mellen Press               The Edwin Mellen Press
          Box 450                                     Box 67
      Lewiston, New York                 Queenston, Ontario
     USA 14092-0450                     CANADA L0S 1L0

               The Edwin Mellen Press, Ltd.
               Lampeter, Ceredigion, Wales
             UNITED KINGDOM SA48 8LT

        Printed in the United States of America

**DEDICATION**

The Editors would like to dedicate this collection of essays to Alan Raitt, who has supported and encouraged the work of several contributors to this volume, as well as having made his own distinguished and distinctive contribution to Flaubert Studies in Britain.

# CONTENTS

| | | |
|---|---|---|
| Foreword | | vii |
| Commendatory Preface | | ix |
| Tony Williams | Introduction: Flaubert Studies 1983–96 | 1 |
| Timothy Unwin | *Novembre* and the Paradox of the New in Flaubert's Early Work | 32 |
| Mary Orr | Reversible Roles: Gender Trouble in *Madame Bovary* | 49 |
| Anne Green | Flaubert and the Sleeping Beauty: An Obsessive Image | 65 |
| Paul Tipper | Flower Figures and the Generation of Irony in *Madame Bovary* | 81 |
| Michael Wetherill | Genetics and Incompletion | 104 |
| Tony Williams | History in the Making: A Genetic Approach to the Tuileries Episode in *L'Éducation sentimentale* | 130 |
| Diana Knight | Whatever happened to Bouvard and Pécuchet? | 170 |
| Steven Beigbeder | Gender Roles in the Novels of Flaubert | 175 |

| | | |
|---|---|---|
| Larry Duffy | Mobility in Flaubert's Fiction: Dynamics, Disorder, Discontinuity | 179 |
| Stephen Goddard | Flaubert: the Classical Dimension | 183 |
| Mary Neiland | *La Tentation de saint Antoine* and the Works of Flaubert: an Intertextual Study | 186 |
| Marion Schmid | Processes of Literary Creation: Flaubert and Proust | 191 |
| Mary Orr | Conclusion: New Lamps for Old? | 195 |
| David Colwell | Bibliography: Flaubert Studies, 1989–97 | 207 |
| Timothy Unwin | A Report on Flaubert and the New Technologies | 235 |

## FOREWORD

The present volume grew out of a conference held at the Institute of Romance Studies in the University of London on 22 November 1996. The main aim of the conference was to take stock of the principal developments in "Flaubert Studies" since the publication of *Flaubert: La Dimension du texte* (Manchester University Press, 1982), with particular reference to the way in which the canonical view of Flaubert has changed in response to the emergence of gender studies, genetic studies and the systematic analysis of symbolic motifs. In addition to the six papers which were read, there was extensive discussion of broader critical issues, both at the end of each session and in the *Table Ronde*, with participation from a number of well-known Flaubert scholars and postgraduate students working on Flaubert. Unlike the previous conference which brought together French as well as British specialists and was conducted entirely in French, the present conference was limited to British specialists and was held in English. Potentially parochial these arrangements may have been, but they did allow the preoccupations of a particular group of scholars to emerge more clearly and the views of a new generation of 'Flaubertistes' to be aired more fully.

September 1998

Tony Williams
Mary Orr

# PREFACE
# Alan Raitt

The centrality of Flaubert's position in the history of the novel, indeed, in the evolution of modern literature generally has long been recognised and is amply attested by the presence of over 7000 titles up to 1988 in the splendid *Bibliographie des Études sur Gustave Flaubert* by D. J. Colwell, to which a valuable supplement is appended in the present volume. It is especially noteworthy that, in addition to academics, there are so many eminent men and women of letters among those who have paid tribute to him by devoting books, major articles and lectures to him, by producing prefaces to his works, by translating him, by making the pilgrimage to Croisset or even by smuggling direct but unacknowledged quotations from his writings in their own publications. The incredibly long list includes authors as varied and distinguished as (in no particular order) Émile Zola, Guy de Maupassant, Henry James, Paul Bourget, Turgeniev, Lafcadio Hearn, Remy de Gourmont, Somerset Maugham, Anatole France, Arthur Symons, Hugo von Hofmannsthal, André Maurois, Raymond Queneau, Marcel Schwob, Jean-Paul Sartre, Nathalie Sarraute, Félicien Marceau, Michel Tournier, Georges Perec, Michel Butor, Mario Vargas Llosa, Julian Barnes, Franz Kafka and Carl Sternheim. That this preoccupation with Flaubert is as lively on this side of the channel as anywhere else is demonstrated by a glance at Meryl Tyers's *Current Research in French Studies at Universities in the United Kingdom and Ireland*, which shows that there are more scholars here working on Flaubert than on any other single French writer of any period.

Introducing the colloquium held at the Grand Palais in 1980 to mark the centenary of Flaubert's death, Professor Pierre-Georges Castex observed that he could only recall two other years since the war when authors had been honoured with celebrations of similar amplitude: 1950 for Balzac — but that was for his birth in 1799 as well as his death in 1850, and 1978 for Voltaire and Rousseau, but there were two of them to be commemorated simultaneously. It may be true, as Diana Knight suggests, that the 1970's and 1980's form the period of the most intense fervour for Flaubert, and it is probably also the case that, nowadays, after over a century of research, there are, strictly speaking, no totally new approaches to Flaubert. But there are certainly new angles on old approaches and new applications of old approaches. There can be no doubt that the Flaubert we see and read in the 1990's is a very different figure from the one who so appealed to Zola and his naturalist disciples of the Groupe de Médan. It is of course a measure of Flaubert's inexhaustible greatness that he has to be invented anew for each successive generation and that his reputation has never suffered from those temporary or permanent eclipses which have affected the standing of so many other nineteenth-century authors, and this despite the fact that the size of his production is no more than a fragment of that of novelists such as Balzac, Zola and Dickens.

The contributors to this volume, in their diversity of method, of age, of institution, all bear witness to the fascination Flaubert continues to exercise over a century after his death, and many neglected or unexpected facets of his genius are illuminated by their studies, and I am happy to have the honour of presenting them to what is sure to be a wide and appreciative readership.

# INTRODUCTION: FLAUBERT STUDIES, 1983–96
## Tony Williams

This collection of essays, which originated in a conference held at the Institute of Romance Studies at the University of London in November 1996, sets out both to assess and to illustrate some of the more significant changes that have taken place in the last fifteen years in the way the work of Flaubert has been approached. It was widely felt that the moment for such an assessment was long overdue, since a period of almost fifteen years had elapsed since the publication of the last major review of Flaubert studies, undertaken by Alan Raitt,[1] and also of the proceedings of *Flaubert: La Dimension du Texte*,[2] the last conference devoted to Flaubert in this country, organised by Michael Wetherill and Bernard Jean. In order to set the context for the essays which follow, this introduction sets out to take stock of the major developments in what could loosely be designated "Flaubert Studies" that have occurred between 1983 and 1996. During this period, the works of Gustave Flaubert, in particular *Madame Bovary* and *L'Éducation sentimentale*, have continued to attract a considerable amount of critical interest, as is attested by the remarkably large number of books and articles listed in the last volume of the *Bibliographie des études sur G. Flaubert*, covering the years 1983 to 1988, published by David Colwell, and the more selective bibliography covering the years 1989 to 1997 at the end of this volume. The comment made by Sartre in 1971, cited by Alan Raitt in 1982, that "Flaubert, créateur du roman 'moderne', est au carrefour de tous nos problèmes littéraires d'aujourd'hui"[3] retains much of its validity.[4] Even if, as Diana Knight argues in her contribution to this volume, we have come a long way from the heady days when all the major intellectual figures in France were drawn to his work and Flaubert was at the height of critical fashion as a result of such fundamental revaluations as those of Jonathan Culler[5] and Jean-Paul Sartre,[6] the major assumption implicit in the title of this collection of essays, and the conference upon which it is based, is that significant changes have, indeed, taken place in the way the work of Flaubert has been approached in the last fifteen years. This assumption is based in part upon the strong conviction held by Flaubert scholars that the novels' potential for generating new meaning is far from exhausted, and also in part upon the recognition that a number of developments within literary studies more generally necessitate a revaluation of established views of Flaubert. In particular, although genetic studies and gender studies may have begun to emerge before 1982, they could not be said to have enjoyed a wide currency and the extent to which Flaubert's work would contribute to their development and be affected by them was still not clear.

Perhaps not surprisingly, given the amount of previous work already completed,[7] there are areas in which there have not been major new developments. Significantly, there has been no new edition of the complete works to replace those published by the Club de l'honnête homme or the Éditions du Seuil.[8] Individual works, however, have been published in new editions. Claudine Gothot-Mersch's widely acclaimed edition of *Madame Bovary* is now complemented by that of Pierre-Marc de Biasi, and important new editions of *L'Éducation sentimentale* have been produced by Michael Wetherill, Claudine Gothot-Mersh and Pierre-Marc de Biasi.[9] There have also been valuable new editions of the *Trois Contes* by Michael Wetherill and Pierre-Marc de Biasi. One of the characteristics of these new editions is the inclusion of genetic material, which has brought to an end as far as the general reading public is concerned the glorious isolation of the final version, in line with a major shift in Flaubert Studies which has been the systematic introduction of a genetic perspective into the analysis of all his works.[10] Complementing these new editions of the fictional works, the third volume of the definitive edition of the *Correspondance* edited by Jean Bruneau, was published in 1991 and the fourth volume has recently appeared.[11] The importance of this superb edition is reflected in the fact that a conference was held to commemorate the publication of the third volume in 1991.[12]

As our understanding of the richness and complexity of Flaubert's life and works has grown, so it has become increasingly difficult to grasp them in their totality. Sartre's three-volume study of Flaubert may not always be based upon historically attested data, but it has a sweep and penetration that dwarfs all other attempts at understanding Flaubert the man. The recent biographies of Jacques-Louis Douchin, Henri Troyat and Herbert Lottman[13] do not add anything appreciably new to our understanding. Likewise, although there have been useful presentations of the work as a whole, such as Claude Mouchard & Jacques Neefs's *Flaubert* and David Roe's *Gustave Flaubert*, they are essentially syntheses of previous work rather than new interpretations. Arguably the most original attempt to encompass the Flaubertian sensibility can be found in Julian Barnes's *Flaubert's Parrot*. Although more concerned with the life than the works, this fictional account of an Englishman's obsession with Flaubert presents some of the most fundamental features of Flaubert's outlook on life in terms which chime remarkably well with our modern sensibility and in asking the question "Is the writer any more than a sophisticated parrot?".[14] Geoffrey Braithwaite articulates one of the most persistent preoccupations of recent criticism.

It would be wrong to conclude from the dearth of works which offer some kind of overview that interest in Flaubert is declining. Rather it has increasingly tended to be more narrowly focused. Critical studies of individual works have often been of an extremely high quality;[15] the major works, in particular *Madame Bovary*, *L'Éducation sentimentale* and the *Trois Contes*, have proved themselves to be inexhaustible, lending themselves to different kinds of critical approach and giving rise to a wide variety of interpretations. Although no single new, readily identifiable, consensus view of Flaubert has emerged, a number of broad trends are apparent.[16] The first is a retreat from the view of Flaubert as literary saboteur extraordinaire, which was widely expressed in the seventies and developed most systematically by Jonathan Culler in *Flaubert, The Uses of Uncertainty*. As the study of the *avant-texte* has progressed, and the different accretions surrounding the final version have revealed a wide variety of literary tactics, the view that Flaubert is simply writing *against* literature as an institution cannot be sustained. A curious aspect of "Flaubert Studies", however, is the strength of the reactions that Culler's study continues to provoke.[17] A second trend is a widespread recognition of the importance in Flaubert's work of a process which can be summed up as the "collapse of oppositions", a process already identified by Culler.[18] Thirdly, a sharper awareness has developed of Flaubert's profoundly ironical attitude to language. Language is constantly on display in Flaubert's works in all its problematic derivativeness and "bêtise" from which there appears increasingly to be no refuge.[19] A new way of framing the central problem of language is developed in Timothy Unwin's chapter in this volume.

A number of works have examined Flaubert's philosophical outlook. Claire-Lise Tondeur in *Flaubert critique. Thèmes et structures* has refined Charles Carlut's analysis of the *Correspondance* and provides a compendium of his views on various subjects, all of them familiar. The drawback of viewing the *Correspondance* as the repository of Flaubert's "philosophy" is that his most deep-seated convictions are not necessarily articulated in letters or even consciously held. At the other extreme Eugenio Donato, in a work of impressive speculative thrust, *Flaubert and the Script of Decadence*, offers a bold and perceptive analysis of some of Flaubert's fundamental intuitions on history, religion and science, as they inform *Salammbô* and *Bouvard et Pécuchet*, in particular. There is, however, a sense in which Flaubert, in his refusal of any absolutist position and his collapsing of oppositions, anticipates the "end" of philosophy whose knell has been sounded by Jacques Derrida. The "ideas" of Flaubert, as abstracted from the *Correspondance* or inferred from the fictional works, have been well worked over. All that remains is for us to "receive" them.[20] The question which perhaps needs to be asked is the one posed by Timothy Unwin: Why does Flaubert express his vision of life in a literary form? Is there an element in his philosophy which makes him turn to literary representation?[21] In the final analysis it is Flaubert's qualities as a writer not as a "thinker" that matter.

Broadly speaking, it is precisely the specificity of Flaubert's writing which has been at the top of the critical agenda in recent years, rather than his philosophical or political outlook. It is no exaggeration to say that Flaubert virtually single-handed, and with a clear understanding of what he was doing, undertook a complete overhaul of the novel as a genre which laid the basis for what we now call "the modern novel". Much of the best critical work of recent years has focused on his shaping and manipulation of the basic constituents of the novel — plot, character, dialogue, description, and symbolism. Michal Ginsburg has perceptively explored the strategies he employs in the plots of his major novels, always, she suggests, a problematic aspect of the novel for Flaubert.[22] In a fine essay in *Reading for the Plot*, Peter Brooks has explored the originality of the plot of *L'Éducation sentimentale*, paying particular attention to the ending, which has baffled generations of readers. Margaret Lowe in *Towards the Real Flaubert* has stressed the importance of the mythological sub-structure which underpins the plot of *Madame Bovary*. More recently, Claire Addison in *Where Flaubert Lies* has set out to decode the hidden significance of dates in Flaubert's work. Whilst plot in all its aspects has always provoked a good deal of interest among French critics, in particular those of structuralist persuasion, character, though continuing to constitute for most readers the principal focus of the reading experience, suffered comparative neglect in the seventies, often seeming in danger of being reduced to a mere aspect of plot. It had perhaps always seemed unlikely that Flaubert could be drafted into the "Death of Character" movement, and Diana Knight's study, *Flaubert's Characters*, represented a successful attempt to qualify Culler's view that Flaubert's characters can be seen as "a ploy for setting up an indeterminate space of meaning". In a not dissimilar vein, D.A.Williams in *"The Hidden Life at its Source"* attempted to show that Frédéric, for all his apparent nullity, could still be considered to function as a coherent character. In both of these works a desire to recuperate character is accompanied by an attempt to demonstrate the originality of the ends to which it was used, either as a vehicle for "essential aspects of Flaubert's aesthetic"[23] or the exploration of a complex psychological state.[24]

The function of dialogue in Flaubert has also received close scrutiny in Stirling Haig's *Flaubert and the Gift of Speech*, in which the subtlety of Flaubert's use of dialogue and awareness that it needed to be carefully rationed are perceptively explored.[25] The complexities of the narrative techniques employed by Flaubert have long fascinated critics. Alan Raitt has re-examined the problematic use of the first person in the opening of *Madame Bovary*[26] and Flaubert's use of *style indirect libre* has continued to be the focus of criticism.[27] Long recognised as highly innovative, Flaubert's use of description has attracted a good deal of attention, from the elegant and lucid analyses of Raymonde Debray-Genette in *Métamorphoses du récit* to the more recent study of James Reid, *Description and Narration in the Nineteenth-Century French Novel*, which explores the way the interplay between "imperfective" description and "perfective" narration can lead to the obliteration of the past and of history. Since Don Demorest's *L'Expression figurée et symbolique dans l'œuvre de Gustave Flaubert*, critics have been attentive to the rich and complex symbolic patterns in Flaubert's work. Although, apart from Margaret Lowe's *Towards the Real Flaubert*, there has been no major new study of Flaubertian symbolism, the intricacies of particular patterns and motifs continue to attract extremely subtle close analysis. The contributions of Paul Tipper and Anne Green to this volume provide good demonstrations of the way significant new patterns can be detected in Flaubert's work, when the analysis is sufficiently closely focused. The continuing confidence of a number of British and American critics that Flaubert's works are capable of generating rich symbolic meaning contrasts with the more sceptical view of several French critics for whom symbolic effects are either pleonastic or problematically stereotyped.

The representational or mimetic dimension of Flaubert's work has long been a topic of critical debate with the structuralist critic's denial of the possibility of referentiality being opposed by the traditional critic's insistence that literary works could meaningfully be considered as having some kind of purchase upon external reality. The debate has been considerably advanced by Christopher Prendergast's illuminating survey, *The Order of Mimesis*, which examines the various cases against mimesis, noting how often they continue to rest upon some notion of reference. Prendergast seeks to detach Flaubert from the context of nineteenth-century Realism and the naïve reflectionist aesthetics associated with it.[28] Central to his analysis is the emphasis on the fraught relationship between Flaubert's texts and "bêtise" as embodied in stereotypes and clichés. Flaubert's attempts to undo cliché and spike stupidity are shown to culminate in the literary "délire" of *Bouvard et Pécuchet*. Within the context of an analysis of the failure of these attempts, the possibility of any secure hierarchy of discourse in the Flaubertian text is effectively scuttled: "The citational play of the language swallows up narrator and character alike, immerses both in the *doxa*."[29] Mimesis undergoes a similar deconstruction in H. Meili Steele's *Realism and the Drama of Reference*. What is re-enacted in this drama is the "failure of realism and positivism to link sense and reference in an ontologically certain world".[30] At the heart of the problem of reference is the problem of language. Flaubert, as Julian Barnes puts it, "saw the underlying inadequacy of the Word".[31] He is, as Donato suggests in *Flaubert and the Script of Decadence*, a linguistic nihilist who undertakes a critique of representation similar to that of Nietzsche.[32] In a full-scale study of his attitude to language, *Flaubert et le Pignouf*, Dufour suggests that, given his despairing sense that language no longer corresponds to reality, all he can do is demonstrate that man "n'est pas maître de son langage" through a repeated presentation of various kinds of "langage en situation".[33] The possibility of aesthetic transcendence of the limitations of language seems to have receded: a profound scepticism about the material he is manipulating is now perceived to lie at the very heart of Flaubert's artistic endeavours.

Flaubert's intense preoccupation with, and reworking of, the formal properties of fiction have ensured that he occupies "une place-charnière dans l'histoire du roman".[34] A good deal of recent criticism has focused on the place of Flaubert within the development of the novel and significant links or affinities with the major trends and movements of nineteenth- and twentieth-century literature can be readily identified. Flaubert's work looks back as well as forward. The large question of his relationship to Balzac has been explored by Guy Sagnes and Graham Falconer, with a process of "debalzaciénisation" being exposed in the *avant-texte*.[35] More recently close comparisons between Flaubert and contemporary writers such as Champfleury and Feydeau have been made by Bill Overton.[36] However, Flaubert is more frequently seen as a writer who anticipates subsequent trends. There has been a shift away from the earlier trend of the seventies to see him as a new novelist *avant la lettre*. One area which has been particularly well-worked is Flaubert's relationship to Naturalism. David Baguley has argued that *Madame Bovary* and *L'Éducation sentimentale* provided two very different models of what the Naturalist novel might be and that Flaubert cast a long shadow over literary production until the end of the century.[37] The account of Flaubert's links with modern novelists writing in English, which previous critics had drawn attention to, has been supplemented by comparisons with Henry James and Conrad.[38] The question of Flaubert's links with the "nouveau roman", fully aired in the sixties, has received less attention, but the list of writers who have been strongly influenced by him continues to grow. In particular, following his insistence on his indebtedness to Flaubert,[39] George Perec's affinities with Flaubert have been examined by critics such as Claude Burgelin and Jacques Neefs.[40] Most recently, Flaubert has been seen as a significant writer within the context of postmodernism, as is attested by the various contributions in *Flaubert and Postmodernism*. As Jonathan Culler succinctly observes, postmodernists relish in Flaubert "the collision and the collusion of the representational and the antirepresentational".[41]

All the developments discussed above can be seen essentially as extensions or logical continuations of earlier critical activity. There have undoubtedly been a number of significant shifts in the way Flaubert has been perceived, in particular in relation to the whole question of mimesis, but "new" in the sense of totally different from anything that has gone beforehand does not seem the most appropriate word to qualify the various interpretations so far mentioned. However, within literary studies more generally, a number of major new approaches have evolved in the last fifteen years, some of which, when applied to Flaubert, have revealed intriguingly "new" facets of his work. One of the most significant of these is undoubtedly what can loosely be called Gender studies, often viewed as an offshoot of feminist criticism. Feminist criticism has reset the agenda in literary studies in all kinds of ways, in particular through its exposure of the patriarchal assumptions frequently embedded in literary works, its emphasis on gender as something constructed rather than given, its attempt to identify and promote a certain way of writing or "écriture féminine", and its insistence on the gendered position of the reader.[42] There are, of course, significant differences between the critical practices of French, British and American feminists and it is clearly impossible to do justice here to the wide range of ideas coming out of feminism as a whole. What is significant is that most if not all the issues debated within feminist criticism in general and Gender studies in particular have a direct bearing on the work of Flaubert and have opened up new ways of viewing his novels. The first point to be made is that even the most brilliant criticism of Flaubert has often suffered in the past from certain blindspots. Naomi Schor makes a crucial claim that Riffaterre skirts the issue in his major article on Flaubert's Presuppositions: "retracing the fatal sequence of the adulteress's plot, he demonstrates the mechanisms of presupposition, while stopping short of exposing the workings of ideology in the service of sexual stereotypes"[43] and more recently Rosemary Lloyd has referred to the accumulated distortions of male-centred readings of *Madame Bovary*.[44] One of the earliest feminist accounts of Flaubert's work, Lucette Czyba's *Mythes et idéologie de la femme dans les romans de Flaubert*, insisted on the extent to which the novels appeared to be in complicity with patriarchal ideology, whilst recognising that they also subverted it. Subsequently it has been widely felt that in Flaubert — perhaps more than in any other nineteenth-century French novelist — gender is a crucial issue and he has mounted in his works a sustained critique of conventional, that is to say patriarchal, notions of both masculinity and femininity. Ever since Baudelaire claimed that masculine blood flows through Emma's fictional veins, critics have been fascinated by the ambiguous mixture of traits in her, but only recently has the extent to which Flaubert in *Madame Bovary* implicitly accepts the relativity of gender stereotypes been clearly recognised. Emma's so-called "masculine" traits have been analysed from a "gender studies" theoretical perspective by Schor,[45] Kelly,[46] Heath[47] and others and this has done much to bring out the counter-ideological thrust of the novel. In a similar vein, the presentation of a "feminine" element in male characters is also being explored. Mary Orr's analysis of Lheureux in this volume is part of the most recent wave of feminist criticism which deconstructs male-authored representations of masculinity.[48] The collapse of oppositions, which is one of the themes of recent work on Flaubert, manifests itself perhaps most spectacularly in the sphere of gender.[49] Flaubert's correspondence with Louise Colet and George Sand has proved a rich source of ideas on writing as in some respects a gendered activity, in particular in Janet Beizer, *Ventriloquised Bodies. Narratives of Hysteria in Nineteenth-Century France*. Flaubert's attempts to define different modes of expression as "male" or "female" anticipates the debate about "écriture féminine" and the claim that a form of "écriture féminine" can be found in his work[50] should be carefully assessed. Lastly, the whole question of reading as a "gendered" activity has a bearing upon the reception of Flaubert's works. Feminist criticism has alerted us to the characteristic blindspots and bias of the male reader and of "phallic" criticism. However, the issue of what reading as a woman might entail is a complex one. Undoubtedly in patriarchal society women have often found themselves coerced into reading "as a man" and reading as a woman can perhaps never be unproblematic.[51] Nor should male critics imagine that it might be possible to accede to an alternative way of reading which would allow them to transcend the limitations of "phallic" criticism.[52] In this context, it is significant that the responses of women to Flaubert have, from the outset, been more favourable than those of male readers and Flaubert often claimed to have written for a female reader. The process of unmasking, if not overcoming, gender bias is now well underway but needs to take account of the slipperiness of the Flaubertian text. Michael Danahy's insistence on the gender bias of the narrator in *Madame Bovary* is well-made [53] but to what extent does the narratorial perspective dominate the novel? If there are other textual agencies operative, such as the "implied author", are they also tainted by gender bias or is it possible for a writer to transcend at a fundamental level a sexually partisan approach?

The extraordinary rise of genetic studies in the last fifteen or more years[54] has been closely associated with a process of renewal and enrichment in Flaubert Studies. As a result of the intense focus on the *avant-texte*, what we understand by "the work of Flaubert" has been transformed in both quantitative and qualitative terms. As indicated above, modern editions of Flaubert's work frequently include a substantial amount of genetic material. There have also been a large number of "dedicated" genetic editions of various kinds of material. Pierre-Marc de Biasi's edition of Flaubert's *Carnets* was a major event, bringing to the attention of the general reading public as well as that of a more specialist audience, the wealth of material, much of it previously unpublished, in Flaubert's notebooks. Editions of the "scénarios" of *Madame Bovary* and *L'Éducation sentimentale* have also been published.[55] The first of these, which places diplomatic transcriptions alongside facsimile reproductions of manuscript material, has set a new standard in the publication of genetic material. There have also been editions of the *avant-textes* of specific sections of fictional works, ranging from the "Comices agricoles" chapter of *Madame Bovary*[56] to the whole of "Un Cœur simple" and "Hérodias".[57] Even now, however, with the notable exception of two of the *Trois Contes*, there is still a considerable amount of the *avant-texte* which is unpublished. In future, new methods of disseminating material, in particular Hypertext, will need to be exploited if the genetic dossiers of the major works are going to be complete. Such is the abundance of genetic material now published that the context in which Flaubert's works are read has changed irretrievably: it is probably no longer possible or desirable for the critic to engage with the "final" version in a way which is unmediated or unaffected by its elaborate process of production as this manifests itself in the *avant-texte*. Much of the manuscript material has considerable intrinsic interest and has provided the basis for a wide range of genetic studies of individual works or episodes.[58] The contribution of Tony Williams to this volume presents a genetic *dossier* which allows the development of a single episode of *L'Éducation sentimentale*, occupying no more than a page of the final version, to be closely followed in all its complexity. Significant advances have been made in the analysis of the genesis of *Madame Bovary*,[59] *Salammbô*,[60] *L'Éducation sentimentale*,[61] and the *Trois Contes*.[62] The corollary has been a good deal of theoretical debate about the relationship between the *avant-texte* and the definitive version, a debate to which the chapter by Michael Wetherill in this volume makes an important contribution. For some, the reconstitution of the *avant-texte* poses a threat to the authority and finality of the definitive version.[63] Ironically, however, the very notion of *avant-texte* depends logically on the existence of a final text to which it is anterior.[64] Raymonde Debray-Genette has pointed out that if "la notion de texte a été fragilisée par celle d'avant-texte", the reverse is also true: "[la notion d'avant-texte] n'est, à son tour, pas moins délicate de par son hétérogénéité et l'insoumission théorique de la matière."[65] Genetic analysis does more, however, than emperil our notions of what constitutes a text or an *avant-texte*: "la connaissance génétique aboutit au paradoxe de tout fragiliser dans le temps même où elle enrichit tout."[66] The recent critique of genetic studies by Pierre Bourdieu rests on the belief that the principle of genetic change is to be found outside the *avant-texte* itself which means that "l'analyse des versions successives d'un texte ne revêtirait sa pleine force explicative que si elle visait à reconstruire la logique du travail d'écriture entendue comme recherche accomplie sous la contrainte structurale du champ et de l'espace des possibles qu'il propose."[67] However, as was pointed out most trenchantly by Raymonde Debray-Genette, "L'étude des manuscrits est [...] bien ce à partir de quoi il faut relire une œuvre. C'est à leur lumière que s'éclaire le rôle de l'environnement culturel, et non l'inverse."[68] In this respect the *avant-texte* might be thought to mediate between the broad literary, social, ideological and biographical contexts from which literary works spring and those works themselves. But the *avant-texte* has more than explanatory force. The appeal of manuscripts undoubtedly contains a fetishistic element, but, more importantly, it can illuminate the sheer complexity of Flaubert's writing viewed as process of production. Flaubert may at times have regretted the endless trouble writing required,[69] and lamented the fact that nobody would ever appreciate the lengths to which he went,[70] but it is perhaps no accident that so much of the manuscript material has survived, ensuring that as much blood has been sweated by genetic critics in deciphering the manuscripts as Flaubert lost in producing them.

The sheer volume of genetic material does, inevitably, pose a serious problem and the time required to compile a genetic *dossier* can at times seem disproportionate to the revelations it contains. However, once established, the *avant-texte* enters into a fascinating relationship with the final version, part conflictual, part parasitic and part ornamental, a relationship which seems designed to keep literary critics on their mettle.

Psychoanalytic approaches in literary studies have a long pedigree[71] but recent debates have tended to focus on the complexities of the relation between psychoanalysis and literature. Some critics have seen in psychoanalysis a way of plugging gaps in literary texts: "The data of consciousness are defective, 'lacunary'; the unconscious is what allows us to reestablish a coherent sequence, an intelligent relation, when we interpolate the unconscious acts which we infer",[72] whilst others have rejected the effect of closure implied by such an approach. In a classic statement of this position, in her discussion of Henry James's *The Turn of the Screw*, Shoshana Felman "seeks not so much to capture the mystery's solution but to follow the significant path of its flight".[73] This broad division is reflected in recent psychoanalytic approaches to Flaubert. In his monograph on *Madame Bovary* Ion Collas sets out to reveal "the hidden psychological structure of the novel"[74] through the analysis of small notations with symbolic value. In order to "explain" the frustrations of Emma's adult existence, Collas adduces a putative unsatisfactory relationship with her mother, for which there is very little direct textual evidence, but this has the effect of reducing the suggestiveness of the novel. The approach of M. Grimaud & W.J. Berg in the analysis of "La Légende de Saint Julien l'Hospitalier" is more persuasive. Julien's cruelty is clearly linked in the text to his upbringing, providing a solid basis for the demonstration that his parricide is "the result of pent-up rage which has finally returned upon its original objects after a lengthy and circuitous route".[75] The security of this oedipal reading is questioned, however, by Pierre-Marc de Biasi, who, adopting the classic "the tale won't tell" position, detects in the *avant-texte* of the story a clear movement towards "l'indécidable".[76] More recently Freud's theory of the fetish, in conjunction with Marxist commodity theory, has also proved effective in opening up a new approach to fetishism in *L'Éducation sentimentale*,[77] and, combined with Derridean views on "différance", a new perspective on the symbolism of the veil in *Salammbô*.[78] Psychoanalytic theory has, arguably, proved most fruitful when used to explore textual processes rather than the "unconscious" of the writer or his characters.

Like psychoanalytic criticism, Marxist approaches to literature have evolved considerably, particularly in the sphere of the analysis of ideology in literary works.[79] A number of significant theoretical advances have been made, in particular by Richard Terdiman[80] and Frederic Jameson,[81] in accounting for the relationship between the ideology prevalent in French society and the ideological or counter-ideological positions developed in nineteenth-century literary texts. Detailed work has been done on the ideological context of Flaubert's works by Nicholas Harrison[82] and Yvan Leclerc,[83] both of whom focus on the trial of *Madame Bovary*. Henri Mitterand has added to his earlier work on "le discours social"[84] and, more recently, Jean-Marie Privat, adopting an ethnographic approach to *Madame Bovary*, has explored the "complexe culture charivarique qui [...] hante le texte".[85] A comprehensive study of Flaubert's literary practice in relation to the social and ideological possibilities of his age can be found in Pierre Bourdieu's ambitious *Les Règles de l'Art*. A number of critics have analysed closely Flaubert's use of cliché in this context[86] but the extent to which it is possible to characterise this practice as counter-ideological is not altogether clear.

One of the most striking features about Flaubert's novels is the way they seem to have something significant to say in relation to a wide range of broader issues and have been enthusiastically taken up by critics whose primary interest is not in Flaubert as an individual writer. Prompted by Tony Tanner's claim that *Madame Bovary* is "the most far-reaching novel of adultery in Western literature",[87] a number of critics have attempted to determine the significance of Flaubert's novel within the canon of the nineteenth-century novel of adultery. Naomi Segal in *The Adulteress's Child*, following up the insight of Naomi Schor that "representational fiction has from its origins figured the particularly inexorable repression to which female desire is subject under patriarchy",[88] suggests that "the adulteress is the woman who, by placing desire where maternity should belong, in her 'inside body', incarnates a scandal to both fathers and sons: that is the scandal of their own, never autonomous desire and its relation to a never quite subordinated other."[89] This concealed but central perception dictates a pattern in male-authored texts, never before so clearly highlighted, which entails the adulterous woman having a difficult relationship with a daughter, who, by virtue of the fact that she is female, is both reproof and punishment. In contrast, the wife whose adultery is forestalled, is typically locked in a closer relationship with a sick son. The replication of this pattern, not just in French novelists but throughout the European novel, is striking and raises important issues relating to the scope for any male novelist, however resistant to the concealed value-system of patriarchy, to duck below its fundamental presuppositions. Flaubert's treatment of adultery, which many have found more enlightened than that of other writers, is shown to conform to a pattern, with the result that some of the singularity of Emma Bovary in particular may seem to be compromised. A complementary perspective is opened up by Alison Sinclair's *The Deceived Husband*, which places the nineteenth-century novel of adultery in a broader context which extends back to Restoration Drama and the Spanish Drama of Honour and uses Kleinian categories to characterise the distinctiveness of Flaubert's treatment: "In the very unsatisfactoriness of the marriage relationship created in this novel, and its antithesis with the idea of Romantic love entertained by Emma, there is the action of the author to force the reader, if bluntly, to an appreciation that love is not ideal, nor marriages likely to be happy. In psychoanalytic terms the absence of illusions can be interpreted as a working towards the depressive position."[90] More recently Bill Overton[91] has shown how, in systematic comparison with other French novelists, in particular contemporary writers such as Champfleury and Feydeau, *Madame Bovary* marks a highpoint which would support the claim that the "novel of female adultery" has come of age. An alternative way of framing Flaubert's treatment of adultery is to explore the indebtedness of Naturalist writers to his work, as Bernard Gallina[92] and, in a more sophisticated way, Nicholas White do.[93] Although it is possible to see *Madame Bovary* as a summation of trends and insights relating to female adultery, it is also possible to see it as the novel in which a kind of rot sets in, with adultery as subject already beginning to show signs of becoming tired of itself. The broad ideological implications of *Madame Bovary*, first explored by Dominick La Capra,[94] are also highlighted by Stephen Heath, who expands Proudhon's claim that "Adultery is seen as a crime against the family, a crime which in itself contains all the others." Heath clearly exposes the ideological stakes which are raised by female adultery: "The reality is that marriage is the allowed expression of the sexual (as love) defined in terms of the function of reproduction [...] and the sexual (as desire) is also to be contained in marriage."[95] Given the importance of these stakes it is debatable whether adultery has become "platitude, as flatly oppressive as all the rest", as Heath asserts.[96] What all this critical discussion highlights is the way *Madame Bovary* continues to occupy centre stage in the ongoing debate about the broad cultural and literary significance of female adultery.

Flaubert's work has also been singled out as central to the exploration of a number of other broad issues straddling traditional literary studies and cultural studies. Considerable attention has been devoted to Flaubert's distinctive treatment of revolution in *L'Éducation sentimentale*,[97] to his presentation of the city,[98] to his view of prostitution,[99] to Orientalism in his work,[100] and to his view of travel. Although Flaubert Studies may not have quite the centrality that they enjoyed in the seventies, on a number of fronts important developments are taking place. These are evidence of the capacity of Flaubert's works to yield new meanings and to bend themselves to new concerns. It is significant that as well as providing abundant material for a continuation of "traditional" critical activity, Flaubert's work has also proved a fertile testing ground for a wide range of new critical approaches and concerns with broader cultural issues. It would be foolish to privilege any one of the different facets of Flaubert's literary output. The fact that no single widely received "new" view of Flaubert has emerged in recent years can, in part, be explained by the variety and complexity of his work, and it is the pluralist spirit, reflected in the title of this volume, which increasingly seems the appropriate critical response. In so far as the essays in this volume are representative, they also herald a movement away from certain characterisitic features of the postmodernist readings of the eighties. Naomi Schor stresses in the Introduction to *Flaubert and Postmodernism* a number of features of the contributions: a waning concern with the production of meaning and a growing concern with undecidability; a valorisation of the marginal; an irreverence towards canonised texts and the eroticisation of the reader's response. The present volume tends to reverse several of these trends: there is a widespread concern to establish a degree of intelligibility in the Flaubertian text; the attention focuses primarily on those texts the postmodernist critics neglected, *Madame Bovary* and *L'Éducation sentimentale*; and the contributors all tend to maintain an attitude of aesthetic admiration for what is perceived to be superb literary craftsmanship. Whilst the postmodernist elaborates a view of the Flaubertian text as "a sort of hermeneutic quicksand where origins and stable meanings vanish, covered up by the shifting sands of difference",[101] the readings we propose strive to tease out the multiple meanings of a text which bears a closer resemblance to the proverbial widow's cruise than a hermeneutic quicksand. The emphasis of this volume falls initially on the complex and controlled suggestivity of the Flaubertian text. Timothy Unwin finds in *Novembre* a rich and coherent exploration of the dialectics of novelty and sameness, with particular reference to the problematics of language. Mary Orr's close account of the presentation of Lheureux demonstrates that *Madame Bovary* mounts a powerful critique of patriarchal values, whilst Anne Green shows how several of Flaubert's works are partly structured by a reworking of elements of the Sleeping Beauty story and Paul Tipper suggests that the rich network of references to flowers in *Madame Bovary* helps to underpin the major opposition between illusion and reality. It is striking that in each of these essays there is a strong presupposition that an intrinsic textual dynamics, which is not necessarily consciously controlled, operates in such a way as to create a degree of thematic coherence. The emphasis then shifts to the *avant-texte*: Michael Wetherill contests the non-teleological approach implicit in early *prises de position* in genetic studies, suggesting that it is only in relation to the end-point represented by the final version that each and every stage of the elaboration process of production assumes its full significance, whilst Tony Williams, in tracing the development of the Tuileries Palace episode in *L'Éducation sentimentale*, exposes a constant process of artistic manipulation of documentary material. These detailed studies of both text and *avant-texte* engage in a common critical practice: the extraction of meaning from complex aesthetic structures. Collectively, it might appear that the various contributors to this volume have moved away from the larger theoretical concerns that preoccupied Flaubert specialists in a earlier period, as Diana Knight suggests, but there seems no limit to the fascination that the fine detail of the Flaubertian text continues to exert, albeit one that is accompanied by a certain amount of ironic awareness of the limitations of the interpretative frames which the critic seeks to clamp on to the works. We have also, however, sought to look forward as well as backward: the brief accounts of PhD work recently completed or in progress provided by postgraduate students point to future approaches, and the question of the direction Flaubert Studies in Britain might take is addressed by Mary Orr in the Conclusion. The volume concludes with a bibliography which supplements the major four-volume bibliography produced by David Colwell and a report by Timothy Unwin on Flaubert and the new technologies which, more than any other contribution, resolutely looks to the future.

## Notes

[1] "État présent des études sur Flaubert", *L'Information littéraire*. See also Enzo Caramaschi, "A Travers un demi-siècle de critique flaubertienne".

[2] *Flaubert: La Dimension du texte*, ed. by P. M. Wetherill.

[3] Sartre, *L'Idiot de la famille*, I, 8; Raitt, art. cit., 24.

[4] See also Naomi Schor, Introduction to *Flaubert and Postmodernism*, xi: "Flaubert has been canonised as the patron saint of modernity."

[5] *Flaubert: The Uses of Uncertainty*.

[6] *L'Idiot de la famille*.

[7] The two volumes of David Colwell's Bibliography covering the period 1921–1982 list over 4500 titles. The four volumes covering the period 1837–1988 list more than 7000 titles. The point has been reached where it is impossible for the mass of Flaubert criticism to be assimilated by even the most diligent of literary scholars.

[8] The first volume of the new Pléiade edition of the Complete Works, edited by Claudine Gothot-Mersch and Guy Sagnes, has been completed for publication.

[9] Full details of the editions referred to can be found under Works Cited at the end of this introduction. It is striking that the "modern" novels have attracted a good deal more attention than *La Tentation de saint Antoine*, *Salammbô* and *Bouvard et Pécuchet*. In addition to the editions of the major works mentioned, there have also been new editions of *Par les Champs et par les grèves*, the 1845 version of *L'Éducation sentimentale* and the *Dictionnaire des Idées reçues*. For a full list of all new editions of Flaubert's work since 1983, see David Colwell's *Bibliographie des études sur G. Flaubert (1983–1988)* and the Bibliography at the end of this volume.

[10] The genetic material is most abundant in Michael Wetherill's editions of *L'Éducation sentimentale* and the *Trois Contes*.

[11] The third volume of the *Correspondance*, covering the years 1859–1868, contains extensive extracts from letters from Maxime du Camp and Louis Bouilhet, as well as over 600 pages of "Notes et variantes". The fourth volume, covering the period 1869 to 1875, was published in 1998.

[12] See *L'Œuvre de l'œuvre. Études sur la "Correspondance" de Flaubert*, ed. Raymonde Debray-Genette & Jacques Neefs.

[13] Jacques-Louis Douchin, *La Vie érotique de Flaubert*; Henri Troyat, *Flaubert*; Herbert Lottman, *Flaubert*.

[14] *Flaubert's Parrot*, 18

[15] For a full list of critical studies of individual works, see David Colwell's *Bibliographie de études sur G. Flaubert (1983–1988)* and the Bibliography at the end of this volume. Major studies in English of *Madame Bovary* are those of Rosemary Lloyd and Stephen Heath, of *L'Éducation sentimentale* those of William Paulson and D. A. Williams, and of the *Trois Contes* that of Alan Raitt. Critical studies in French have been published on *Madame Bovary* by Gérard Gengembre and on *L'Éducation sentimentale* by Pierre Bourdieu and Jean Borie. There have also been a number of collections of articles relating to *Madame Bovary*: *Emma Bovary*, edited by Harold Bloom, and *Approaches to Teaching Flaubert's "Madame Bovary"*, edited by Laurence M. Porter & Eugene F. Gray. For a full list of articles on individual works, see David Colwell's *Bibliographie des études sur G. Flaubert (1983–1988)* and the Bibliography at the end of this volume.

[16] See also Naomi Schor (Introduction to *Flaubert and Postmodernism*, xii), who identifies as current concerns the status of the referent, the performative aspect of language, the revaluation of the marginal, the production of undecidability, and the pleasure of the text.

[17] See for instance Marc Girard, *La Passion de Charles Bovary* and Diana Knight's comments in her contribution to this volume. Culler is not really claiming that the emperor has no clothes but his approach has touched many a raw nerve, since it appears to some to suggest a scandalous emptiness at the heart of the Flaubertian enterprise.

[18] See Eugenio Donato, *The Script of Decadence. Essays on the Fiction of Flaubert and the Poetics of Romanticism*: "For Flaubert, the death of the Gods is nothing more than the abolishment of differences and their general dissolution in the quicksands of similarity" (22); "For Flaubert, the end of history means a general collapsing of all differences — racial, social, political — into mediocrity." (43)

[19] Amongst the critics who have been most attentive to this aspect of Flaubert's work one might mention Christopher Prendergast, Philippe Dufour and Anne Herschberg-Pierrot.

[20] See Jacques Derrida, " 'Une Idée de Flaubert' ", 671: "La philosophie a eu lieu, il n'y a plus rien à attendre d'elle, elle a déjà saturé son champ et notre culture; tout ce qui reste à faire, pour faire autre chose enfin, c'est peut-être la recevoir, comme un énorme héritage d'idées reçues, la lire et la traduire."

[21] *Art et Infini. L'Œuvre de jeunesse de Gustave Flaubert*, 91.

[22] *Flaubert Writing: A Study in Narrative Strategies*, 1: "His early difficulty in sustaining a narrative [...] is not entirely overcome in his mature works. [...] Unlike such authors as Balzac and Stendhal, Flaubert seems to have a problem generating his text and keeping it going."

[23] Diana Knight, *Flaubert's Characters*, 5: "Flaubert's characters [...] should be seen as exemplary, since they acquire aesthetic status and are central to the operation of Flaubert's value-system. This privilege is won through their special role in relation to essential aspects of Flaubert's aesthetic: the opaqueness of language, experience, stupidity, repetition and fascination and rêverie as the aim of art."

[24] D. A. Williams, "*The Hidden Life at its Source*", 8: 'In Flaubert a growing awareness of the complexity of the psychology of modern man [...] makes possible the creation of totally new characters — shadowy, uncertain, vacillating — and the exploration of a new kind of psychological state — intractable, contradictory, self-defeating."

[25] See also Marie-Thérèse Mathet's, *Le Dialogue romanesque chez Flaubert*.

[26] " 'Nous étions à l'étude' ".

[27] Vaheed K. Ramazani, *The Free Indirect Mode. Flaubert and the Uses of Irony*.

[28] *The Order of Mimesis*, 181.

[29] Ibid., 202.

[30] *Realism and the Drama of Reference*, 34.

[31] *Flaubert's Parrot*, 19.

[32] *The Script of Decadence*, 13: The ironic quest of Bouvard and Pécuchet stems from their incapacity to recognise that language is incapable of grasping the nature of things.

[33] *Flaubert et le Pignouf*, 12.

[34] Alan Raitt, "État présent des études sur Flaubert", 23.

[35] Guy Sagnes, "Tentations balzaciennes dans le manuscrit de *L'Éducation sentimentale*"; Graham Falconer, "Travail de 'débalzaciénisation' dans la rédaction de *Madame Bovary*".

[36] Bill Overton, *The Novel of Female Adultery. Love and Gender in Continental European Fiction*.

[37] *Naturalist Fiction. The Entropic Vision*.

[38] M. Conroy, *Modernism and Authority. Strategies of Legitimation in Flaubert and Conrad*; G. Falconer, "Flaubert, James and the problem of undecidability".

[39] "Emprunts à Flaubert".

[40] Claude Burgelin, "Perec, lecteur de Flaubert" and Jacques Neefs, "De Flaubert à Perec".

[41] "The Uses of Madame Bovary", 9.

[42] For a review of trends in feminist criticism see Toril Moi, *Sexual/Textual Politics. Feminist Literary Theory* and Mary Eagleton, ed., *Feminist Literary Criticism*.

[43] Introduction to *Flaubert and Modernism*, xv.

[44] *Madame Bovary*, 172: "a gendered reading might begin to unravel many of the male-centred misinterpretations that have grown up ever since Baudelaire depicted as masculine all Emma's positive and active attributes."

[45] In *Breaking the Chain. Women, Theory and French Realist Fiction*, 17, Schor argues that what Emma "envies in a man is not so much the possibility of traveling, but the possibility of writing; what she needs in order to write are neither words nor the pen, but a phallus".

[46] In *Fictional Genders. Role and Representation in Nineteenth-Century Narrative*, Dorothy Kelly, in an attempt to account for the view that there is something in Emma that does not match the "feminine" identity she is under pressure to assume, examines the way her attitude to language, in particular to signifiers as possessing rich meanings, evolves from one typical of a woman to one typical of a man.

[47] In *Flaubert: "Madame Bovary"* Heath focuses on hysteria which, central to patriarchy's ideological construction of femininity, is seen to "articulate, however inarticulately, an opposition to society", provides a way of glossing Emma's apparent virilization ("refusing her identity, the hysteric runs against the terms of her identification as a woman and so is forced into the terms of male identification"), and is shown to be recast by Flaubert to provide both "a new social-sexual representation" and a metaphor for his own condition as a writer.

[48] See also Mary Orr, "Reading the other. Flaubert's *L'Éducation sentimentale* revisited".

[49] See, in particular, Dorothy Kelly's comments in *Fictional Genders* (16): "Derrida shows that the systematization of gender in a hierarchical opposition entails a moment of aporia, an illogical place where the system can be shown to undo itself. In Derrida's theory [...] traditional gender concepts are studied and assumed, but, when one follows their logic to its conclusions, gender self-destructs."

[50] Hélène Cixous & Catherine Clément, *La Jeune Née*.

[51] See Jonathan Culler, *On Deconstruction. Theory and Criticism after Structuralism*, 43–64 for a perceptive review of the attempts of feminist critics to grapple with the problem.

[52] For a clear statement of the problematics of "male feminism", see Stephen Heath's essay in *Feminist Literary Criticism*, 193–225.

[53] See "*Madame Bovary*: A Tongue of one's own", in *Emma Bovary*, ed. Harold Bloom.

[54] For a lucid presentation of genetic studies see Almuth Grésillon, *Éléments de critique génétique*. The special issue of *Yale French Studies* entitled *Drafts* (ed. Michel Contat, Daniel Hollier & Jacques Neefs) contains a good range of articles on the principal issues facing genetic studies.

[55] *Plans, notes et scénarios de "Madame Bovary"*, ed. Yvan Leclerc; *L'Éducation sentimentale. Les scénarios*, ed. Tony Williams.

[56] *Les Comices agricoles de Flaubert*, 2 vols, ed. Jeanne Goldin.

[57] *Corpus Flaubertianum. Édition des manuscrits d'"Un Cœur simple"*, ed. Giovanni Bonaccorso et al; *Corpus Flaubertianum. Édition des manuscrits d'"'Hérodias"*, 2 vols, ed. Giovanni Bonaccorso et al. See also *O manuscrito en Flaubert. Trancriçao, classificaçao e interpretaçao do proto-text do conto "Hérodias"*, ed. Philippe Willemart.

[58] For details of genetic studies see the annual "Flaubert, Biblio" which has been prepared since 1991 by Odile de Guidis on behalf of the Programme Flaubert, Institut des Textes et Manuscrits Modernes.

[59] See in particular the analysis of Jeanne Goldin, Vol. I and the more recent work of Raymonde Debray-Genette.

[60] See in particular Bernard Gagnebin, *Flaubert et "Salammbô". Genèse d'un texte*.

[61] See in particular Kazuhiro Matsuzawa, *Introduction à l'étude critique et génétique des manuscrits de "L'Éducation sentimentale" de Gustave Flaubert* and Eric le Calvez, *Flaubert topographe: "L'Éducation sentimentale". Essai de poétique génétique*.

[62] See in particular Raymonde Debray-Genette, *Métamorphoses du récit* and Philippe Willemart, *Dans la Chambre noire de l'écriture: "Hérodias" de Flaubert*.

[63] See Robert Melançon, "Le Statut de l'œuvre", 57: "La reconstitution de l'avant-texte implique-t-elle la destruction du texte?"

[64] See Daniel Ferrer, "Clementis's Cap: Retroaction and Persistence in the Genetic Process" in *Drafts. Yale French Studies* for a vigorous argument in support of this view and the question relating to the *avant-texte* raised by Robert Melançon (art. cit., 55): "De quoi est-il l'avant si le processus de genèse est appelé à se poursuivre indéfiniment dans le surgissement des variantes?"

[65] *Métamorphoses du récit,* 81.

[66] *Ibid.,* 85.

[67] *Les Règles de l'art,* 277.

[68] "Esquisse d'une méthode", in *Métamorphoses du récit,* 26.

[69] Letter of 16 April 1853: "Que c'est bête de se donner tout ce mal-là et que personne n'appréciera jamais cela" (*Correspondance*, II, 308).

[70] Letter of 6 April 1853: "Et qui est-ce qui s'apercevra jamais des profondes combinaisons que m'aura demandées un livre si simple?" (*Correspondance*, II, 296).

[71] See Elizabeth Wright, *Psychoanalytic Criticism: Theory in Practice*.

[72] J. Laplanche & S. Leclaire, "The Unconscious; a psychoanalytic study", 125.

[73] S. Felman, "Turning the Screw of Interpretation".

[74] *"Madame Bovary". A Psychoanalytical Reading,* 20.

[75] See W. J. Berg, G. Moskos & M. Grimaud, *Saint Oedipus. Psychocritical approaches to Flaubert's Art,* 155. See also for an equally circumspect approach Charles Bernheimer, *Flaubert and Kafka. Studies in Psychopoetic structure*.

[76] "Flaubert et la poétique du non-finito".

[77] Diana Knight, "Object Choices: Taste and Fetishism in Flaubert's *L'Éducation sentimentale*".

[78] Andrew J. McKenna in "Flaubert's Freudian Thing" argues that violence and desire are inseparable in the novel and that, through the use of the veil as a representation of language as founding reality, "we witness a process in which static oppositions crumble".

[79] For a review of different approaches see Terry Eagleton, *Ideology. An Introduction*.

[80] *Discourse/Counter-Discourse. The Theory and Practice of Symbolic Resistance in Nineteenth-Century France*.

[81] *The Political Unconscious. Narrative as a Socially Symbolic Act*.

[82] *Circles of Censorship*.

[83] *Crimes écrits. La Littérature en procès au XIXe siècle*.

[84] "Sémiologie flaubertienne. Le Club de l'Intelligence".

[85] *Bovary, Charivari. Essai d'ethno-critique*.

[86] See in particular the work of Anne Herschberg-Pierrot.
[87] *Adultery in the Novel*, 235.
[88] N. Schor, *Breaking the Chain. Women, Theory and French Realist Fiction*, x.
[89] *The Adulteress's Child*, 11.
[90] *The Deceived Husband*, 185.
[91] *The Novel of Female Adultery. Love and Gender in Continental European Fiction, 1830–1900.*
[92] *Eurydices fin de siècle, Emma Bovary et le roman naturaliste.*
[93] "Carnal Knowledge in French Naturalist Fiction".
[94] "*Madame Bovary*" *on trial.*
[95] *Flaubert: "Madame Bovary".*
[96] As Stephen Heath (op. cit., 84) puts it, "[Flaubert] exhausts the platitudes of the novel of adultery, leaving no hold for its habitual framework of reference and value."
[97] See G. T. Harris & P. M. Wetherill, eds, *Littérature et Révolutions*; Priscilla Parkhurst Ferguson, *Paris as Revolution. Writing the Nineteenth-Century City.*
[98] See Christopher Prendergast, *Paris and the Nineteenth Century.*
[99] Charles Bernheimer, *Figures of Ill Repute*; Jan Matlock, *Scenes of Seduction.*
[100] See in particular Giovanni Bonaccorso, *L'Oriente nella narrativa di Gustave Flaubert*, Jeanne Bem, "L'Orient ironique de Flaubert", in *Le Texte traversé*, and Beryl Schlossman, *The Orient of Style.*
[101] Naomi Schor, Introduction to *Flaubert and Postmodernism*, xiii.

**Works Cited**

Flaubert, Gustave, *Carnets de travail*, ed. Pierre-Marc de Biasi (Paris: Balland, 1988)

Flaubert, Gustave, *Les Comices agricoles de Flaubert*, 2 vols, ed. Jeanne Goldin (Geneva: Droz, 1984)

Flaubert, Gustave, *Corpus Flaubertianum. Édition des manuscrits d'"Un Cœur simple"*, ed. Giovanni Bonaccorso et al (Paris: Les Belles Lettres, 1983)

Flaubert, Gustave, *Corpus Flaubertianum. Édition des manuscrits d'"Hérodias"*, ed. G. Bonaccorso et al (Vol.1, Paris: Nizet, 1991; Vol. 2, Paris: Sicania, 1995)

Flaubert, Gustave, *Correspondance*, ed. Jean Bruneau, 4 vols, (Paris: Gallimard, 1973–98)

Flaubert, Gustave, *L'Éducation sentimentale*, ed. Peter Michael Wetherill (Paris: Garnier, 1984)

Flaubert, Gustave, *L'Éducation sentimentale. Les scénarios*, ed. Tony Williams (Paris: José Corti, 1992)

Flaubert, Gustave, *L'Éducation sentimentale*, ed. Pierre-Marc de Biasi (Paris: Seuil,1993)

Flaubert, Gustave, *Madame Bovary*, ed. Gérard Gengembre (Paris: Magnard, 1988)

Flaubert, Gustave, *Madame Bovary*, ed. Pierre-Marc de Biasi (Paris: Seuil, 1992)

Flaubert, Gustave, *Madame Bovary*, ed. Pierre-Marc de Biasi (Paris: Imprimerie Nationale, 1994)

Flaubert, Gustave, *"Mémoires d'un fou", "Novembre" et autres textes de jeunesse*, ed. Yvan Leclerc (Paris: Flammarion, 1991)

Flaubert, Gustave, *Œuvres complètes,* 2 vols ed. Bernard Masson (Paris: Seuil, 1964)

Flaubert, Gustave, *Œuvres complètes*, 16 vols (Paris: Club de l'honnête homme, 1971–75)

Flaubert, Gustave, *Par les Champs et par les grèves*, ed. Adrianne J. Tooke (Geneva: Droz, 1987)

Flaubert, Gustave, *Plans, notes et scénarios de "Madame Bovary"*, ed. Yvan Leclerc (Paris: CNRS, 1995)

Flaubert, Gustave, *Pour Louis Bouilhet*, ed. Alan Raitt (Exeter: University of Exeter Press, 1994)

Flaubert, Gustave, *Le Sottisier*, ed. Bruno de Cessole (Paris: NIL, 1995)

Flaubert, Gustave, [Trois Contes] *O manuscrito en Flaubert. Trancriçao,classificaçao e interpretaçao do proto-text do conto "Hérodias"*, ed. Philippe Willemart (San Paolo: Universidade de Sao Paolo, 1984)

Flaubert, Gustave, *Trois Contes,* ed. Pierre-Marc de Biasi (Paris: Flammarion, 1986)

Flaubert, Gustave, *Trois Contes*, ed. Peter Michael Wetherill (Paris: Garnier, 1988)

Flaubert, Gustave, *Trois contes*, ed. Pierre-Marc de Biasi (Paris: Seuil, 1993)

Flaubert, Gustave, *Voyage en Égypte*, ed. Pierre-Marc de Biasi (Paris: Grasset, 1991)

Addison, Claire, *Where Flaubert Lies. Chronology, Mythology and History* (Cambridge: Cambridge University Press, 1996)

Baguley, David, *Naturalist Fiction. The Entropic Vision* (Cambridge: Cambridge University Press, 1990)

Barnes, Julian, *Flaubert's Parrot* (London: Jonathan Cape, 1984)

Beizer, Janet, *Ventriloquized Bodies. Narratives of Hysteria in Nineteenth-Century France* (Ithaca and London: Cornell University Press, 1994)

Bem, Jeanne, *Le Texte traversé* (Paris: Librairie Honoré Champion, 1991)

Berg, W. J., Moskos, G. & Grimaud, M., *Saint Oedipus. Psychocritical Approaches to Flaubert's Art* (Ithaca and London: Cornell University Press, 1982)

Bernheimer, Charles, *Flaubert and Kafka. Studies in Psychopoetic Structure* (New Haven: Yale University Press, 1982)

Bernheimer, Charles, *Figures of Ill Repute: Representing Prostitution in Nineteenth-Century France* (Cambridge, Mass.: Harvard University Press, 1989).

Biasi, Pierre-Marc de, "Flaubert et la poétique du non-finito", in *Le Manuscrit inachevé. Écriture, création, communication* (Paris: CNRS, 1986), 45–73

Bloom, Harold, ed., *Emma Bovary* (New York: Chelsea House Publishers, 1994)

Bonaccorso, Giovanni, *L'Oriente nella narrativa di Gustave Flaubert* (Messina: Antonio Sfameni, 1981)

Bourdieu, Pierre, *Les Règles de l'art. Genèse et structure du champ littéraire* (Paris: Seuil, 1992)

Brooks, Peter, "Retrospective Lust, or Flaubert's perversities", in *Reading for the plot. Design and Invention in Narrative* (Oxford: Clarendon Press, 1984)

Burgelin, Claude, "Perec, Lecteur de Flaubert", in *Flaubert, et après*, ed. Bernard Masson (Paris: Minard, 1984), 135–71

Caramaschi, Enzo, "A Travers un demi-siècle de critique flaubertienne", in *Flaubert e il pensiero del suo secolo* (Messina: Facoltà di lettere e filosofia, 1985), 105–47

Carlut, Charles, *La Correspondance de Flaubert. Étude et répertoire critique* (Paris: Nizet, 1968)

Cixous, Hélène and Clément, Catherine, *La Jeune Née* (Paris: Union générale d'éditions, 1975)

Collas, Ion, K., *"Madame Bovary". A Psychoanalytical Reading* (Geneva: Droz, 1985)

Colwell, David John, *Bibliographie des études sur G. Flaubert (1983–88)* (Egham: Runnymede Books, 1990)

Conroy, Mark, *Modernism and Authority. Strategies of legitimation in Flaubert and Conrad* (Baltimore: John Hopkins University Press, 1985)

Contat, Michel, Hollier, Daniel & Neefs, Jacques, eds, *Drafts. Yale French Studies*, 89 (1996).

Culler, Jonathan, *Flaubert: The Uses of Uncertainty* (London: Elek, 1974)

Culler, Jonathan, "The Uses of *Madame Bovary*", in *Flaubert and Postmodernism*, ed. N. Schor & H. F. Majewski, 1-12.

Culler, Jonathan, *On Deconstruction. Theory and Criticism after Structuralism* (London: Routledge and Kegan Paul, 1983)

Czyba, Lucette, *Mythes et idéologie de la femme dans les romans de Flaubert* (Lyon: Presses universitaires de Lyon, 1983)

Danahy, Michael, "*Madame Bovary*: A Tongue of one's own", in *Emma Bovary*, ed. Harold Bloom.

Debray-Genette, Raymonde, *Métamorphoses du récit* (Paris: Seuil, 1988)

Debray-Genette, Raymonde & Neefs, Jacques, *L'Œuvre de l'œuvre. Études sur la "Correspondance" de Flaubert* (Saint-Denis: Presses universitaires de Vincennes, 1993)

Debray-Genette, Raymonde, "Hapax et paradigmes, Aux frontières de la critique génétique", in *Genesis*, 6 (1994), 79–92

Demorest, Don L., *L'Expression symbolique et figurée dans l'œuvre de Gustave Flaubert* (Paris: Les Presses modernes, 1931)

Derrida, Jacques, "Une Idée de Flaubert: 'La lettre de Platon'", *Revue d'histoire littéraire de la France*, 81 (1981), 658-76.

Donato, Eugenio, *The Script of Decadence. Essays on the Fiction of Flaubert and the Poetics of Romanticism* (New York and Oxford: Oxford University Press, 1993)

Douchin, Jacques-Louis, *La Vie érotique de Flaubert* (Paris: Pauvert, 1985)

Dufour, Pierre, *Flaubert et le Pignouf* (Saint-Denis: Presses universitaires de Vincennes, 1993)

Eagleton, Mary, ed., *Feminist Literary Criticism* (London: Longman, 1991)

Eagleton, Terry, *Ideology. An Introduction* (London: Verso, 1991)

Falconer, Graham, "Flaubert, James and the problem of undecidability", *Comparative Literature* 39 (1987), 1–18

Falconer, Graham, "Travail de 'débalzaciénisation' dans la rédaction de *Madame Bovary*", in *Flaubert 3. Mythes et religions (2)* (Paris: Minard, 1988), 123–56

Felman, Shosana, "Turning the Screw of Interpetation", *Yale French Studies*, 55/56 (1977), 94-207

Ferguson, Priscilla Parkhurst, *Paris as Revolution. Writing the Nineteenth-Century City* (Berkeley, Los Angeles, London: University of California Press, 1994)

Gagnebin, Bernard, *Flaubert et "Salammbô". Genèse d'un texte* (Paris: Presses universitaires de France, 1992)

Gallina, Bernard, *Eurydices fin de siècle, Emma Bovary et le roman naturaliste* (Udine: Aura editrice, 1992)

Girard, Marc, *La Passion de Charles Bovary* (Paris: Imago, 1995)

Ginsburg, Michal Peled, *Flaubert Writing: A Study in Narrative Strategies* (Stanford: Stanford UP, 1986)

Grésillon, Almuth, *Éléments de critique génétique* (Paris: Presses universitaires de France, 1994).

Griffin, Robert, *Rape of the Lock. Flaubert's Mythic Realism* (Lexington: French Forum, 1988)

Haig, Stirling, *Flaubert and the Gift of Speech. Dialogue and Discourse in Four "Modern" Novels* (Cambridge: Cambridge University Press, 1986)

Harris, Geoffrey T. & Wetherill, Peter Michael, eds, *Littérature et Révolutions* (Amsterdam: Rodopi, 1990)

Harrison, N., *Circles of Censorship: Censorship and its Metaphors in French History, Literature, and Theory* (Oxford: Clarendon Press, 1995)

Heath, Stephen, *Flaubert: "Madame Bovary"* (Cambridge: Cambridge University Press, 1992)

Herschberg-Pierrot, Anne, *Le "Dictionnaire des Idées reçues" de Flaubert* (Lille: Presses universitaires de Lille, 1988)

Jacquet, Marie-Thérèse, *Les Mots de l'absence, ou Du "Dictionnaire des Idées reçues" de Flaubert*, (Paris: Nizet, 1987)

Jameson, Frederic, *The Political Unconscious. Narrative as a Socially Symbolic Act* (London: Methuen, 1981)

Kaplan, Louise J., *Female Perversions. The Temptations of Emma Bovary* (New York: Doubleday, 1991)

Kelly, Dorothy, *Fictional Genders. Role and Representation in Nineteenth-Century Narrative* (Lincoln and London: University of Nebraska Press, 1989)

Knight, Diana, *Flaubert's Characters* (Cambridge: Cambridge University Press, 1985)

Knight, Diana, "Object Choices: Taste and Fetishism in Flaubert's *L'Éducation sentimentale*", in *French Literature, Thought and Culture in the Nineteenth Century. A Material World*, ed. Brian Rigby (London: Macmillan, 1993), 198–217

La Capra, Dominick, *"Madame Bovary" on trial* (Ithaca: Cornell University Press, 1980)

Laplanche, J.& Leclaire, S. "The Unconscious; a psychoanalytic study", *Yale French Studies*, 48 (1972), 118–75

Le Calvez, Éric, *Flaubert topographe: "L'Éducation sentimentale". Essai de poétique génétique* (Amsterdam: Rodopi, 1997)

Leclerc, Yvan, *Crimes écrits. La Littérature en procès au XIX$^e$ siècle* (Paris: Plon, 1991)

Lloyd, Rosemary, *Madame Bovary* (London: Unwin Hyman, 1989)

Lottman, Herbert, *Flaubert* (London: Methuen, 1989)

Lowe, Margaret, *Towards the real Flaubert. A Study of "Madame Bovary"* (Oxford: Clarendon Press, 1984)

McKenna, Andrew J., "Flaubert's Freudian Thing. Violence and Representation in *Salammbô*", *Stanford French Review*, 12 (Fall–Winter 1988), 305–25

Masson, Bernard, *Lectures de l'imaginaire* (Paris: Presses universitaires de France, 1993)

Mathet, Marie-Thérèse, *Le Dialogue romanesque chez Flaubert* (Paris: Aux Amateurs de livres, 1987)

Matlock, Jan, *Scenes of Seduction: Prostitution, Hysteria, and Reading Difference in Nineteenth-Century France* (New York: Columbia University Press, 1994)

Matsuzawa, Kazuhiro, *Introduction à l'étude critique et génétique des manuscrits de "L'Éducation sentimentale" de Gustave Flaubert*, 2 vols, (Tokyo: Librairie-Éditions France Tosho, 1992)

Melançon, Robert, "Le statut de l'œuvre", *Études françaises*, 28, 1 (Autumn 1992), 49–66

Mitterand, Henri, "Sémiologie flaubertienne. Le Club de l'Intelligence", in *Flaubert et après*, ed. Bernard Masson (Paris: Minard, 1984), 61–77

Moi, Toril, *Sexual/Textual Politics. Feminist Literary Theory* (London: Methuen, 1985)

Mouchard, Claude & Neefs, Jacques, *Flaubert* (Paris: Balland, 1986)

Neefs, J., "De Flaubert à Perec", in *T.L.E. Théorie, Littérature, Enseignement*, 5 (1987), 35–47

Orr, Mary, "Reading the other. Flaubert's *L'Éducation sentimentale* revisited", *French Studies*, 46 (1992), 412–23

Overton, Bill, *The Novel of Female Adultery. Love and Gender in Continental European Fiction, 1830–1900* (London: Macmillan, 1996)

Paulson, William R., *Sentimental Education. The Complexity of Disenchantment* (New York: Twayne, 1992)

Perec, George, "Emprunts à Flaubert", *L'Arc*, 79 (1979), 49-50

Prendergast, Christopher, *The Order of Mimesis. Balzac, Stendhal, Nerval, Flaubert* (Cambridge: Cambridge University Press, 1986)

Prendergast, Christopher, *Paris and the Nineteenth Century* (Oxford: Blackwell, 1994)

Privat, Jean-Marie, *Bovary, Charivari. Essai d'ethno-critique* (Paris: CNRS, 1995)

Raitt, Alan W. "État présent des études sur Flaubert" in *L'Information littéraire*, 34 (1982), 198-206 and 35 (1983), 18-25

Raitt, Alan W., " 'Nous étions à l'étude' ", in *Mythes et religions (1)*, ed. Bernard Masson (Paris: Minard, 1986)

Raitt, Alan W., *Trois Contes* (London: Grant & Cutler, 1991)

Ramazani, Vaheed K., *The Free Indirect Mode. Flaubert and the Uses of Irony* (Charlottesville: University Press of Virginia, 1988)

Reid, James H., *Narration and Description in the French Realist Novel. The Temporality of Lying and Forgetting* (Cambridge: Cambridge University Press, 1993)

Roe, David, *Gustave Flaubert* (London: Macmillan, 1989)

Guy Sagnes, "Tentations balzaciennes dans le manuscrit de *L'Éducation sentimentale*", *L'Année Balzacienne*, 2 (81), 53–64

Sartre, Jean-Paul, *L'Idiot de la famille*, 3 vols, (Paris: Gallimard, 1971–2).

Schor, Naomi & Majewski Henry F., *Flaubert and Postmodernism* (Lincoln: University of Nebraska Press, 1984)

Schor, Naomi, *Breaking the Chain. Women, Theory and French Realist Fiction*, (Columbia: Columbia University Press, 1985)

Schlossman, Beryl, *The Orient of Style* (Durham and London: Duke University Press, 1991)

Segal, Naomi, *The Adulteress's Child. Authorship and Desire in the Nineteenth-Century Novel* (Oxford and Cambridge, MA: Polity Press, 1992)

Sinclair, Alison, *The Deceived Husband: A Kleinian Approach to the Literature of Infidelity* (Oxford: Clarendon Press, 1993)

Steele, Meili M., *Realism and the Drama of Reference. Strategies of Representation in Balzac, Flaubert and James* (University Park and London: The Pennsylvania State University Press, 1988)

Tanner, Tony, *Adultery in the Novel* (Baltimore and London: The John Hopkins University Press, 1979)

Tipper, Paul Andrew, *The Dream Machine. Avian Imagery in "Madame Bovary"* (Durham: University of Durham, 1994)

Terdiman, Richard, *Discourse/Counter-Discourse. The Theory and Practice of Symbolic Resistance in Nineteenth-Century France* (Ithaca: Cornell University Press, 1995)

Tondeur, Claire-Lise, *Flaubert critique. Thèmes et structures,* (Amsterdam, Philadelphia: John Benjamins, 1984)

Troyat, Henri, *Flaubert* (Paris: Flammarion, 1988)

Unwin, Timothy, *Art et Infini. L'œuvre de jeunesse de Flaubert* (Amsterdam: Rodopi, 1992)

Wetherill, Peter Michael, ed., *Flaubert: La Dimension du texte* (Manchester: Manchester University Press, 1982)

White, Nicholas & Segal, Naomi, eds, *Scarlet Letters. Fictions of Adultery from Antiquity to the 1990s* (London: Macmillan, 1997)

White, Nicholas, "Carnal Knowledge in French Naturalist Fiction", in *Scarlet Letters. Fictions of Adultery from Antiquity to the 1990s* (London: Macmillan, 1997), 123–33

Willemart, Philippe, *Dans la Chambre noire de l'écriture: "Hérodias" de Flaubert* (Toronto: Éditions Paratexte, 1996)

Williams, David Anthony, *"The Hidden Life at its Source": A Study of Flaubert's "L'Éducation sentimentale"* (Hull: Hull University Press, 1987)

Wright, Elizabeth, *Psychoanalytic Criticism: Theory in Practice* (London: Methuen:1984)

# *NOVEMBRE* AND THE PARADOX OF THE NEW IN FLAUBERT'S EARLY WORK
## Timothy Unwin

The questions raised by the concepts of novelty, revival, originality, or indeed by the more general notion of modernity, are so fundamental to Flaubert's project as a writer that, as we seek at the dawn of the millenium to find new approaches to his work, we are forced to begin by problematising our own gesture. My purpose is to do precisely that, suggesting that new readings of Flaubert's work must start by asking questions about their own assumptions. Why is the "new" held to be of value? What expectations of "novelty" does the Flaubertian text promote or undermine? And is its meaning in some way dependent on this process? These are in some respects old questions, but — importantly — they underline a very Flaubertian irony about the quest for novelty. The enquiry which is to be pursued here will seek, not to resolve such irony, but to enter into it and perhaps to exploit it.

From the point of view of that famous "blague supérieure", can we even be sure that novelty exists? Is our belief in it merely the result of artistic manipulation? Should we consign novelty to the dustbin together with its sister concept originality, doing what the *Dictionnaire des idées reçues* advises under the entry "original"? — "Rire de tout ce qui est original, le haïr, le bafouer, et l'exterminer si l'on peut" (*Œuvres complètes,* II, 312).[1] Given Flaubert's complex treatment of the relationship between the original and the commonplace (as described notably by Felman, 1975, 191–213), any attempt to revive or renew our outlook on his work must of course expect to encounter major obstacles. Certainly, there is almost universal agreement that interpretations which do *not* propose something new must be of limited value, yet as any seasoned reader of Flaubert knows, almost every possible "new" stance seems to have been pre-empted, indeed sabotaged, by the ironies of texts which seem to have been arranged "de telle manière que le lecteur ne sache pas si on se fout de lui, oui ou non" (*Correspondance,* I, 679).[2] However, the view that Flaubert's work systematically undermines *all* attempts to make sense of it — fashionable in the seventies, in the wake of Sartre, Culler and others — might in the nineties seem overly, indeed almost quaintly, pessimistic. Similarly, to argue that all has been said and that we are merely condemned (alongside the writer himself and those famous two *copistes* of his last novel) to the final irony of repetition may itself be no more than a critical cliché. Though it is clear that we must take account of the "dark side" of Flaubert, I shall be suggesting here that there are insights to be gained through a self-conscious engagement with the relationship that exists in his work (and by extension in our reading of it) between the new and the old, the original and the commonplace. Such insights must, of course, come at a price, and it will be necessary in this discussion of *Novembre* to revisit ground covered in somewhat different ways by Felman (1975), Brombert (1981), and Castelein (1986). Yet that very act of revisitation is peculiarly appropriate to the subject of this paper, which is about Flaubert's own quest to find the new in "common" places. It has often been said that *Novembre* marks a crucial turning point in Flaubert's career.[3] The question of why and how this is the case has not however been exhausted, and there is perhaps no better starting point for a more general revisitation and reassessment of Flaubert's work than this richly self-conscious text.

More explicitly than earlier texts, *Novembre* stages not only the question of the "writing" of experience — and of that possibly spurious relationship between some lived reality and its textual copy — it also focuses explicitly on how the text gets read (as we see most clearly in the intervention of the second narrator who, at the end of the story, characterises himself as a reader of the earlier text and discusses its merits and failures). But *Novembre* is also a text which is written in, and into, the very space of repetition, echo, uniformity. It explores the artistic possibilities of that realm, in the mode of metafictional enquiry, and asks constantly how such a narrative of sameness and banality *might* be read. The unexceptional nature of the story's content is constantly stressed. "J'étais donc ce que vous êtes tous," the narrator tells us, "un certain homme qui vit, qui dort, qui mange, qui boit, qui pleure, qui rit [...]" (*OC*, I, 252). Thus *Novembre* views itself — and indeed views its viewing — as rooted in the ordinary, the hackneyed, the recycled, acknowledging that maybe everything is, after all, a copy, that there is nothing original or new to be discovered, that we are left only to say what is not, or to say what might have been. Yet its claim to novelty — and novelty is implicitly held to be a worthwhile, even fundamental, value by the young Flaubert — is precisely because it looks into the abyss of artistic hopelessness and faces the darkness. In so doing, it invites its reader to participate in this dangerous gesture, suggesting that novelty, and any meaning which accompanies it, is that which is salvaged from eternal sameness and constructed out of that sense of near defeat which is so powerfully inscribed in the text. But unlike, say, Felman, I wish to argue here that far from deconstructing its own relationship with the "lieu commun", *Novembre* tries — though sometimes fails — to construct sense and significance essentially *against* the "lieu commun", the latter being recognised as pervasive, omnipresent and threatening, yet also paradoxically accepted and integrated into the text. For *Novembre* is the site of a twofold struggle by the young Flaubert: first, a struggle against the destructive power of cliché, and second, a struggle to come to terms with cliché and exploit it meaningfully.

The idea of novelty is, as Flaubert is well aware by the time he writes *Novembre*, fraught with paradox. Antoine Compagnon points out in *Cinq paradoxes sur la modernité* that the discovery of the new — a value which enters definitively into the collective artistic credo in the nineteenth century — is destined, by the very logic of its own belief-system, to be eclipsed in its turn by yet newer discoveries, just as it replaced previous forms which, once new, came to be seen as outmoded. Self-destruction is implicit in the belief in novelty.[4] This inescapable logic of evolution and replacement recalls those endless "défilés" from

Flaubert's early mystical works through to the final *Tentation*, where systems, ideologies, heresies or gods eternally strive for transcendence, only to be transcended in their turn. It is indeed, as Compagnon argues, with writers like Baudelaire and Flaubert that the "tradition of the new" is first established, with all the contradictions that such a term implies. And just as Baudelaire, in that famous final line of "Le Voyage", seeks to plunge "au fond de l'inconnu, pour trouver du nouveau", so too in Flaubert the quest to break away and discover novelty — at almost any price — is present from the earliest works. As he is composing *Smarh*, early in 1839, Flaubert writes to Chevalier of his sense that something new and different, by definition unknown and obscure, is emerging in his style: "Et je sens pourtant, mais confusément, quelque chose s'agiter en moi, je suis maintenant dans une époque transitoire et je suis curieux de voir ce qu'il en résultera" (*Corr.*, I, 37–8). Some fourteen years later, talking about *Novembre* in a letter to Louise Colet of 29 October 1853, Flaubert interestingly starts his comments about the text by saying that on a re-reading it had indeed seemed *new* to him (though only because — ironically perhaps — he had forgotten it in the intervening years): "Cela m'a paru tout nouveau, tant je l'avais oublié." But, he continues, "ce n'est pas bon, il y a des monstruosités de mauvais goût, et en somme l'ensemble n'est pas satisfaisant. Je ne vois aucun moyen de le réduire, il faudrait tout refaire [...]." And then the famous final comment "Ah! quel nez fin j'ai eu de ne pas le publier! Comme j'en rougirais maintenant!" (*Corr.*, II, 460). If there is self-condemnation here, then there is also a belief in his own progress as an artist, his ability to write better in 1853 than in 1842, the year *Novembre* was completed. But the harsh overall judgement on that work which was, in another, earlier line, the "clôture de [sa] jeunesse" (*Corr.*, I, 410) — in other words, the point of transition to his maturity — ironically re-enacts that of the second narrator of *Novembre*, echoing the drama of self-judgement and self-transcendence that has already been staged within both this work and others. Indeed, throughout Flaubert's early work we find such interventions which denounce the style that had earlier been considered original or new, and by implication suggest that a yet newer and better approach is possible. The movement of transcendence, the denunciation of previous perspectives or forms, thus ironically also foreshadows its own future relegation in some further totalising vision at the very moment in which it underpins the belief in novelty.

In the early works, this recurrent paradox translates itself into a conflict between the idealistic visionary and the cynical outsider, the first being a believer in novelty or originality and the second a denouncer of cliché. Although cliché and originality seem to be mutually exclusive properties, they nonetheless find themselves in an enforced state of cohabitation in Flaubert's early work, even if the pattern of their interaction is largely one of alternation and replacement. For just as the intense quest for novelty seems inevitably to lead to a later denunciation of its clichés, so too the cynical later judgement is dependent on an implicit recognition of the value of novelty (if only because the author understands that he has failed to achieve it). The one voice never quite exists without the other, and there is already a foreshadowing of that fascinating interaction of novelty and cliché in the works of Flaubert's maturity. Yet importantly, prior to *Novembre*, these are primarily in a state of conflict rather than of continuum or interrelation. On the one hand, there is an ongoing attempt to re-empower language (seen as a poor and finite reflection of the infinite subtleties of the poet's soul) and return it to some innocent, pristine, edenic state. On the other hand, the writer inevitably concludes that such a hope was misguided and misplaced. Central to the young author's quest is the affirmation that a vision of artistic sublimity has been glimpsed, and yet, time and again, he recognises the futility of his own attempts to reach it.[5] True, a richly anxious sense of paradox emerges on occasions, with a hint of recognition that language as degraded copy has its fascinations; but the dominant note is one of defeat and despair, a failure to match up in language to the vision of poetic splendour, rather than a sense of the depth of this relationship between the old and the new.[6] This is important, because it suggests that Flaubert's instinctive reflex in the early works is to escape from the restrictions imposed by language, to transcend its clichés, rather than to accept its power and its hold over him. His pessimism is always accompanied by a belief that originality might be possible, or might have been possible, even where he has failed to achieve it. Yet his selfcondemnations are no less harsh for this realisation. In *Mémoires d'un fou* (where the text is systematically punctured with the cynical interventions of a harsher literary judge) there is a constant sense that the desire to transcend the clichés of ordinary life, far from leading to the renewal and rejuvenation of art, may itself be a sign of degeneration, and the hopelessness of the text's opening line — "Pourquoi écrire ces pages? A quoi sont-elles bonnes?" — seems to re-echo throughout it. More grandiosely in *Smarh*, the author who re-reads himself and composes an epilogue entitled *Réflexion d'un homme désintéressé à l'affaire et qui a relu ça après un an de façon* is amazed to discover how far his actual achievement was from what he had hoped for:

> Ce que tu admirais il y a un an est aujourd'hui fort mauvais; j'en suis bien fâché, car je t'avais décerné le nom d'un grand homme futur, et tu te regardais comme un petit Goethe. L'illusion n'est pas mince, il faut commencer par avoir des idées, et ton fameux mysère en est veuf. [...] Adieu, le meilleur conseil que je puisse te donner, c'est de ne plus écrire. (*OC*, I, 218).

The early works consistently dramatise this struggle to capture a vision of infinite poetic splendour, which the writer firmly believes he has glimpsed. Ironically, however, the belief in this vision is underlined by emphasis on the failure of the attempt. The process of putting the vision into words itself becomes at once a stumbling block and a reason for greater conviction, as the author recognises the bluntness of the instrument at his disposal.

So, if the late 1830s see Flaubert grappling seriously with the demon of the "lieu commun" for the first time, the duality between the would-be poet-mystic and the sceptical, disabused literary judge remains nonetheless largely unresolved before the writing of *Novembre*. It translates itself as an oscillation between (at least) two different perspectives or modes of writing (see Ginsberg, 1986, 16–32, for an analysis of the narrative crises provoked by such clashes in both *Mémoires d'un fou* and *Novembre*), and the sense of disappointment and failure is dominant. Although *Novembre* marks a clear step forward, what nonetheless remains a constant is the hope, expressed time and again by Flaubert up to and including the writing of *Novembre*, of finding some innovating and regenerating power in language, of transcending the "lieu commun", of reinvesting the word with something more than just verbal power, giving it a dynamic impact upon the realities it evokes. The young Flaubert believes emphatically in the power of language. One of the clearest and most striking examples of his desire to escape from the anxiety of influence and create a new language, free of the shackles of banality, is a passage in *Smarh* where he stops and promises, some day, the ultimate and perfect page, a page which will not be a copy of reality, but which will itself somehow "generate" reality, or new realities, giving to readers of it the elixir of life and the elucidation of all mysteries — as well, perhaps, as the fulfilment of all libidinous desires:

> Un jour que j'aurai de l'imagination, que j'aurai été penser à Néron sur les ruines de Rome, ou aux bayadères sur les bords du Gange j'intercalerai la plus belle page qu'on ait faite; mais je vous avertis d'avance qu'elle sera superbe, monstrueuse, épouvantablement impudique, qu'elle fera sur vous l'effet d'une tartine de cantharides, et que, si vous êtes vierge, vous apprendrez de drôles de choses, et que, si vous êtes vieillard, elle vous fera redevenir jeune; ce sera une page qui passera en prodigalité la poésie de M. Delille, en intérêt les tragédies de M. Delavigne, en exubérance le style de J. Janin, et en fioritures celles de P. de Kock; une page, enfin, qui, si elle était affichée sur les murs, mettrait les murs en chaleur eux-mêmes, et ferait courir les populations dans les lupanars devenus désormais trop petits, et forcerait hommes et femmes à s'accoupler dans la rue [...]. (*OC*, I, 211)

Clearly, there are traces here of the *Garçon* speaking, with his mockery of bourgeois respectability and his cynical deflation of ideals. Yet there is a serious message being expressed as well. Language is no longer, at this point, a tool to convey reality — though it is, interestingly, a self-reflexive instrument. Rather it aspires to alter and recreate reality through its own linguistic power. We have here the ideal of a style which would, even more than a "manière absolue de voir les choses", itself be a mode of being — not copy or simulacrum, but the essential principle from which all things flow, a kind of infinitely divisible and infinitely proliferating matter as in Saint Antoine's vision in the text written ten years later.

Despite the fact that *Novembre* shows the author shifting towards an acceptance of cliché, and refusing to place exaggerated hopes on the potentially liberating properties of his own style, something of this vision of a stylistic absolute returns in certain pages of the text and indeed remains implicit throughout. It is most notably the case in the passage describing the writer's pantheist vision, where a state akin to verbal ecstasy is reached:

> l'esprit de Dieu me remplissait, je me sentais le cœur grand, j'adorais quelque chose d'un étrange mouvement, j'aurais voulu m'absorber dans la lumière du soleil et me perdre dans cette immensité d'azur, avec l'odeur qui s'élevait de la surface des flots; et je fus pris alors d'une joie insensée, et je me mis à marcher comme si tout le bonheur des cieux m'était entré dans l'âme. [...] Et je compris alors tout le bonheur de la création et toute la joie que Dieu y a placée pour l'homme; la nature m'apparut belle comme une harmonie complète, que l'extase seule doit entendre; quelque chose de tendre comme un amour et de pur comme la prière s'éleva pour moi du fond de l'horizon, s'abattit de la cime des rocs déchirés, du haut des cieux; il se forma, du bruit de l'Océan, de la lumière du jour, quelque chose d'exquis que je m'appropriai comme d'un domaine céleste, je m'y sentis vivre heureux et grand, comme l'aigle qui regarde le soleil et monte dans ses rayons. (*OC*, I, 256–7)

Now although this passage does not explicitly reflect on the question of a literary style, there is an important sense in which style, or words, are its centre. As in the passage in *Smarh*, the implication is that in the end it is not language which copies reality (whatever "reality" might be), but reality which copies — or flows outwards from — language. For the vision of nature here is generated by the power, the precision, the pleasure and indeed the abundance of words. It is self-consciously textual, poetically contrived in its choice of terms and its rhythmic sonorities. As I have argued elsewhere (Unwin, 1992, 133–51), it would therefore be putting things the wrong way round to look upon this passage, as have a number of commentators, as some kind of "transcription" of experience. Words themselves are the locus of any so-called "mystical" experience, the image of nature deriving from them rather than being at their origin. And in that sense, the passage is a fulfilment of the promise of *Smarh*. Words and their object seem, for this brief moment in *Novembre*, to exist in some stylistic equilibrium. Cliché is transcended, a sense of escape becomes possible, and the narrator gives the impression that his language at last catches up with the vision it wishes to convey, perhaps indeed because the vision is nothing other than the words themselves. Novelty and regeneration are achieved — or at least, the fleeting sense of them — as language creates and generates its own stylistic ideal. In a text which so clearly articulates a sense of artistic despair and hopelessness, it is important to remember this optimistic dimension.

Yet although we find this belief in a linguistic regeneration in *Novembre*, it seems now to exist as an extreme which the author perceives as being at the outer limit of his possibilities — his real subject being how to articulate a meaningful message in the face of the disappointment and despair which is his usual artistic condition. The writing of the text moves between these two poles and, after the pantheist passage, the sceptical narrator interrupts the flow and detaches himself quite deliberately: "Puis ce fut tout; bien vite je me rappelai que je vivais, je revins à moi, je me mis en marche, sentant que la malédiction me reprenait. [...] Il y a des jours où l'on a vécu deux existences, la seconde n'est déjà plus que le souvenir de la première" (*OC*, I, 257). We find here something more than that movement of oscillation so familiar in Flaubert's early works, from "inside" to "outside", from ideal to real, from the sense of novelty to the awareness of the commonplace.[7] This time, it seems, the narrator is deliberately returning to and facing his sense of despair, setting himself outside the experience of poetic regeneration in order to view it coldly and not fall victim to its illusions. The real task of writing, it is now implied, is to face up to its own derivative status — though importantly, writing henceforth derives not from some original "experience", but from the vision of stylistic energy which has just been described. Intuition of that artistic ideal must now remain implicit, being contained within the act of writing as it seeks stylistic plenitude not by some magical escape from the constraints of style, but by concentration on the reality of the commonplace. Even though there remains in *Novembre* an element of nostalgia for the sublime that will later be more fully contained, we now see Flaubert moving towards the position that will be outlined at the end of the first *Éducation sentimentale*, where Jules concentrates his attention exclusively on the objective realities of the world, steadfastly refusing his art the possibility of escape, and discovering the poetry of the real ("il apprit la géographie et ne plaça plus le climat du Brésil sous la latitude de New-York" (*OC.*, I, 354) ).

However, a sense of duality, indeed of contradiction — the old jostling with the new, the clichéd with the original, the emptiness of words with the vision of plenitude — is still apparent in *Novembre*. Alternating with the quest for artistic transcendence is the recognition of banality, both in life and in art. Yet, importantly, this duality is now also negotiated as a more or less explicit reflection on writing itself. By stepping back from his quest for artistic transcendence, the narrator perceives this not as an escape into another poetic realm, but as a form of nourishment for that very act of writing which he is now carrying out. Emotions are cultivated, for the first time in Flaubert's work, in a spirit of detachment, held in check, maintained in some precarious equilibrium that emphasises first and foremost their artistic potential, as in the young narrator's sensual dreams: "Pour ce qui était de la beauté des passions et de leurs bruits sonores, les poètes me fournissaient des thèmes à ma rêverie [...]" (*OC*, I, 257). To realise his sensual dreams would, of course, to be to deny their poetic richness and their multiplicity, so as he contemplates and desires women it is "ni celle-ci, ni celle-là [...] mais toutes, mais chacune, dans la variété infinie de leurs formes et du désir qui y correspondait" (*OC*, I, 259). Through writing, there is a coming to terms with the illusory nature of desire, yet a concomitant cultivation of its virtual status. And illusion is now also seen from the perspective of the ordinary and the everyday. This is different from earlier texts which had viewed the banality of daily life as an unwelcome and untimely interference, a diversion from the real subject — as when, in *Mémoires d'un fou*, the dreaming young schoolboy was suddenly confronted with the derision of his classmates (*OC*, I, 232). *Mémoires d'un fou* is a fitful and jerky text, reflecting such alternations between dream and reality. *Novembre* — though still punctured by crisis points showing the writer's difficulty in coping with his paradoxical subject — is generally more fluid and uniform, a text in which words beget words and language itself is the structuring and defining principle.

The opening pages of *Novembre* focus in particular on the poeticisation of experience. The narrative presents itself predominantly as a workshop on language, a text at one remove from text — perhaps not as clearly as the 1845 *Éducation*, but sufficiently so for one critic (Castelein, 1986) to have argued forcefully that *Novembre* is also a novelist's novel, a work about the vocation of the writer and the place of writing. And whereas the 1845 *Éducation* ends as a reflection on art, *Novembre* begins as one. The narrative self-consciously gives textual validity to experience whilst it denies the significance of real life, cultivating failure in order to articulate it and produce writing: "Mes désirs n'avaient point d'objet, ma tristesse n'avait point de cause immédiate; ou plutôt, il y avait tant de buts et tant de causes que je n'aurais su en dire aucun" (*OC*, I, 253). The truth of inner experience is impossible to speak, implies the author, yet here he is articulating it nonetheless — as though its impossibility were in some way the guarantee of the effectiveness, or at least of the validity, of his efforts. Thus does the text thematise monotony, repetition and the banal, and the dream of stylistic transcendence starts by delving into those very values from which it hopes to liberate itself. The opening chapters emphasise the monotony of the narrator's existence, and look for the poetry of unfulfilled hopes and desires. Striking a clearly Baudelairean note almost at the outset, the narrator writes: "J'ai à moi des souvenirs nombreux dont je me sens accablé, comme le sont les vieillards de tous les jours qu'ils ont vécus" (*OC*, I, 248).

Inevitably, given this attempt to articulate paradox, *Novembre* is shot through with tensions. But where critics like Felman saw in *Novembre* signs of Flaubert's mastery of the subversive power of the signifier, turning sense inside out through its multiple ironies, perhaps we can now afford to be simpler and see signs of an old Flaubertian contradiction of the 1830s which lingers on into the 1840s and remains unresolved — the contradiction between the desire for poetic transcendence, on the one hand, and the narrator's recognition of his artistic limits on the other. For while the nostalgia for a linguistic paradise remains, it must be said that it is not quite integrated into the aesthetic of the commonplace which is now being developed. The narrator's quest to find equilibrium between the old and the new frequently stumbles upon the dejected realisation that a poetics of the banal must itself be subject to contamination by the subject it deals with. The text is shot through with this contradiction between the sense of the ordinary and the desire to transcend it artistically, and the contradiction attempts to resolve itself precisely through a reflection on failure as one of the fundamental issues of writing. Now if this alone were the defining character of *Novembre*, it would not be significantly different from earlier texts (*Mémoires d'un fou*, for example, in which the narrator emphasises the failure of words to come up to his own expectations of them). However, alongside the reflection on failure there is an additional dimension, for life itself, though not always seen as amenable to a transposition into art, becomes the subject of a reflection about how art *might* henceforth be achieved. The text operates at a further remove than was previously the case, including in its vision its own attempt to wrest from life those words which will turn it into text: "Je tâchais de découvrir, dans les bruits des forêts et des flots, des mots que les autres hommes n'entendaient point, et j'ouvrais l'oreille pour écouter la révélation de leur harmonie" (*OC*, I, 251). The text is indeed written not only at a remove from reality, but also at a remove from itself and its status as text, in that shadowy and difficult realm of the self-reflexive. Poetic power is sought, and discovered, through a reflection on how poetic power might be achieved, a purposefully tautological gesture which of course foreshadows the attitude of Jules at the end of the first *Éducation sentimentale*, where the artistic process becomes a "panthéisme immense, qui passe par lui et réapparaît dans l'art" (*OC*, I, 370). And it clearly marks out *Novembre*, not the first *Éducation* as has so often been stated, as the first text by Flaubert in which the principle of "impassibilité" is truly developed — if at least "impassibilité" is to be understood as the quest for an aperceptive stance which includes its own modes of representation as part of its totalising perspective.

The ironies of "impassibilité" — with its dual movement of detachment and totalisation — are elsewhere apparent in *Novembre*. As Felman and Castelein have both pointed out, *Novembre* is also a text poised between the "je" of earlier Flaubertian narratives and the "il" of later ones (Felman, 1975, 209–11; Castelein, 1986, 135–6). Two episodes literally mark out this state of pronominal in-betweenness: first, the episode with the prostitute Marie, and second, the intervention of the second narrator at the conclusion of the text. In a sense, each of these episodes achieves the same goal but by precisely contrary routes, the first leading further into the diegesis, the second leading out from it. Yet in each case, the difference of perspectives between the homodiegetic narrator and his replacement ultimately reveals their identity. The "new" perspective turns out to be the same as the old, built out of it and leading back into it. The combined effect of these two episodes is, then, to suggest that cliché is both within and without, present both in the naïve gesture to express feelings, but also in the harsh artistic judgement which coldly evaluates such expression. There is no transcendent perspective, containing the clichés of another one and remaining uncontaminated by them. The expression of cliché and the recognition of cliché are co-terminously present in each perspective offered.

The episode with Marie is framed, at the outset, in terms of cliché, and it initially appears that the prostitute can be considered a purveyor and a recycler of linguistic commonplaces, safely held at a distance by the "superior" hero-narrator. Marie, as the "fille publique", is very precisely a symbol of sameness and "overuse" (as has been argued persuasively by Brombert). Her speech is constituted quite explicitly of clichés. And yet, as has so often been pointed out, what she says has a clear relationship of specularity to the narrator's own discourse, and so it is therefore the relationship and similarity between the narrator's and the prostitute's discourses which focus our interest. On the one hand, the narrator maintains a silent distance as Marie narrates her story, and often he participates only through perfunctory gestures. This refusal to respond seems to underline the clichéd and risible nature of Marie's appeals, which are not dignified by any verbal reaction from the narrator. And yet, even as he remains silent, she is underlining their similarity ("Ne sommes-nous pas faits l'un pour l'autre? Tes espérances ne vont-elles pas bien avec mes dégoûts?" (*OC.*, I, 269) ). It is ironically Marie who suggests, again through her clichés, the sameness of their experience, so that the narrator finds himself admitting (and thus ironically recycling Marie's already derivative ideas): "Sans nous connaître, elle dans sa prostitution et moi dans ma chasteté, nous avions suivi le même chemin [...]" (*OC*, I, 268).[8] And of course, despite the narrator's apparent aloofness in the face of Marie's appeal to him, and his disappearance from her life, there is his own subsequent poeticisation of this banal experience. Cliché, the cliché of the prostituted, is turned into the poetry of despair when, in the final specular twist in the tale, the narrator himself regrets the absence of Marie in his life and expresses the same despairing desire for the absolute as she had. It is a kind of retrospective transmutation, built powerfully out of its own sense of being poised on the abyss of the ridiculous. Thus does style include within itself this speculation on its own sense of failure: "C'est pour me la rappeler que j'ai écrit ce qui précède, espérant que les mots me la feraient revivre; j'y ai échoué [...]" (*OC*, I, 271).

The same is true of the intervention of the second narrator, anticipating (as do so many of the elements of this novel) the ending of the first *Éducation* where Jules achieves an artistic stance through the recognition of his own failure. But just as Jules will delve back into his life rather than try simply to escape into some new form of art in which he can slough off the dross of existence, so too the second narrator of *Novembre* turns into the "reflection" of the first. What Sartre says of this episode — when he argues that it is a deliberate distancing act by the young Flaubert from himself, a kind of last-ditch attempt to achieve a new identity before the crisis of 1844 — must surely be wrong (Sartre, 1973, 1711–56). For Sartre underplays the identity of perspective between the second and first narrator, and where he does acknowledge evidence of it, suggests that this is Flaubert's realisation that total escape from himself, a "killing-off" of his previous self, is not quite possible. Yet there is much more than this, for what is most striking about this passage is that, although it starts out by adopting a judgemental perspective on the first narrator, it very rapidly progresses towards a sympathetic sharing of that narrator's view on the world. What was initially an "outside" view, a dissociation from the earlier narrator's mystical reveries, silly ideas and stylistic excesses, becomes in the space of a few paragraphs a kind of eulogy, certain phrases of which could figure in the descriptions of Jules at the end of the 1845 *Education*: "Il était plein de scrupules délicats et de vraie pudeur [...] Mais on le trouvait cynique, parce qu'il se servait des mots propres et disait tout haut ce que l'on pense tout bas" (*OC*, I, 273). Indeed, what is most striking here is the blending of different perspectives. The initial momentum towards detachment from the first narrator (which seems to have influenced Sartre's reading of the entire conclusion of the novel) quickly stalls, and there is a rebirth of his style and perspective. The killing-off of the old becomes very clearly its revival. Within the antitheses, it is suggested, lies identity, and at the risk in my turn of uttering a cliché, I would suggest that the whole of Flaubert's art lies here.

So the ending of this novel seems finally to reinforce the paradox of the whole text, and to underline its central quest to find novelty through its very recognition of cliché. Thus does the author seem at last to find a way forward, through his discovery of the poetic power of cliché. This, indeed, is the novelty of *Novembre*, which is a rich and complex novel despite and even because of its obvious stylistic excesses and structural failings. It is the site of a reflection about stylistic novelty which will nourish and inform all of Flaubert's later work. It is very much a laboratory in which the artist formulates, for the first time, the view that his dreamed-of language might only exist in and through the banality of human experience, indeed that novelty may ultimately not exist at all. But the discovery of nothingness — if indeed it is that — is still a discovery. Novelty is not the end product. It is, rather, to be found in the artistic process itself. *Novembre* is a crucial turning point. It is a portrait of the artist as a young man, an emerging credo, and a manifesto which will nourish not only the 1845 *Éducation sentimentale*, but the entire Flaubertian corpus.

**Notes**

[1] References giving volume and page number are to "L'Intégrale" edition of the *Œuvres complètes* (Paris: Seuil, 1964, 2 vols.).

[2] References giving volume and page number are to the "Pléiade" edition of the *Correspondance* (Paris: Gallimard, 1973–98).

[3] Felman describes *Novembre* as a "texte décisif qui marque un tournant non seulement pour l'écriture flaubertienne mais pour l'impact que Flaubert a laissé sur la conscience littéraire et critique" (Felman, 192–3).

[4] As Compagnon points out in the opening chapter of his study, modernity, though based on the idea of a break with the past, now establishes itself paradoxically as a "tradition" — a tradition whose precarious status is maintained by a constant process of self-transcendence, or breaking with itself (Compagnon, 1990, 7-13). Compagnon also points out, importantly, that this tradition of modernity only becomes possible in the wake of the French Revolution, which gives a dramatic model of rupture with the past and establishes the idea of quest for the new. Thus he stresses the historical nature of this transition: "La tradition moderne commença avec la naissance du nouveau comme valeur, puisqu'il n'a pas toujours été une valeur" (Compagnon, 9).

[5] See, for example, the following passage in *Mémoires d'un fou* (1838): "J'avais un infini plus immense, s'il est possible, que l'infini de Dieu, où la poésie se berçait et déployait ses ailes dans une atmosphère d'amour et d'extase; et puis il fallait redescendre de ces régions sublimes vers les mots, — et comment rendre par la parole cette harmonie qui s'élève dans le cœur du poète, et les pensées de géant qui font ployer les phrases, comme une main forte et gonflée fait crever le gant qui la couvre?" (*OC*, I, 231).

[6] The uncompleted *Agonies* (1838) confirms the young writer's feeling of failure to capture in language the infinite subtleties of poetic sentiment: "Oh! si j'étais poète, comme je ferais des choses qui seraient belles! Je me sens dans le cœur une force intime que personne ne peut voir. Serai-je condamné toute ma vie à être comme un muet qui veut parler et écume de rage?" (*OC*, I, 158).

[7] This oscillation from the ideal to the real occurs not only with the author's artistic ideals, but also with his amorous ones. The "poetry" of love is replaced by a mood of execration of the ideal, as in the description of the developing attitude towards Maria in *Mémoires d'un fou*, when the narrator imagines her in conjugal intimacy with her husband: "Je me mis à rire, car la jalousie m'inspira des pensées obscènes et grotesques; alors je les souillai tous les deux, j'amassai sur eux les ridicules les plus amers, et ces images qui m'avaient fait pleurer d'envie, je m'efforçai d'en rire de pitié" (*OC*, I, 239).

[8] See Brombert for a fascinating discussion of the link between images of the road, prostitution and the reflection on language in *Novembre*.

**Works Cited**

Flaubert, Gustave, *Correspondance*, ed. Jean Bruneau, 4 vols, (Paris: Gallimard, Bibliothèque de la Pléiade, 1973-98)

Flaubert, Gustave, *Œuvres complètes*, 2 vols (Paris: Seuil, 1964)

Brombert, Victor, "De *Novembre* à *L'Éducation*: communication et voie publique", *Revue d'Histoire Littéraire de la France*, 81 (1981), 563–72

Castelein, Machteld, "*Novembre* de Gustave Flaubert: un récit funèbre", *Les Lettres Romanes*, 40 (1986), 133–45

Compagnon, Antoine, *Cinq Paradoxes sur la modernité* (Paris: Seuil, 1990)

Felman, Shoshana, *La Folie et la chose littéraire* (Paris: Seuil, 1975)

Ginsberg, Michal Peled, *Flaubert Writing: A Study in Narrative Strategies* (Stanford: Stanford UP, 1986)

Sartre, Jean-Paul, *L'Idiot de la famille* (Paris: Gallimard, Vol. II, 1972)

Unwin, Timothy, *Art et infini: l'œuvre de jeunesse de Gustave Flaubert* (Amsterdam: Rodopi, 1992)

# REVERSIBLE ROLES: GENDER TROUBLE IN *MADAME BOVARY*

## Mary Orr

There has been much debate surrounding Emma's supposed "masculinity" or Charles's "feminine" attributes, and the gender stereotypes both characters mirror or subvert, as Tony Williams and others have shown so effectively.[1] It is not only the main protagonists, however, who demonstrate problematic gender behaviour. What I will seek to demonstrate is that the same is true of the male secondary figures, most importantly Lheureux, whose gender identity is very much in question. His carefully calculated strategies of cloaking and doubling his real nature and intentions are not simply economic or counter-doses of reality to Emma's love intrigues as seen in his purveying to Emma of the manteau *doublé* and the trunk for her elopement which he makes a double order. Lheureux manifests the very sinister other face of gender-bending hitherto unnoticed in the novel, primarily because the masculine power at work in him as *homo economicus* has been taken as read.[2] It is time to reveal what lies behind his double nature of merchant-usurer to uncover what hides in his closet. As Lheureux's grip over Emma tightens and his ploys all succeed, our discovery of his real nature will go some way to explaining why the reading experience of the third part of *Madame Bovary* is so distressing and harrowing, especially its ending.

Lheureux is very much the face and interface of the commodity cult which treats women as things within the male economic system of nineteenth-century France and its marriage relations. Yet the reader's first introduction to him frames him according to a behaviour more usually required of women: subservience, desire to please, desire to oblige, deference, humility, knowledge of his station. A cloth dealer à la Uriah Heep, he uses these traits as a disguise. As he will pull out endless bales of cloth to secure a sale, he comforts Emma with stories about lost dogs who eventually find their owners. His entrepreneurial nose sniffs out a potential new customer, so he turns on all the charm he possesses. His "shaggy dog" stories range over the full trawl of the exotic (Constantinople to Paris), the mythic (dogs covering a distance of fifty leagues and four rivers), and the personally verifiable which is the most incredible story of all: a dog returning after an interval of twelve years. While it is a rare comic moment in the depiction of this character (we will see a second, more calculated "joke" presently), Lheureux's interventions here do more than offset humorously the tragic loss of Emma's greyhound bitch on her journey to Yonville. The scene offers a deep insight beyond Lheureux's consolations into his real character. He is a danger to the vulnerable, for he will always turn others' loss to his own gain. Totally conversant with the laws of patriarchal economics (he knows money is power),[3] he is both calculating in his responses to women, and as we will see to men, and an adept calculator for his own *overtly* financial interests. It is these which will be shown to have an even more sinister impetus than feeding on others' yearnings or unfulfilled desires.[4] The catch-all dog stories betray increasing numerical details (his forte) and the ability to cover questionable facts with a veneer of mathematical (therefore true) evidence designed to deflect the unsuspecting from pursuing any countercheck. Accuracy we will see operates as multiplication for Lheureux: exaggerated subtraction of his real powers cloaked by deference brings ultimate addition to them. Desire to serve covers his real, and hidden, desire to dominate "customers" of every persuasion and taste. Those who prefer exotic, or practical, goods can all be lured into his double web of merchant-usurer. Then as pawnbroker, he breaks his pawns.

Lheureux's chameleon capacity to conform to any client's colour is made manifest in the later physical description of him when he goes to see Emma. He appears, as if by magic, at dusk, a time calculated for shady deals in the half-light between night and day and when Charles is not at home:

> Né Gascon, mais devenu Normand, il doubla sa faconde méridionale de cautèle cauchoise. Sa figure grasse, molle et sans barbe, semblait teinte par une décoction de réglisse claire, et sa chevelure blanche rendait plus vif encore l'éclat rude de ses petits yeux noirs. On ignorait ce qu'il avait été jadis: porteballe, disaient les uns, banquier à Routot, selon les autres. Ce qu'il y avait de sûr, c'est qu'il faisait, de tête, des calculs compliqués à effrayer Binet lui-même. Poli jusqu'à l'obséquiosité, il se tenait toujours les reins à demi courbés, dans la position de quelqu'un qui salue ou qui invite. (pp. 167–8)[5]

Like Homais, the only other rival in his power game to sew up the community, Lheureux has a dubious past, but instead of covering this up, as Homais does,[6] his tactic is to display, exhibit and confuse with a range of possibilities and doublings which are designed to mask his actual intentions.[7] His very body language smacks of the ambiguities and double intentions of his character designed to flatter and yet gain control, a body language which matches his southern "patter" soldered to a manipulative guile. Guile and wiles are of course normally associated with women as embodiments of Eve, the seductress. This character "cross-dresses" in the codes of seduction to disarm. His calculated civilities blend with a carefully chosen word designed to flatter Emma; his shop is not worthy of an *"élegante"*.[8] He has already summed Emma up and has pre-selected items which he calls "rares", designed to appeal to her vanity and frivolousness, and taste for luxury and the exotic. His appearance highlights the same play on seductive ("female") appearances. His almost "feminised" face, because beardless, appears open. The effect is compounded by its roundness and the startling effect of his white hair and contrasting beady black eyes. This black and white ex-huxter gives a dazzling verbal display made up of references to what is perceived normally as a women's world: "mercerie [...] lingerie, bonneterie ou nouveautés". However, his knowledge of such "female" things is a bluff for the altogether male business connections and suppliers he uses whose names mirror the range of his dog stories:

*Trois Frères, Barbe d'Or, Grand Sauvage.* The overall effect is designed to dazzle, as his numbers will later when Emma has fallen into debt, and into his clutches.[9]

Although it is the case that he also has male clients, Lheureux's overt market is female. Knowing that women under the *Code Civil* have no independent means, he uses their dependence on men to his own advantage, indeed to manipulate men through their wives. In Emma's case, he has already singled out her vulnerability, her penchant for whatever is non-utilitarian, assessed her probable irresponsibility and childish response to glittery objects. Like a magician who plucks items out of a hat, Lheureux has his "carton vert" whereby he combines "porteballe" and "banquier" by introducing his second profession as usurer in its "portable" form. In his ability to procure anything Emma desires from anywhere, he mirrors that magic quality of the omnipotent Parent who provides and gives everything. The reality is the negative double of the good father or the sugar daddy. As merchant *and* usurer, when his own merchandise cannot be paid for, he is the purveyor of bitter pills with sugar coatings. His obsequiousness, overemphasis of the word *"élégante"*, overrepetition of "Madame" in the whole first interview reveal him as cunning copyist of female behaviour patterns. Lheureux's imitation is therefore the *insincerest* form of flattery, betraying his real contempt of women and the feminine.

Lheureux's misogyny however goes deeper than derision of frivolous, spendthrift women. His desire is to humiliate, to subordinate, and in this we begin to glimpse the sexual ramifications of his financial power. As Rodolphe in due course, his beady black eyes spot Emma's vulnerability to seduction: "Puis ses deux mains sur la table, le cou tendu, la taille penchée, il suivait, bouche béante, le regard d'Emma qui se promenait indécis parmi ces marchandises" (p. 168). The looker is looked at, greedily, sexually. Indeed one might already begin to detect his disarticulation of her as a woman as he fragments her person into hands, neck, waist. In mock-deferential familiarity he accepts her rebuff of business that day in thinly veiled threat:

> — Eh bien! nous nous entendrons plus tard; avec les dames je me suis toujours arrangé, si ce n'est avec la mienne, cependant!
>
> Emma sourit.
>
> — C'était pour vous dire, reprit-il d'un air bonhomme après sa plaisanterie, que c'est pas l'argent qui m'inquiète... Je vous en donnerais, s'il le fallait.
>
> Elle eut un geste de surprise.
>
> — Ah! fit-il vivement et à voix basse, je n'aurais pas besoin d'aller loin pour vous en trouver; comptez-y! (p. 169)

Lheureux's "joke", his confident, soft and intimate tone, betray his real interests. These are contained in his words of alleged generosity, the giving of money to a woman. Tanner's limp interpretation of Lheureux, that he is "trying to transform the vagueness and indistinctness of erotic-emotional desire into a specific greed for an infinity of unnecessary commodities",[10] fails to grasp the *male* erotic desire also on full display in this scene. The double meaning and innuendo of Lheureux's words are extremely clear: the transaction of prostitution. He is also openmouthed, panting, enjoying the seemingly non-physical contact in close proximity with a woman (at sunset!).[11] The covert titillation and perversity of his desire are revealed in the objects he puts on display:

> Alors M. Lheureux exhiba délicatement trois écharpes algériennes, plusieurs pacquets d'aiguilles anglaises, une paire de pantoufles en paille, et, enfin, quatre coquetiers en coco, ciselés à jour par des forçats. [...] De temps à autre, comme pour en chasser la poussière, il donnait un coup d'ongle sur la soie des écharpes, dépliées dans toute leur longueur; et elles frémissaient avec un bruit léger, en faisant, à la lumière verdâtre du crépuscule, scintiller, comme de petites étoiles, les paillettes d'or de leur tissu. (p. 168)

Lheureux is the purveyor of the fetish and the fetishist *par excellence*.[12] His manipulation of the silky fabrics, female garments and sensuous ornaments is designed to fit women into sexual-erotic stereotypes of the prostitute, so that he can achieve arousal, but at one remove from engaging with the humanity of the woman who is his victim. This passage really needs to be read aloud to allow the sibilants and plosives to echo the swish of the fabric, its fall, its glittering fascination and sensuousness. Lheureux's treatment of Emma is therefore "pornographic" in so far as his real purchase of her fragments her and thereby uses her female body for his own masturbatory ends.

Lheureux's *volupté* however is as complex as his gender-blurred social behaviour and duplicated identities already discussed. His perversion derives from a blend of fetishism, exhibitionism and muted transvestism. Ordinary female garments are his trade; exotic accoutrement is the stuff of his excitement.[13] These are a special selection of his more general stock, the clothing of the brothel, of the *cocotte* in both western and eastern iconography. The "écharpes *algériennes*" tap into cliché stereotypes of the middle-eastern belly dancer. In the verbal richness of this passage, Lheureux's "coquetterie" and use of Emma as a "cocotte" emerge clearly from the items in "coco". The irony is that she will indeed use the most expensive of Lheureux's scarves, bought as consolation at Léon's departure, as "seraglio" attire, posing like an odalisque: "elle se la nouait à la taille par-dessus sa robe de chambre; et, les volets fermés, avec un livre à la main, elle restait étendue sur un canapé, dans cet accoutrement" (p. 190). Furthermore, the complex of male-female gender positions in Lheureux's "coquetterie" reverberates in that "coco" or liquorice water which Flaubert has used to describe Lheureux's face from the very outset: "teinte par une décoction de réglisse claire". Lheureux wears his double "coco" nature on his face literally and metaphorically for he is all the dictionary ramifications of a "vilain coco", the "zèbre" in all its black and white markings.

Like Rodolphe who views the female as other, foreign, as a slave ("forçat") to his desires, Lheureux represents Don Juanism, but in its more sinister guise. His design to humiliate women, watch them writhe in his clutches, then find pleasure in brutal rejection when he tires of them, actually calls for their annihilation. The chill the reader experiences as the third part of the novel unfolds, and Emma is forced to pay with her life, can now be explained by the sadism underpinning Lheureux's behaviour. However, his rapacious vampirism on female weakness, and its related dependence on men which patriarchy has constructed, co-exists with his constant need for self-assertion in that same patriarchal world. Female idealisation and veneration of powerful men who are seen to be able to give love, pleasure, or material comfort, are transsexualised by Lheureux in his thrill of making debts so large that financial repayment is impossible, and thus humiliated, the victim pays him (the powerful man) with their life.

But there are more doubles to Lheureux's vilainy and male power complex. Not only does he make a fetish of the female body: money too is a fetish designed to enhance his feeling of male potency. His perversion of male sexuality strikes against men and is thus not merely misogynistic, but misanthropic. Let us return to that crucial opening "shot" of Lheureux plying his trade:

> Et il se mit à demander des nouvelles du père Tellier, le maître du *Café Français,* que M. Bovary soignait alors.
>
> — Qu'est-ce qu'il a donc, le père Tellier?... Il tousse qu'il en secoue toute sa maison, et j'ai bien peur que prochainement il ne lui faille plutôt un paletot de sapin qu'une camisole de flanelle? *Il a fait tant de bamboches quand il était jeune! Ces gens-là, madame, n'avaient pas le moindre ordre!* il s'est calciné avec l'eau-de-vie! Mais c'est fâcheux tout de même de voir une connaissance s'en aller. (p. 169, my emphasis)

It is obviously Tellier's profligacy and debaucheries which so insense Lheureux, a Lheureux who is self-confessedly sick when he leaves Emma on this occasion ("je ne me sens pas en mon assiette; il faudra [...] que je vienne consulter Monsieur, pour une douleur que j'ai dans le dos"). By railing against Tellier's lifetime of dissoluteness, excesses, dissipation, overindulgence, he does not acknowledge his own sickness and debauchery of restraint. The fetishist has given his game away at every juncture, for he actually despises both the wanton, sexual woman and the spendthrift man. Tellier is the first victim of Lheureux's purge in the novel.[14] In the deeply ironic setting of the Comices, a paean to male economics and victorious husbandry, madame Lefrançois informs Homais of Lheureux's activities:

> On va le saisir cette semaine. C'est Lheureux qui le fait vendre. Il l'a assassiné de billets. [...]

> L'hôtesse donc se mit à lui raconter cette histoire, qu'elle savait par Théodore, le domestique de M. Guillaumin, et bien qu'elle exécrât Tellier, elle blâmait Lheureux. C'était un enjôleur, un rampant.
>
> — Ah! Tenez, dit-elle, le voilà sous les halles; il salue madame Bovary. (p. 201).

Hence, Lheureux deflects all his "male" energy into the "macho" public face of patriarchal power, money. To buy out men via their attractive wives, to buy up potent men, and hold the community purse-strings constitute the motivations of his financial activities and psycho-sexual obsessions where the accumulated coins of avarice outdo Binet's adeptness at calculation and masturbatory activities in making napkin rings.[15] Lheureux refuses the creativity, albeit repetitive and limited, of the wood-turner, but is highly entrepreneurial in cloning wooden objects, which are produced in duplicate or triplicate. I will return to his box fetish later. His delivery of Hippolyte's new wooden leg, a fetishised phallus of some pertinence to our discussion of Lheureux's desire to appear omnipotent, is a further case in point. Its uselessness to the wearer ensures the request for another to make a pair, a more practical leg "for everyday".[16] Lheureux's manipulation of substitute male and female body parts, his hoarded wealth, ally him to the only other sanctioned lone wolf and wealthiest man in the area, the lawyer Guillaumin. His castle is the grandiose outer shell of accumulated wealth and sexual gratification, whereas Lheureux's holdings are all in portable form.[17]

Lheureux's "assassination" of Tellier and purveying of the visible appendage that signals Hippolyte's demasculinisation are but secondary scenarios of the full amplification of his destruction of the *couple*, Emma/Charles, which gathers energy from the Comices episode onwards. Emma's first commission can now be reread with fuller proleptic irony in the context of duplicity, double-takes, double lives and deceptions. The "grand manteau, à long collet, *doublé*" (p. 265, my emphasis) is doubled by the double-order trunk. The double-dealer spots immediately Emma's deception and thus springs his trap; to indebtedness for his assistance as accomplice he will add debt, big debt: "Décidément, pensa Lheureux, il y a du grabuge là-dessous." It is at this point that Emma chains herself to him, literally and metaphorically:

> — Et tenez, dit madame Bovary en tirant sa montre de sa ceinture, prenez cela: vous vous paierez dessus.
>
> Mais le marchand s'écria qu'elle avait tort; ils se connaissaient; est-ce qu'il doutait d'elle? Quel enfantillage! Elle insista cependant pour qu'il prît enfin la chaîne, et déjà Lheureux l'avait mise dans sa poche et s'en allait. (p. 265)

Lheureux's haste to have Emma's chain in the intimacy of his pocket is explained when she comes to him much later with the bailiff's demand:

> Contre le mur, sous des coupons d'indienne, on entrevoyait un coffre-fort, mais d'une telle dimension, qu'il devait contenir autre chose que des billets et de l'argent. M. Lheureux, en effet, prêtait sur gages, et c'est là qu'il avait mis la chaîne en or de madame Bovary, avec les boucles d'oreille du pauvre père Tellier, qui, enfin contraint de vendre, avait acheté à Quincampoix un maigre fonds d'épicerie, où il se mourait de son catarrhe, au milieu de ses chandelles moins jaunes que sa figure. (pp. 358–9)

The chain is obviously another trinket to add to his collection. Not only do we have final proof of the connections between Tellier and Emma; this report of Tellier's demise is Emma's death knell. We are witnesses to the symbolic "coffin" of all Lheureux's victim debtors, whose fetish-like tokens are all buried in this strongbox. These are the "gages" of Lheureux's perversions, his personal sexual trophies. They are perverse doubles of the goods he put on display to sell to Emma, and the goods in his shop below. This "coffre-fort" is also the secret alter ego of the man, the deceiver who deals in "leurres".[18] Feeding on the secret vices of others (père Tellier's drink problems and Emma's "voluptés"), Lheureux finds happiness only in his own almost necrological perversions. His male pandora's box is his secret mainspring, whose transference to others is the need to provide them with the boxes (trunks and "paletots de sapin", coffins singular or tripled as is Charles's order) that define their earthly coil and his unassailability.

In complete repetition of his earlier sales strategy of ingratiation and insinuation, and, as we can now see, from his perverse love of the morbid, Lheureux next strikes when Bovary père dies. This time, however, he plays for Charles through Emma's guilt. With careful calculation, he arranges the sale of material to make mourning clothes and suggests power of attorney for her, to prevent worrying Charles at such a difficult time. He misses no opportunity to do business in person if it doubles his profit from misery. "Il n'envoya point l'étoffe, il l'apporta. Puis il revint pour l'aunage; il revint sous d'autres prétextes, tâchant cette fois de se rendre aimable, serviable, s'inféodant, comme eût dit Homais, et toujours glissant à Emma quelques conseils sur la procuration. Il ne parlait point du billet" (p. 327). Emma learns not only his lessons on finances parrot fashion. She practises and masters deception by insinuation, hinting that Guillaumin's drawing-up of the power of attorney might be unreliable, so that she gets the doubly gullible Charles not only to authorise an unlimited spending spree, but also to authorise her to see Léon. There rapidly follow the new furnishings and her piano lessons, both requiring the money that only Lheureux can supply. Like a wicked fairy, Lheureux turns up in Rouen and sees her with Léon. Now Lheureux adds threats and less veiled blackmail to his repertoire to add Charles's inheritance to her portfolio which he knows is now effectively his. It is only a matter of time, time which is running out fast, for he already has Emma's watch-chain.

The harrowing account of Emma's debts, promissory notes, and Lheureux's computations of compound interest, his accountant's precisions, the torturer's final role as hangman to put an end to fantasy once and for all (pp. 358–61, 367–9) makes the third part of *Madame Bovary* a horror story. It is a rerun of Rodolphe's "billet doux" to break with Emma with all its suicidal aftermath, only now the erotic stakes are Lheureux's, the accomplishment of another "immaculate" kill. Immediately after the revelations of the "coffre-fort", Lheureux's necrophilic and murderous intentions are revealed in his very language and the cloak-and-dagger game he plays by offloading his own ploys on his sidekick, the "mâtin de Vinçart":

— Mais j'ai été forcé moi-même, j'avais le couteau sur la gorge. [...]

— Oh! c'est bien simple: un jugement du tribunal, et puis la saisie...; *bernique!*

Emma se retenait pour ne pas le battre. Elle lui demanda doucement s'il n'y avait pas moyen de calmer M. Vinçart.

— Ah bien, oui! calmer Vinçart; vous ne le connaissez guère; il est plus féroce qu'un Arabe. (p. 359)

— Pensiez-vous, ma petite dame, que j'allais, jusqu'à la consommation des siècles, être votre fournisseur et banquier pour l'amour de Dieu? Il faut bien que je rentre dans mes déboursés, soyons justes!

Elle se récria sur la dette.

— Ah! tant pis! le tribunal l'a reconnue! Il y a jugement! on vous l'a signifié! D'ailleurs, ce n'est pas moi, c'est Vinçart. (p. 367)

Vinçart, Lheureux's "Other" as "Arabe" and "bourreau", is an anagrammatic "cousin germain" of Canivet, the doctor amputator of Hypolyte's foot and a Gallic form of victor (from the Latin "vincere"). The graphic details of this final interview show Lheureux's sadism, his algolagnia, how utterly he despises women, particularly when he turns turncoat and accuses Emma of sexual harrassment. When Emma puts her hand on his leg, he is full of misogynistic righteous indignation: "Laissez-moi donc! On dirait que vous voulez me séduire!" (p. 367).[19] This rejection narrative is but the preface to the final graphic representation of Emma's death throes, the trigger of all her further rejections and last-ditch struggles at the hands of Guillaumin and Rodolphe before her suicide. Significantly, Lheureux is in at the kill, turns up at her funeral, and uses the same pejorative words to hide his revulsion of her under the cloak of respectability: "Cette pauvre petite dame! quelle douleur pour son mari" (p. 414). Such loaded words speak of his design now on her other half, Charles. Even though Lheureux effectively "kills" two Bovarys with one stone, Flaubert does however hide from the reader Lheureux's final dealings with Charles, first via Vinçart (p. 416) and then by the final *coup*, the "saisie" (p. 420). Perhaps Charles has somehow risen above Lheureux by his naive, uncomplicated, but indubitable masculinity, because he was caught in Emma's web, not Lheureux's. But in this age ruled by money and power, Lheureux's public masculinity (like Homais's and Guillaumin's) will ensure him such an omnipotently secure place that his private, perverse, sexual proclivities will remain unchecked. Although Homais gets his "croix", he was indeed right to evaluate Lheureux as his rival in his manner of "s'inféodant". Homais's own death as a result of Lheureux's schemes and empire-building is very much suggested, for Lheureux has just opened a rival establishment to the *Lion d'or*, *Les Favorites du Commerce*, and sewn up all the trading routes in commissions. This not only literally overlays Tellier. It strikes at Madame Lefrançois and also Homais. Lheureux, then, is Flaubert's answer to Vautrin. His diabolical machinations and control of the economies of money and desire make him the "carton vert" copy of patriarchy's underbelly.

Where male critics have failed to see such licence and licentiousness, a gender-conscious optic reveals that this "minor" character is lethal and especially so in his protean manipulations of gendered behaviours.[20] Flaubert has created a character whose male pandora's box unleashes the miasma of patriarchy's male sicknesses as well as those female maladies male critics have concentrated in Emma. Flaubert is posing some awkward questions concerning male sexual insecurity, even paranoia in this text. I would go further and claim that patriarchy's own fear of impotence is under threat of exposure even though Lheureux's fear of emasculation is carefully wrapped in silks and exhibited in male economic terms. On the scale of patriarchy's abuse of woman, he doubles by day the Jekyll who wants woman to be decorative to ensure her wispy insubstantiality; by night (or dusk) he lives the Hyde who feeds on woman to provide a fetishistic sexual release; and in secret, he is the sadean Don Juan, the pornographer who seeks necrophilic release, whereby the victim is simply snuffed out and kept as a voodoo trophy in his special strongbox. What is of course even more sinister is his overinflated sense of invincibility (via Vinçart), whereby men too are his victims for having too much of the real potency he desires so that his own tenuous ego requires a circumscribed space all to itself, bound with iron and carefully guarded. Parasite and vampire, seducer and destroyer, those roles specially favoured in decadent representations of Woman, find their male model in this shape-, money- and sex-changer, Lheureux. His "coffres" reveal not only a lethal box of tricks, but conceal the "restes" of his victims in an all-encompassing coprophilia, a desire which links the liquorice stain on his face with this "coco" 's discourse.

### Notes

[1] Tony Williams, "Gender Stereotypes in *Madame Bovary*". See also Stephen Heath, *Flaubert: Madame Bovary* and Diana Festa-MacCormick, "Emma Bovary's masculinisation: Conventions of Clothes and Morality of Conventions"; J-L. Mercier, "Le sexe de Charles".

[2] Heath, op. cit., 58, dismisses the character thus: "(Lheureux after all is just a minor capitalist swindler, clever enough for Yonville-L'Abbaye)." More recently, in his study of characters in relation to "le Beau", Girard, 1995, 76, sees Lheureux quintessentially as the "marchand de nouveautés", the dealer in transient fashions; and 51, "Cupide et non lubrique, il ne perçoit leur pouvoir [des femmes] qu'au travers des folies auxquelles elles s'abandonnent quand elles sont amoureuses [...]. Le créancier d'Emma mesure l'attrait d'une femme à sa prodigalité." Picard, 1973, 93 is one of the few critics to take Lheureux to task as more than just a clever and ruthless financial operator: "Toujours est-il que, dans la mesure où l'on accepte de considérer une structure romanesque comme une succession d'*épreuves de la réalité*', lesquelles de ramènent toujours [...] à un affrontement initiatique, le véritable partenaire d'Emma ne saurait être ni Charles, ni Rodolphe, ni Léon, comparses châtrés, ni Homais, ni Bournisien, doubles et spectateurs: c'est Lheureux, détenteur d'argent (et d'ailleurs fournisseur des cravaches et jambes de bois)."

[3] Neefs, *Madame Bovary de Flaubert*, 39 notes the huge influence the usurer had during the Second Empire and quotes Sorlin to verify the lynchpin position of such a figure in the circulation of wealth in the provinces. The "lent travail occulte et corrosif de Lheureux" has another face that male critics have overlooked, as we shall discover.

[4] Kaplan, *Female Perversions*, 514–5 writes that "L'heureux [sic] [...] was a master of figuring out just how far and how much he could transform Emma's sexual hunger into a hunger for material goods [...] he understood concretely that he could turn a healthy profit from the unsatisfied yearnings of Emma Bovary."

[5] Page references are to *Madame Bovary* (Paris: Garnier Flammarion, 1986), as this edition is readily available to students.

[6] "Il avait enfreint la loi du 19 ventose an XI, article 1$^{er}$, qui défend à tout individu non porteur de diplôme l'exercice de la médecine; si bien que, *sur des dénonciations ténébreuses,* Homais avait été mandé à Rouen, près M. le procureur du roi, en son cabinet particulier. Le magistrat l'avait reçu debout, dans sa robe, hermine à l'épaule et toque en tête. C'était le matin,

avant l'audience. On entendait dans le corridor passer les fortes bottes des gendarmes, et comme un bruit lointain des grosses serrures qui se fermaient. Les oreilles du pharmacien lui tintèrent à croire qu'il allait tomber d'un coup de sang; il entrevit des culs de basse-fosse, sa famille en pleurs, la pharmacie vendue, tous les bocaux disséminés; et il fut obligé d'entrer dans un café prendre un verre de rhum avec de l'eau de Seltz, pour se remettre les esprits.

Peu à peu, le souvenir de cette admonition s'affaiblit, et il continuait, comme autrefois, à donner des consultations anodines dans son arrière-boutique. Mais le maire lui en voulait, des confrères étaient jaloux, il fallait tout craindre; *en s'attachant M. Bovary par des politesses, c'était gagner sa gratitude, et empêcher qu'il ne parlât plus tard,* s'il s'apercevait de quelque chose" (151–2, my emphasis to highlight the parallels with Lheureux's appearance and behaviour).

[7] Neefs, *op. cit.*, 80 notes the phonic doublings which match his double roots, "doublant sa faCOnde méridionale de CAUtèle CAUchoise, drôle de 'COCO' comme le dit la réitération phonique, et qui retire d'ailleurs, quand il le faut derrière sa doublure, le nommé Vinçart de Rouen". I would point out the material verification of this wonderful observation. Among the many items Lheureux shows Emma are doubles doubled: "enfin, quatre COQUEtiers en COCO" (my emphasis).

[8] Such flattery matches Rodolphe's later verbal seduction of Emma at the Comices agricoles.

[9] See 346, for example.

[10] Tanner, *Adultery in the Novel*, 297.

[11] Note how similar this meeting is to the one Emma has with Guillaumin where she does ask for money.

[12] Kaplan, op. cit., 34–6: "A fetish is designed to keep the lies hidden, to divert attention away from the whole story by focusing attention on the detail [...] a complex symbol that expresses and yet conceals all the forbidden and dangerous wishes, all the losses, abandonments, anxieties, and terrors of childhood [...]. A sexual fetish is significantly more reliable than a living person. It expects neither commitment nor emotional engagement [...]. The French analyists say the term *fetish* originates in the French word *factice*, meaning 'ficitious' [sic] or 'artificial'. The sexual *fetish*, of course, represents artificial or imaginary genitals, and sexual fetishism is about the creation of fictitious and artifical genitals. The mighty penis in eternal erection, the phallus, is as fictionalized as the shortchanged clitoris or mutilated vagina that the phallus is meant to repair and compensate for. [...] Whereas the French would like to claim the fetish as an emblem of their tolerance for sexual diversity, it is generally held that the word derives from the Portuguese *feitiço*, meaning 'false' or 'worship of false values'. The word is said to have come into existence to describe 'the veneration for, and precious status of, seemingly useless objects

that the Portuguese explorers had found in various African religions'. Marx spoke of 'commodity fetishism' to describe capitalism, with its worship of useless commodities as though they were sacred objects."

[13] I will leave it to more qualified psychoanalysts to discuss, but there is much which might suggest deep transsexuality in Lheureux, that combination of cross-dressings which is designed to mask, with as many layers of gender-stereotyping as possible, a "female" within and hence goes some way to explaining his misogyny. Kaplan's discussion of transvestism helps to elucidate these complex perversions, but not explain them all in Lheureux's case, which is intensely complex. "Transvestism is a variation on fetishism. The basic requirement for sexual arousal is that the person dress in the clothes of the opposite sex, literally cross-dressing. Transvestism was found in many ancient cultures and was labeled a disease by Hippocrates. But until the recent past, around 1930, the medical profession could not decide which variety of cross-dressing was 'true' transvestism and which was perhaps an aspect of homosexuality or which perhaps a symptom of sex-gender dissonance, which doctors today label transsexualism. Throughout history women had been cross-dressing as a way of gaining access to educational, social, and political powers that would otherwise be denied them. [...] Very few females cross-dress as a means of enabling sexual arousal. [...] When the impulse to cross-dress is quiescent, the transvestite dresses in hyper-masculine clothing. [...] They enjoy participating in the macho activities that fortify them against the feminine wishes and tendencies that impel them to act out their perverse fantasy." *(op. cit.,* 23–5)

[14] Picard, *art.cit.*, 95 acknowledges Tellier's place as Lheureux's first victim in the novel, but assumes that, as debtor, this is why the innkeeper is evicted. Later, on page 96, Picard gives an explanation for Lheureux's motives in destroying Emma in terms of class and economic differences: "Emma, finalement, a bien rencontré l'autre-de-classe en Lheureux, dans la mesure où *elle a cessé d'appartenir à la même classe* que lui; la pauperisation et la prolétarisation des Bovary les renvoient au peuple d'où ils viennent de sortir."

[15] Tanner, *op. cit.*, 257 has noted that "Binet's hobby is solipsistic, masturbatory, yet it pervades society (he is after all the tax collector)." I would argue that his solipsistic activity is like Lheureux's but at a further remove from encounter with flesh-and-blood women for the symbolisation of women makes it non-destructive.

[16] "Le pilon en était garni de liège, et il avait des articulations à ressort, une mécanique compliquée recouverte d'un pantalon noir, que terminait une botte vernie. Mais Hippolyte, n'osant à tous les jours se servir d'une si belle jambe, supplia Madame Bovary de lui en procurer une autre plus commode" (256–7). This is a male member with a mechanical spring action *par excellence*. Lheureux also uses the opportunity of buying the second leg — a "curiosité masculine" — to seduce Emma into more Parisian "curiosités féminines".

[17] Lheureux's wares, the "paquets d'aiguilles anglaises, une paire de pantoufles en paille", find their reincarnation in Guillaumin's projections of his legal omnipotence, his English furniture and the embroidered slippers Emma wears when he sexually harrasses her.

[18] Both senses of the French are highly pertinent: illusions and decoys to snare his prey.

[19] We have now seen that Lheureux's behaviour towards Emma is but the perverse form of sexual harassment.

[20] It seems no accident that social mimicry is further emphasised in the ending through the actions of truly "minor" characters. As Privat, *Bovary Charivari*, 29-30, has pointed out, Félicité (Emma's maid) elopes wearing Emma's clothes and "en volant tout ce qui restait de la *garde-robe*" (my emphasis). It is highly significant that her name is as much an antinomic signifier as *Lheureux* and operates as its female "match". Furthermore, her partner is none other than Théodore, servant to Guillaumin, Lheureux's co-evil equivalent, but negative re-embodiment of Emma's father, Théodore Rouault. The wheels have come full circle, but in a downwards spiral.

**Works Cited**

Flaubert, Gustave, *Madame Bovary* (Paris: Garnier Flammarion, 1986)

Festa-MacCormick, D., "Emma Bovary's masculinisation: Convention of Clothes and Morality of Conventions", in *Gender and Literary Voice,* ed. J. Todd, (New York: 1980)

Kaplan, L. J., *Female Perversions* (London: Penguin, 1991)

Mercier, J.-L., "Le sexe de Charles", *Nouvelle Revue Française*, 309 (1978), 47–62

Neefs, J., *Madame Bovary de Flaubert* (Paris: Classiques Hachette, 1972)

Picard, M., "La prodigalité d'Emma Bovary", *Littérature,* 10 (1973), 77–97

Privat, J-M., *Bovary Charivari: essai d'éthno-critique* (Paris: CNRS Éditions, 1994)

Tanner, T., *Adultery in the novel: contract and transgression* (Baltimore & London: The Johns Hopkins University Press, 1979)

Williams, Tony, "Gender Stereotypes in *Madame Bovary*", *Forum for Modern Language Studies*, 28 (1992), 130–9

# FLAUBERT AND THE SLEEPING BEAUTY: AN OBSESSIVE IMAGE

## Anne Green

"Voilà encore une de mes ambitions! Écrire un conte de fées", confided Flaubert to Louise Colet in 1853.[1] A close reading of his work reveals that one fairy tale in particular haunted Flaubert, and so pervasive is its presence in his work that in a very real sense he may be said to have carried out his ambition. This article aims to show that a remarkable relationship between clusters of details and images associated with *La Belle au bois dormant* recurs in one novel after another, and that Flaubert exploited and transformed the fairy tale with an almost obsessive persistence.[2] Echoes of the Sleeping Beauty are clearly present as early as *Novembre* and continue to appear in his writing, repeatedly, for the rest of his life.

The reader hardly needs to be reminded that the essentials of that fairy tale are the good and evil wishes bestowed on the Princess at birth, the enchanted hundred-year-long sleep into which she and her household fall when she pricks her finger, and the impenetrable forest of trees and thorns which springs up around her castle and conceals all but the tops of its turrets; then, one hundred years later, the arrival of the Prince for whom the thickets part, his entry into the castle and his progression upstairs, past sleeping courtiers, into the golden bedchamber where he bestows the magic kiss on Beauty; and finally the celebrations as the household awakes and the Prince and Princess are married. It also goes without saying that the tale is usually interpreted as a metaphor for an awakening to sexual and social maturity and for the period of passivity that precedes it.[3] But Perrault's version (which Flaubert knew and admired)[4] continues the story beyond the familiar ending. His second part carries an undercurrent of terror that is absent from twentieth-century retellings: the Prince is warned that the castle is haunted by evil sorcerers or by a child-eating ogre, and there is a brief moment of horror as he enters the castle courtyard and finds apparently lifeless bodies everywhere. Furthermore, in Perrault's version the story continues after the Prince's marriage, and describes how his wicked mother plots to kill and eat his wife and their two young children before she comes to a satisfactorily gruesome end in a vat of serpents.

In Flaubert's earlier works, however, this element of horror is largely absent. What is particularly retained from the fairy tale plot is the Prince figure's enchanted progress towards the upstairs room where the Princess awaits his kiss. In *Novembre*, for example, we find the hero making his way, alone and with mounting desire, through deserted streets[5] and forests until finally, after a journey which "dura un siècle", he reaches his goal — a mysterious and apparently deserted house with shuttered windows. As in the fairy tale, all obstacles melt away: "personne ne passait, je m'avançai, je m'avançai; je sens encore le contact de la porte que je poussai de mon épaule; elle céda; j'avais eu peur qu'elle ne fût scellée dans la muraille, mais non, elle tourna sur un gond, doucement, sans faire de bruit." Just as the Prince climbs the staircase and passes by silently occupied rooms before he comes to Sleeping Beauty's golden chamber,[6] so does the hero of *Novembre*: "Je montai un escalier [...] je montais toujours [...] personne ne me parlait" and he enters a room bathed in pale golden light where he finally gazes in wonderment at "une figure d'une adorable beauté", and bestows his "premier baiser d'amour" (*OC*, I, 259). In this text, Flaubert makes the fairy tale association quite explicit: the hero's dreams of his future are described as being "comme dans les contes de fée" (*OC*, I, 249), and he returns for more of the beautiful woman's "magie terrible" (*OC*, I, 261). But Flaubert is here exploiting the well-known story in contradictory ways. While its essential quality of innocence and desire enhance that aspect of his own narrative, the absence of the fulfilment and happy ending associated with the fairy tale is stressed. "Ce n'était donc que cela, aimer! ce n'était donc que cela, une femme!" says the hero, adding that "l'illusion évanouie laisse en nous son odeur de fée, et nous en cherchons la trace par tous les sentiers où elle a fui" (*OC,* I, 261). Later, he contemplates Marie's beauty as she sleeps, but the Sleeping Beauty image is undermined when she wakes and warns him that she is no Princess (*OC,* I, 264). Marie, of course, is a prostitute rather than an innocent young girl, while the hero, unlike his forceful counterpart in the fairy tale, is repeatedly described as passive, waiting, dreaming, sleeping. So in *Novembre* the reader's attention is repeatedly drawn to a fairy-tale subtext which helps to evoke a dreamlike state of desire and innocence and expectation while at the same time undermining those ideals and highlighting a theme of disenchantment which is summed up by the hero at the end: "'Pourquoi ne suis-je pas resté là-bas?' Et il pensa avec amertume à la joie de son départ" (*OC,* I, 276).

The second chapter of *Madame Bovary* carries similar resonances. Charles sets off for Les Bertaux alone, travelling past trees and hedges and clumps of thorns,[7] and finally arrives at the courtyard, where his horse shies in unexplained terror (echoing the moment of horror as the fairy-tale Prince enters the courtyard of the castle). Like the hero of *Novembre*, Charles is here presented in a double perspective, identified not only with the active Prince who wins through to the castle, but also with the passive qualities of the sleeping Princess. But as Bruno Bettelheim has pointed out, the characteristics projected onto the male and female heroes of fairy tales are in fact two artificially separated aspects of a single process: "even when a girl is depicted as turning inward in her struggle to become herself, and a boy as aggressively dealing with the external world, these two *together* symbolise the two ways in which one has to gain selfhood: through learning to understand and master the inner as well as the outer world."[8] Flaubert appears to have understood this well for his own characters often share traits with more than one of the fairy tale's stereotypes. Thus Charles sleeps for most of the journey, and the narrative draws attention both to his somnolent passivity, and to his active, professional side: "Encore endormi par la chaleur du sommeil, il se laissait bercer au trot pacifique de sa bête. [...] Charles, de temps à autre, ouvrait les yeux; puis, son esprit se fatiguant et le sommeil revenant de soi-même, bientôt il entra dans une sorte d'assoupissement où, ses sensations récentes se confondant avec des souvenirs, lui-même se percevait double, à la fois étudiant et marié, couché dans son lit comme tout à l'heure, traversant une salle d'opérés comme autrefois" (*OC*, I, 578). This double perspective continues as Charles enters the farmhouse and goes upstairs to the bedroom where he suddenly falls under Emma's spell at the moment when she pricks her finger on a needle.[9] The narrative moves swiftly to another room where (somewhat incongruously in the farmhouse context) there is a small table set for two, with silver goblets, standing next to a surprisingly grand canopied and curtained bed[10] — an account which echoes the swift movement from royal table to royal bed in Perrault's version of the fairy tale.[11]

Clearly Charles is no fairy-tale Prince, and he cannot "awaken" Emma. On the contrary, when Félicité later compares Emma to M. Guérin's daughter who suffered from "une manière de brouillard qu'elle avait dans la tête" that vanished after she married, Emma retorts that her own lethargy came on after her marriage: "Mais, moi, reprenait Emma, c'est après le mariage que ça m'est venu"(*OC*, I, 611).

As the novel continues, the essential elements of the fairy story are repeated and reworked. Part I ends with Emma again pricking her finger, this time on her wedding bouquet whose dusty and discoloured orange blossom conveys the disillusionment of her marriage to Charles, and this second pricking alerts us to the fact that she is now waiting for another lover. But Emma's next love affair also fails to conform to the fairy tale, which Flaubert evokes in ironic fragments in his description of Homais's Sunday gathering: everyone present falls asleep, leaving Emma alone with Léon who subsequently, in a farcically suggestive moment, pricks his fingers on the cactus plant he carries in his lap for her but finds it impossible to declare his love (*OC*, I, 607–8).

With the introduction of Rodolphe, however, the rhythm of the fairy story reasserts itself more strongly, although perhaps not in the way one might expect. For Emma now plays the Prince's role, while Rodolphe is cast as the Sleeping Beauty: Emma, who "entrait dans quelque chose de merveilleux"(*OC*, I, 629), is suddenly overwhelmed by a desire to see Rodolphe, and she sets off when everyone is asleep, swiftly crossing the countryside without glancing behind her, seeing only the tips of the château's weather vanes silhouetted against the sky. She enters the château with the dreamlike ease that is so characteristic of the fairy story: "Elle y entra, comme si les murs, à son approche, se fussent écartés d'eux-mêmes"; she goes upstairs, pushes open a door, and "tout à coup, au fond de la chambre, elle aperçut un homme qui dormait. C'était Rodolphe. Elle poussa un cri." And she kisses him (*OC,* I, 629). In this passage full of fairy-tale resonances the apparent reversal of male and female stereotypes is less significant than the fact that Flaubert goes on to subvert the uniqueness of the fairy tale's climax. After this first magical visit, each time that Charles goes out early in the morning the episode is repeated and is progressively stripped of its magic. On subsequent occasions Emma's journey across country is impeded by a range of obstacles (including an encounter with Binet, whose comment to her, "*ça pique*", has a special resonance in the context of the fairy tale)[12] and by the time she arrives in the room bathed in golden light where Rodolphe lies asleep[13] she is muddy, dishevelled and out of breath. And, of course, there is no fairy-tale ending.[14]

Whereas a subverted Sleeping Beauty subtext seems perfectly in keeping with the story of Emma Bovary's disappointed dreams of romance, its presence in Flaubert's Carthaginian novel is perhaps more surprising. Yet the same elements recur in *Salammbô* in a series of variations on the fairy tale. Mâtho, the Prince figure, is determined to enter the impregnable castle which houses the object of his desire, but in contast to the effortlessness of the Prince's entrance his attempts to find a way in repeatedly and dramatically fail.[15] It is only with Spendius's help that he does finally penetrate into Carthage, but their journey still lacks the dreamlike ease of the fairy story: instead it is a spectacularly arduous expedition during which both are injured and almost drown (*OC,* I, 715). Once they emerge from the aqueduct, however, the fairy-tale element starts to take over. The two men move silently and effortlessly through undergrowth and pass with ease through one defensive wall after another while "la ville entière dormait"(*OC,* I, 716). They step past women sprawled asleep on the ground, and observe the play of light on the faces of other sleeping figures *(OC,* I, 717). The moment of horror that occurs in

Perrault's version of the fairy tale as the Prince is about to enter the castle is echoed and protracted in *Salammbô* as the two men encounter chilling monstrosities "confondues les unes par-dessus les autres dans un désordre mystérieux qui épouvantait"(*OC*, I, 718) during their passage through the outer chambers: "La terreur, plus que les murs, défendait les sanctuaires. Mâtho, à chaque pas, s'attendait à mourir"(*OC*, I, 717).[16] But whereas the magical ease of the Prince's progress is interrupted only for a moment, the journey of Mâtho and Spendius towards their Sleeping Beauty is now no longer effortless and resolute: they become lost in the labyrinthine passages, Mâtho wants to run away, and it is only when Spendius has found the sacred veil and given it to him that Mâtho seems to reassume the Prince's role: "Tout à coup il s'écria: — Mais si j'allais chez elle? Je n'ai plus peur de sa beauté? [...] Me voilà plus qu'un homme maintenant. Je traverserais les flammes, je marcherais dans la mer! Un élan m'emporte!" (*OC*, I, 718). It is an essential feature of the Sleeping Beauty tale that the Prince must act alone: he is the chosen one for whom the trees part. Mâtho, however, despite his bravura, is not yet ready to go unaccompanied, and with Spendius leading the way the two men set off again, passing more sleeping women. This time their journey is interrupted by a huge monkey which tries to grab the veil from Mâtho who does not dare fight back. This strange encounter contrasts curiously with an incident in the second part of the fairy tale where the precocious courage of the Prince's young son is demonstrated in a sword fight with a great monkey:[17] Mâtho's unwillingness to fight indicates that he is not yet ready for the heroic role.

It is only when he finally leaves Spendius behind and bounds alone up the steps of the palace that Mâtho's quest takes on the fairy tale's dreamlike ease: "à chacun de ses pas une immensité plus large l'entourait, et il continuait à gravir avec l'étrange facilité que l'on éprouve dans les rêves"(*OC*, I, 719). Just as Perrault's Prince passes rooms where courtiers lie asleep before entering the "chambre toute dorée" where the beautiful Princess lies in a bed hung with draperies,[18] so Mâtho passes apartments where "il crut voir [...] des personnes endormies"(*OC*, I, 719) before entering the chamber with its golden floor where Salammbô lies asleep in her curtained bed. At this point, however, the two stories dramatically part company: in the fairy tale the Prince's words of love are perfectly reciprocated by Beauty, and the whole palace wakes for joyful celebrations of the wedding feast, whereas Mâtho's declaration of love is met with incomprehension and horror by Salammbô: "Sans comprendre ce qu'il sollicitait, une horreur la saisit"(*OC*, I, 720). Her screams for help rouse the inhabitants of the palace whose reaction is in stark and parodic contrast to the rejoicings of the awakened household in the fairy tale:

> Un grand tumulte monta en ébranlant les escaliers, et un flot de monde, des femmes, des valets, des esclaves, s'élancèrent dans la chambre avec des épieux, des casse-tête, des coutelas, des poignards. Ils furent comme paralysés d'indignation en apercevant un homme; les servantes poussaient le hurlement des funérailles, et les eunuques pâlissaient sous leur peau brune. (*OC*, I, 720)

Here again, just at the point where we would expect the symbolic kiss, the Sleeping Beauty parallel breaks off: violence and terror intrude, and the narrative reaches a particularly disturbing crisis. This violent disruption of the fairy tale intimates the impossibility of a happy ending. As if to underline the point, Salammbô is here identified less with Sleeping Beauty than with the wicked fairy as she curses Mâtho and invokes his death with such venom that he cries out as if pierced — by a sword rather than a spindle, it is true, although it is surely significant that one of the dreadful injuries that finally bring about his death should indeed be a stab wound from a spindle.[19] The optimism of the Sleeping Beauty fantasy vanishes quickly from this novel. Far more so than Flaubert's earlier works, it is coloured by the dark undercurrents of violence, jealousy, infanticide and cannibalism which run through the second part of Perrault's *Belle au bois dormant*.

In *L'Éducation sentimentale*, on the other hand, the fairy-tale element provides an almost comic underpinning to the relationship between Frédéric and Madame Arnoux. Frédéric feels compelled by fate to make his way to her house — "la fatalité l'ordonnait"(*OC*, II, 31) — but he suffers a series of farcical failures. Flaubert teases the reader by starting to evoke the familiar elements of the journey — the hero makes his way alone, everything falls silent, people fall asleep,[20] — but then interrupting it. At one point Frédéric is even described as standing outside Madame Arnoux's house imagining himself magically transported through its walls to the sleeping beauty within: "il restait les yeux collés sur la façade, — comme s'il avait cru, par cette contemplation, pouvoir fendre les murs. Maintenant, sans doute, elle reposait, tranquille comme une fleur endormie, avec ses beaux cheveux noirs parmi les dentelles de l'oreiller, les lèvres entre-closes, la tête sur un bras." But Frédéric is no Prince: "Il s'éloigna"(*OC*, II, 36).[21]

Shortly after, Madame Arnoux pricks her finger on the pin that Arnoux has inserted into her bouquet, and this creates a new bond between her and Frédéric: "maintenant il y avait entre eux un lien nouveau, une espèce de complicité" (*OC*, II, 39). It is not until the Creil episode, however, that Frédéric finally assumes the role of Prince. After overcoming a number of obstacles he plunges into the countryside, and in the distance he sees "un petit château à tourelles" alongside factory chimneys.[22] He enters the Arnoux building (which, significantly, is surrounded by a garden featuring four spiky cacti),[23] climbs the staircase to the first floor, and finds it strangely deserted: "Il ne rencontra personne dans l'escalier. Au premier étage, il avança la tête dans une pièce vide; c'était le salon. Il appela très haut. On ne répondit pas; sans doute, la cuisinière était sortie, la bonne aussi; enfin, parvenu au second étage, il poussa une porte" — and there is Madame Arnoux looking as if she has just been roused from sleep, in a half-open dressing gown, with her hair hanging loose. As Frédéric enters she thrusts a pin into her hair, cries out, and vanishes.[24] When she reappears, Frédéric is enchanted ("tout l'enchanta", *OC*, II, 78) and this, of course, is the moment in the fairy tale when the kiss should be bestowed. Instead, "Frédéric se retenait pour ne pas la couvrir de baisers"(*OC*, II, 78). When he does dare to talk to her of love (with the help of a volume of Musset) she dismisses his words as "criminel[s] ou factice[s]"(*OC*, II, 80) and in an echo of Marie's warning to the hero of *Novembre* that he must not mistake her for a Princess, Madame Arnoux reminds Frédéric that she is not "une grande dame!"(*OC*, II, 81). So once again, the story of Sleeping Beauty provides an ironic commentary on Flaubert's plot. The fact that the fairy tale has a consistent structure and a plot that moves swiftly towards its familiar and happy ending serves to emphasise the absence of those features in the novel: in *L'Éducation sentimentale* with its "défaut de ligne droite"(*OC*, II, 162) there can be no neatly reassuring resolution.

*La Légende de St Julien l'Hospitalier* offers Flaubert's most complex and revealing reworking of the Sleeping Beauty story, where the full horror of the second part of Perrault's version becomes clear. The fairy tale atmosphere is immediately evident in the opening description of the castle with its pointed turrets and paved courtyard guarded by dragon-gargoyles.[25] It stands in the middle of a forest and is encircled first by a moat, then by a ring of stakes, and finally by "une forte haie d'épines"(*OC*, II, 178). The disused portcullis, the arrow-slits clogged with swallows' nests and the sleeping guard all serve to evoke the fairy tale's sense of suspended animation. Similarly, the apparently gratuitous reference to the fact that the châtelaine "filait à la quenouille" every morning (*OC*, II, 178) is reminiscent of the "bonne Vieille [qui] était seule à filer sa quenouille" in Perrault's version of the fairy tale, and on whose spindle the Princess pricks herself.[26] The parents in Flaubert's story have a baby as a result of praying to God (*OC*, II, 178), just as the King and Queen of Perrault's fairy tale finally produce a daughter after many prayers.[27] The feasting which follows both births is in each case accompanied by extraordinary prophecies about the baby's future, both good and bad. But in Flaubert's story, of course, the baby is a boy, and the unfurling of the tale takes a very different course, although events are always underpinned by the general fairy-tale world which Julien inhabits: "Il délivra des reines enfermées dans des tours. C'est lui, et pas un autre, qui assomma la guivre de Milan et le dragon d'Oberbirbach", and in classic fairy-tale fashion he will refuse any reward for his services until he is finally offered the Emperor's beautiful daughter in marriage (*OC*, II, 182).

In *St Julien* the elements of the fairy tale are even more dispersed than in Flaubert's previous works: details associated with one character in the fairy story are transferred to a different character in the *conte*, and events are separated or multiplied or reversed. There are two different castles and several descriptions of Julien's mysterious progress through the forest towards them. But most importantly, the familiar key details are present once again, more numerous than ever — the prophecies, the piercing, the encircled castle, the deep sleep, the silence, the mysterious arrival at the castle, the kiss — although not, perhaps, in their expected places. Julien's obsession with hunting carries implicit sexual overtones which are quite explicit in the second part of Perrault's fairy story where the Prince's daily hunting expeditions are a cover for his clandestine visits to Beauty and result in the birth of their two children.[28] Julien makes many expeditions into the thorn-filled forests but instead of penetrating them with ease to find a Sleeping Beauty and gain ultimate maturity, he returns "couvert de sang et de boue avec des épines dans les cheveux et sentant l'odeur des bêtes farouches. Il devint comme elles" (*OC*, II, 180). In one description of him entering the forest, making his way across vast distances and following an avenue of tall trees (as in Perrault)[29] which form a triumphal arch to lead him to the place where he massacres the stags, Flaubert draws attention to the dreamlike ease of the hunt which, like the Prince's progress, takes place outside time and space: "Il était en chasse dans un pays quelconque, depuis un temps indéterminé, et par le fait seul de sa propre existence, tout s'accomplissant avec la facilité que l'on éprouve dans les rêves" (*OC*, II, 181). But Julien's quest is also threatening and terrifying, and his sudden, mysterious arrival alone at the castle is no triumph:

> Son cheval était perdu; ses chiens l'avaient abandonné; la solitude qui l'enveloppait lui sembla toute menaçante de périls indéfinis. Alors, poussé par un effroi, il prit sa course à travers la campagne, choisit au hasard un sentier, et se trouva presque immédiatement à la porte du château. (*OC*, II, 181)[30]

Clearly Julien is unready to play the Prince's role to the full, slipping instead into Beauty's passive mode as soon as he arrives at the castle by taking to his bed for three months (*OC*, II, 181). His disturbing journey has brought him back to his parents' castle rather than to one housing an unknown Sleeping Beauty, and the oedipal implications of this twist to the fairy tale are underlined when shortly after this episode Julien comes close to carrying out the piercing prophesy by almost impaling his father with a sword and his mother with a javelin (*OC,* II, 182).

It is fitting that the story's climax should reflect the fullest reworking of the Sleeping Beauty tale. The topos of the penetration through the woods and into the castle recurs, with Julien's wife and parents asleep in his castle and Julien again in the forest, alone: "C'était partout un grand silence [...]. Le bois s'épaissit, l'obscurité devint profonde" (*OC,* II, 184). He carries on, cutting his way through the creepers and accompanied by a nightmarish throng of animals, most of which are associated with stinging or piercing (serpent, porcupine, insects, and monkeys which pinch him) until he sees the rooftops of his castle above the trees. Although this is not the Prince making his magical, dreamlike entry into the castle, nor the usual bewitched sleeping Princess, the tale derives from both. The familiar events unfold, but with added horror and violence: "Sa soif de carnage le reprenait; les bêtes lui manquant, il aurait voulu massacrer des hommes. Il gravit les trois terrasses, enfonça la porte d'un coup de poing" and enters the bedchamber where he bends down to plant the magic kiss on the sleeping Princess — only to feel a beard against his lips. The intensity of horror that this kiss engenders, followed as it is by the murders of his parents, is even greater than in *Salammbô*. The oedipal overtones of the second part of the fairy tale are brought close to the surface here, and as in the fairy tale they are resolved by the mother's violent death. *St Julien* offers the darkest and most troubled reworking of the story. Paradoxically, this tale is the only work discussed to have a "happy" ending, but that is bought at the terrible cost of bypassing the whole central focus of the fairy tale: the wife — who, it must be noted, has never figured as a Sleeping Beauty — is cast off; the beloved parents who lie in her bed and receive the kiss in her place are killed; and Julien spends the rest of his life in isolation from human society.

The essential elements of the Sleeping Beauty story clearly play a vital part in shaping Flaubert's fiction and in forming and challenging the reader's expectations, as well as offering an intriguing insight into the hidden workings of

Flaubert's mind. Just how deeply these fairy-tale images were embedded in his unconscious is indicated by the strange, feverish nightmare recorded by Flaubert in 1856, which he claimed was a recurrence of one he had had eight years earlier.[31] The richly ornamented Louis XIV bed on which he lies motionless in his dream, as if in a trance; the hideous old crone with supernatural powers who has him under her spell; the repeated references to being pricked or pierced; the near-conflation of the lubricious old woman and the loving presence of his mother; the old hag's transformation into a scaly green serpent; and the recurring images of marriage and death, all overlaid with a tone of intense horror — these elements of the nightmare sequence are all easily recognisable as central images in the full Sleeping Beauty story. The obvious sexual content of the nightmare, with its mixture of sexual desire and revulsion and its hints of an unresolved oedipal conflict, seems to be a vivid representation of Flaubert's anxieties about moving from a stage of passive dependence to a fully mature adult life. This problem is one that is dramatised in virtually all his fiction and perhaps helps to explain why the story of Sleeping Beauty, which tells of the successful overcoming of such difficulties, recurs with such obsessive regularity in his work.

On the other hand, as Bettelheim has observed, the Sleeping Beauty story shows that "a long period of quiescence, of contemplation, of concentration on the self, can and often does lead to highest achievement,"[32] and it is interesting to note that, according to Maxime Du Camp, Flaubert himself had a tendency to lapse into long periods of quiescence and passivity until the end of his days. Du Camp's tone reflects his exasperation at his friend's failure to become fully awakened to a normal life: in terms strikingly reminiscent of the fairy tale he writes that Flaubert often seemed to shut himself off from the outside world and float in a permanent dream from which he could barely rouse himself,[33] and his further description of Flaubert in a state of virtual suspended animation within a safe, familiar circle offers us a remarkable image of the writer himself as a Sleeping Beauty.[34] We may therefore conjecture that Flaubert's preoccupation with the Sleeping Beauty story stemmed from his recognition, at some deep level, that remaining in a state of *songe permanent*, however limiting, was necessary if he was to produce great art.

**Notes**

[1] *Correspondance*, II, 376.

[2] Surprisingly, the few critics to have noticed Flaubert's interest in the Sleeping Beauty see its presence only in *Madame Bovary*. Juliette Frølich examines the influence of Perrault on Chapter 2 of *Madame Bovary* in "Charles Bovary et *La Belle au bois dormant*". Michel Picard relates the fairy tale to Emma's dream world which he sees as a refusal to recognise the class struggle.

[3] See Bettelheim, 225–7.

[4] "J'ai lu ces jours-ci les contes de fées de Perrault; c'est charmant, charmant. [...] Et dire que, tant que les Français vivront, Boileau passera pour être un plus grand poète que cet homme là" (*Corr.*, II, 209).

[5] "Il y avait peu de monde dans les rues; [...] il n'y avait pas d'oiseaux autour des clochers" (*OC*, I, 258). References giving volume and page number are to "L'Intégrale" edition of the *Œuvres complètes*, 2 vols (Paris: Seuil, 1964).

[6] Perrault, 247.

[7] "Ces trous entourés d'épines que l'on creuse au bord des sillons"; "un trou de haie"; "Charles se baissait pour passer sous les branches" (*OC*, I, 578).

[8] Bettelheim, 226. The point is clearly borne out in *Novembre*, where the hero says of Marie, "elle dans sa prostitution et moi dans ma chasteté, nous avons suivi le même chemin." (*OC*, I, 268).

[9] "Tout en cousant, elle se piquait les doigts, qu'elle portait ensuite à sa bouche pour les sucer.

Charles fut surpris de la blancheur de ses ongles. Ils étaient brillants, fins du bout, plus nettoyés que les ivoires de Dieppe, et taillés en amande. [...] Ce qu'elle avait de beau, c'étaient les yeux: quoiqu'ils fussent bruns, ils semblaient noirs à cause des cils, et son regard arrivait franchement à vous avec une hardiesse candide" (*OC*, I, 579).

[10] "Deux couverts, avec des timbales d'argent, y étaient mis sur une petite table, au pied d'un grand lit à baldaquin revêtu d'une indienne à personnages représentant des Turcs" (*OC*, I, 579).

[11] Perrault, 249: "Et après souper, sans perdre de temps, le grand Aumônier les maria dans la Chapelle du Château et la Dame d'honneur leur tira le rideau." This point is also made by Juliette Frølich, pp. 204–5. Frølich also identifies the Prince's wicked mother with Charles's first wife (ibid., 207–9).

[12] On one of these occasions she is is confronted by Binet and "le long canon d'une

carabine qui semblait la tenir en joue" (*OC,* I, 630). See also Perrault, 247, where the Prince "entre dans la salle des Gardes qui étaient rangés en haie, la carabine sur l'épaule."

[13] "Rodolphe, à cette heure-là, dormait encore. [...] Les rideaux jaunes, le long des fenêtres, laissaient passer doucement une lourde lumière blonde" (*OC,* I, 630).

[14] Paradoxically, the ending of *Madame Bovary* carries echoes of another set of fairy tales, those which start with a poor young man setting out for market to sell his last cherished possession, and on the way encountering a stranger who will magically transform his life to one of happiness and prosperity. This is surely the topos evoked on the final page of *Madame Bovary* when Flaubert writes of Charles: "Un jour qu'il était allé au marché d'Argueil pour y vendre son cheval, — dernière ressource, — il rencontra Rodolphe"(*OC,* I, 692). But of course no magical transformation takes place, and Charles dies the next day.

[15] "Plus de vingt fois il fit le tour des remparts, cherchant quelque brèche pour entrer. Une nuit, il se jeta dans le golfe et pendant trois heures, il nagea tout d'une haleine. Il arriva au bas des Mappales, il voulut grimper contre la falaise. Il ensanglanta ses genoux, brisa ses ongles, puis retomba dans les flots et en revint" (*OC,* 1, 711).

[16] Cf. Perrault, 247: "tout ce qu'il vit d'abord était capable de le glacer de crainte: c'était un silence affreux, l'image de la mort s'y présentait partout, et ce n'était que des corps étendus d'hommes et d'animaux, qui paraissaient morts."

[17] The theme of the fight with a monkey is a recurrent one in Flaubert's writing. Cf. *La Spirale,* where he refers to "la cour d'un roi — un fils de roi faisant des armes avec un singe" Katherine Singer Kovacs, *Le Rêve et la vie. A Theatrical experiment by Gustave Flaubert,* 100. See also Flaubert's account of dreaming about a monkey, where it is clear that the monkey represents aspects of Flaubert's self: "Je ne sais si c'est moi qui regarde le singe ou si c'est le singe qui me regarde — les singes sont nos aïeux. [...] Et ma mère me dit [...] 'comme il te ressemble!'" (*Voyage en Italie et en Suisse, OC,* II, 460).

[18] Perrault, 247.

[19] *OC,* I, 720, and later "une jeune fille, dissimulant sous sa manche la pointe d'un fuseau, lui fendit la joue" (*OC,* I, 796).

[20] See, for example, "le quartier latin, si tumultueux d'habitude, mais désert à cette époque"; "les grands murs des collèges, comme allongés par le silence"; "ronflement"; "la dame du comptoir bâillait", etc. (*OC,* II, 32).

[21] Paradoxically, he *is* a fairy-tale Prince for Louise Roque: according to a manuscript note Frédéric "lui produit l'effet d'un Prince de Conte de fées" (Nouvelles Acquisitions Françaises 17611, fol. 14, cited Williams, 67).

[22] This castle is a reminder of the castle Frédéric sees from the boat at the beginning of the novel, and which inspires an idyllic fantasy that contains several elements of the fairy story: "Un

peu plus loin, on découvrit un château, à toit pointu, avec des tourelles carrées. Un parterre de fleurs s'étalait devant sa façade; et des avenues s'enfonçaient, comme des voûtes noires, sous les hauts tilleuls. Il se la figura passant au bord des charmilles. A ce moment, une jeune dame et un jeune homme se montrèrent sur le perron, entre les caisses d'orangers. Puis tout disparut" (*OC*, II, 11).

[23] Cf. Léon's cactus (*OC*, I, 607–8) and p. 68 above.

[24] "Et elle avait les deux mains levés, retenant d'une main son chignon, tandis que l'autre y enfonçait une épingle. Elle jeta un cri, et disparut" (*OC*, II, 78).

[25] See the "dragons, dans la cour du château" which pull the Good Fairy's coach (Perrault, 245).

[26] Perrault, 244. Flaubert's description of the amplitude of the châtelaine's costume echoes the kind of effect that he most admired in Perrault: "Les cornes de son hennin frôlaient le linteau des portes; la queue de sa robe de drap traînait de trois pas derrière elle"(*OC*, I, 178); see also Flaubert's letter of 16 December 1852 to Louise Colet: "J'ai lu ces jours-ci les contes de fées de Perrault; c'est charmant, charmant. Que dis-tu de cette phrase: 'La chambre était si petite que la queue de cette belle robe ne pouvait s'étendre.' Est-ce énorme d'effet, hein?" (*Corr.*, II, 209).

[27] See Perrault, 243: "Ils allèrent à toutes les eaux du monde; vœux, pèlerinages, menues dévotions, tout fut mise en œuvre, et rien n'y faisait. Enfin pourtant la Reine devint grosse." Note also that the only named character in Flaubert's tale is the protagonist, a characteristic feature of fairy stories. For further discussion of the absence of naming in fairy tales, see Bettelheim, 40.

[28] Note that, like Julien, the Prince keeps his marriage secret from his parents.

[29] See Perrault, 247: "il marcha vers le Château qu'il voyait au bout d'une grande avenue où il entra, et ce qui le surprit un peu, il vit que personne de ses gens ne l'avait pu suivre, parce que les arbres s'étaient rapprochés dès qu'il avait été passé."

[30] See Perrault, 247: "il vit que personne de ses gens ne l'avait pu suivre, parce que les arbres s'étaient rapprochés dès qu'il avait été passé."

[31] *Corr.*, II, 606–9.

[32] Bettelheim, 226.

[33] "Flaubert s'arrêta; [...] de plus en plus il restreignit son champ d'action et se concentra dans sa rêverie du moment; il restait parfois des mois entiers sans ouvrir un journal, se désintéressant du monde extérieur [...]. Les notions de la vie réelle lui échappaient et il semblait flotter dans un songe permanent dont il ne sortait qu'avec effort" (Du Camp, 201).

[34] "Bien souvent [...] nous avons été surpris de voir que nul progrès ne s'était accompli en lui, que ses facultés déjà considérables n'avaient point acquis l'ampleur qu'elles promettaient et qu'il tournait invariablement dans le même cercle, dans le cercle que nous connaissions, et dont

si souvent nous avions fait le tour avec lui. Il semble avoir eu toutes ses conceptions vers la vingtième année et avoir dépensé sa vie entière à leur donner un corps" (Du Camp, 202).

**Works Cited**

Flaubert, Gustave, *Carnets de Travail*, ed. Pierre-Marc de Biasi (Paris: Balland, 1988)

Flaubert, Gustave, *Correspondance*, 4 vols, ed. Jean Bruneau (Paris: Gallimard, Bibliothèque de la Pléiade, 1973–98)

Flaubert, Gustave, *Œuvres complètes*, 2 vols, ed. B. Masson (Paris: Seuil, 1964)


Bettelheim, Bruno, *The Uses of Enchantment. The Meaning and Importance of Fairy Tales* (London: Penguin, 1978)

Du Camp, Maxime, *Souvenirs littéraires*, ed. Daniel Oster (Paris: Aubier, 1994)

Frøhlich, Juliette, "Charles Bovary et *La Belle au bois dormant*", *Revue Romane*, 12 (1977), 202–9

Perrault, Charles, *Contes*, ed. Marc Soriano (Paris: Flammarion, 1989)

Picard, Michel, "La Prodigalité d'Emma Bovary", *Littérature* 10 (1973), 77–97

Singer, Katherine Kovacs, *Le Rêve et la vie. A Theatrical Experiment by Gustave Flaubert* (Harvard: Harvard Studies in French Literature, no. 38, 1981)

Williams, D. A., *"The Hidden Life at its Source". A Study of Flaubert's "L'Éducation sentimentale"* (Hull: Hull University Press, 1987)

# FLOWER FIGURES AND THE GENERATION OF IRONY IN *MADAME BOVARY*

## Paul Andrew Tipper

As we approach the new millenium and the wheels of the Flaubert industry continue to turn one hundred and twenty years after his death, one might review the shape that critical studies of his works have assumed, with an eye to introducing fresh hermeneutic insights into a field of output that is of necessity becoming more and more narrowly focused and having increasingly only specialist appeal. Exhaustive thematic studies of Flaubert's *œuvre* are in abundance, as are readings both iconoclastic and esoteric; and as for the thematic irrecuperability that was the staple of the 1970s Flaubertian, the swing of the critical pendulum is once again reaffirming Flaubert's mimetic practice, the emphasis being put squarely on his *lisibilité*.[1]

What new things remain to be said? Should we perhaps be approaching the texts in a millenial spirit, boldly widening the ambit of investigation so as to encompass scientific, social and cultural issues in an evaluation of works which are, quite simply, a cornucopia of textual riches? Could we somehow relate the thematic body of Flaubert's writings to an extratextual culture that must have influenced him as he pored over endless volumes before writing a single word of his own? And, crucially, might this relationship uncover a hidden textual dimension that traditional rhetoric cannot capture? It is with these considerations in mind that the present study seeks to explore how textual connotation might be enriched when an aspect of the cultural climate in which Flaubert was writing might be seen to enhance the ironising intent at the core of this frenetic stylist's work. The aspect in question is the language of flowers,[2] a lexicon mingling sentimentality and pseudo-science which grew into a flourishing paraliterary genre in the early part of the nineteenth century and of which, interestingly, Flaubert professed a total lack of knowledge.[3] Whether the man is protesting too much or not we cannot know for certain, nor does it really matter. What will be explored in this study are the ways in which a language of flowers that was in the air at the time Flaubert was writing can be seen to add an ironically suggestive dimension to the already highly-charged floral patterning that permeates the semantic fields of *Madame Bovary*.[4]

The spotlight, then, will still be firmly centred upon textual poetics, but with the inclusion of extra-literary elements in the evaluative process. Any comprehensive study of suggestive motifs or of patterns of deep-structure signifieds must be done in a systematic fashion. When the focus of investigation becomes more complex and refined, then the system employed to process data must in its turn be equally sophisticated if textual amplitude is to be adequately represented. Ever mindful of the charge made against structuralist analysis of narrative that "what started as a powerful protest against ruling critical assumptions ended up as just one more available method for saying new things about well-worn texts",[5] the "millenial" critic will wish to meet such objections by rejuvenating the texts themselves. Such a rejuvenation could imply breathing new life into an old text by using a purpose-built methodology, an analytical framework specifically engineered to assist study of a particular motif, where "scientific" reliability combines with the flair and imagination of an insightful reader to proffer an analysis that is at once both empirically accurate and aesthetically coherent. Over the years, my own work has taught me that the nature of Flaubert's rhetoric lends itself particularly well to structural analyses with its "symphonic organization of themes, the controlled opposition and parallelism of characters and events, the delicately reverberant counterpoint of symbols and images".[6] Meaning in Flaubert is to be abstracted from a subtextual grammar, the study of which should be undertaken *differentially* rather than *referentially*. It is within these *differences* that connotative potential lies, inside the semiological gaps that meaning is born. With specific reference to Flaubert's *style artiste*, Lilian Furst observes the sea change his writing practice introduces into nineteenth-century French literature: "In Flaubert, description is integrated into the action, and tends to diminish in quantity, and change in quality, as density yields to suggestiveness." [7] The present study will now focus on one aspect of this suggestiveness, adopting a formal approach to the analysis of floral topoi in *Madame Bovary*.

Analyses of discrete motifs in *Madame Bovary* are too numerous to chart here and some work has already been done on organic imagery in the novel in Don Demorest's pioneering study[8] and also in an article by Margaret Church,[9] yet no work to date has concentrated on what appears to be a rich source of suggestive patterning — the flower image. Many of Flaubert's symbolic encodings encourage a double reading with regard to Emma's predicament; a subjectivised viewpoint (corresponding to Emma's outlook) and an objectivised viewpoint (corresponding to textual truth), where the latter may be seen in some way to provide a corrective to Emma's distorted self-image. It can be expected, then, that such dichotomous relations should yield ironic tensions in their polarised elaboration. Typically, this is what happens in the myriad differential relations that the text of *Madame Bovary* allows an analyst to establish. Motifs which appear, initially at any rate, to be "innocent" take on a pernicious colouring when evaluated in aggregate. This is because Flaubert's aesthetic patterns of meaning always cohere with the novel's thematic determinism, which involves a shift from misguided subjective optimism to truthful objective pessimism. Jonathan Culler comments on precisely this ironic mechanism that is part and parcel of Flaubert's *modus operandi* in connection with Emma:

> Irony reduces the particular forms of her desire to clichéd illusions and denies them the status of valuable alternatives to a mediocre world [...]. One knows Emma's fate, not because one is given to understand that characters like her in such a situation will necessarily meet a tragic end, but because one gains as one reads a knowledge of how the book will treat her

aspirations and activities. Emma is fated to be destroyed by the irony of Flaubert's prose.[10]

It is the irony underlying an allusive floral semiology that we now wish to explore.

The analysis of flower figures in *Madame Bovary* — and there are some thirty four different varieties — is a complex undertaking for three reasons. Unlike a study of, for example, the novel's references to horses, vehicles, footwear, paper, or liquids, flowers are *a priori* value-charged signifiers carrying a weight of culturally-encoded signifieds which both the text and the analyst are working with. Secondly, flowers carry idealising implications[11] which may not easily be devalorised by internal structuration, where a flower reference is to underpin negation inhering in an episode, a character trait or, indeed, in an overarching theme. And thirdly, flower imagery, as it was widely exploited by nineteenth-century poets and novelists, is synchronous with *Le Langage des fleurs*, a highly sentimentalised system of communication that was popularized by Charlotte de Latour from 1819 onwards.[12] Each of these factors has the potential to generate irony: the irony produced when *a priori* value clashes with textually-established value, whatever the pole of the respective value might be; the irony produced when the text negates a traditionally-encoded idealized flower; the irony, or possible double irony, produced when one bears in mind that *Le Langage des fleurs* was already a Romantic commonplace at the time Flaubert was composing *Madame Bovary*,[13] thus providing him with already culturally ironised sense-units that might undermine Emma's rose-coloured outlook on to her world. Yet these issues, in their turn, require the analyst to decide whether the approach to the evaluation of the floral motif should be, in the words of Northrop Frye, as "an autonomous verbal structure",[14] implying a total disregard of any externally-imposed cultural framework of signification — and a disregard of authorial design — or whether inclusion of the rich possibilities for irony inhering in *Le Langage des fleurs* should be brought to bear on the analysis, irrespective of whether it was consciously or subconsciously exploited by Flaubert in his private poetics. In short, does *our* awareness of the nineteenth-century language of flowers add something to the already suggestive ironies that Flaubert's textually-encoded flower motifs generate? And this is the critical point, for it is present-day reader's reception of the text that allows new interpretations to grow; it is the power of suggestion in the text that *contemporary* scholars are able to highlight that is all-important. It is difficult to assess the extent of Flaubert's knowledge of nineteenth-century flower culture. On the one hand, he could profess total ignorance of it, insisting that the inclusion of some "fleurs significatives" in a birthday letter to Louise Colet was Du Camp's idea, a frivolous gesture which he sees as being somehow beneath his dignity and of which he understands nothing of "le sens symbolique".[15] On the other hand, there is a suggestion in a letter to Du Camp himself that he knew something about conventional flower usage. Roses, everlasting flowers and violets were all placed on Caroline Flaubert's body following her untimely death in childbirth in March 1846. Such flowers, of course, are generally understood by French people to be redolent of death and thus any ascription of precise conscious knowledge to Flaubert regarding "fleurs significatives",[16] or indeed their conventional associations, would be potentially misleading. The ritual use of flowers, both in Flaubert's day and in our own, has been fully documented.[17]

An interesting historical feature of *Le Langage des fleurs* is the extreme popularity of its eleventh edition, which was published in 1847.[18] This date coincides, approximately, with Flaubert's and Louise Colet's initial meeting. He may not have known very much about the popularised flower codes of the day, but Louise's irksome demands for sentimental floral tributes must certainly have been a constant reminder of their saccharine potential.[19] In the *Correspondance* Flaubert draws on the flower figure as a metaphor for inferior Art, in the formula *fleurs blanches*, a shorthand code for the tawdry Romantic verse that was proliferating in the 1850s.[20] So the generic term *fleurs* has negative connotations in Flaubert's pronouncements on aesthetic matters and all verse which is deemed by him to be cloying is perforce branded artistic detritus from which sickly *fleurs blanches* might spring. A possible corollary to this, of course, is the *intent* to present fictional flowers in a similar way, to have the reader see them as other than Emma does, to see them as loaded with a romanticised cargo that masks, temporarily, the reality which she will be eventually led to confront. Flower paradigms contribute to metatextual operations which make this reality an inescapable truth.

Any comments on authorial intention can only ever be conjectural since no manifest acknowledgement of the language of flowers, or of the values a nineteenth-century readership would have recognised in it, is anywhere in evidence in Flaubert's writings. The nineteenth century did see a wealth of works, both poetry and prose, with flowers built into their titles, and which drew on the intrinsic figurative breadth these super-valent signifiers have always enjoyed. But with the exception of an early work, *Un Parfum à sentir* (1836), Flaubert's titles are never obviously florally-encoded; and at the risk of giving yet more hostages to fortune one should remember that green-fingeredness was patently *not* a gift in the Flaubert family. Perhaps its unique claim to floral fame came in the form of Flaubert's mother's maiden name, *Fleuriot*, for it has been well documented that his grandfather — incompetent horticulturalist that he was —, owned a collection of dried flowers, consigned to a supposedly meticulously-labelled *herbier*, but which were, in fact, all incorrectly named.[21] In the face of the circumstancial evidence outlined here, one may be disinclined to accept the possibility of conscious authorial input in relation to culturally-imbued flower systematisation and be inclined, rather, to accept that textual patterning is charged with its own intrinsic dynamic, an artistic goal that Flaubert always aspired to anyway.[22] Any *extra* suggestivity that is produced when *Le Langage des fleurs* is considered concurrently with Flaubertian textual poetics should be noted and vicariously revelled in. The present study, then, will explore floral signifieds as they are produced differentially in *Madame Bovary,* any corroborative or, indeed, new meanings being seen as the product of cross-fertilisation between a private poetics and extra-textual signifieds. One caveat, however, should be noted. The analyst should be wary of the temptation to mobilise culturally-encoded signifieds as a convenient stop to fill a textual gap where it appears that no meaning is produced by internal paradigmatic patterning. And the reverse is also true: cultural values should not be omitted from the discussion simply because they add nothing new or because they conflict with the text's own value-system.

The question of inclusion or non-inclusion of extra-textuality as it is embodied in flower signifiers (*Le Langage des fleurs*) to enhance meaning raises a further methodological problem for a reading of Flaubert and in the context of other literary works. A methodology for flower analyses must incorporate mechanisms whereby meaning can be refined to distinguish the arbitrary from the figurative, the eccentric from the consonant. The remainder of this study will explore how such a methodology can be implemented to tease meaning out of flower paradigms in *Madame Bovary* (or any other text). The treatment will not be exhaustive (only two flower types will be studied) but it is hoped that the "synthetic" approach adopted here will offer an example of how the methodology may be exploited for all other flower figures in the novel.

## MAIN STEPS

(i)  consultation of computer-compiled concordances,[23] where available, to determine the frequency of occurrence and semantic contexts of flower figures

(ii)  organisation of flower figures into paradigms

(iii)  analysis of flower figure distribution by part/chapter/page/paragraph

(iv)  analysis of the metonymic/metaphoric links between flower figure and character

(v)  analysis of result of cross-referencing between dissimilar flower figures in similar semantic contexts

(vi)  analysis of the global symbolic yield of the flower figure (effected after consideration of the 16 variables)

(vii)  evaluation of this yield in the light of the conventional flower figure value

## VARIABLES

### (I) Flowers in extra-fictive space

(i)  flower figure visually striking (e.g. colour/size)?

(ii)  flower figure monochromatic/polychromatic?

(iii)  flower figure delicately/sturdily/coarsely textured?

(iv)  flower figure fragrant/odourless?

(v)  flower figure ephemeral/long-lasting?

(vi)   flower figure indigenous to France/exotic?

(vii)  flower figure wild/cultivated?

(viii) flower figure a spring/summer/autumn/winter blossom?

**(II) Flowers in fictive space**

(i)    flower figure foregrounded in context (e.g. subject of verb)?

(ii)   flower figure overdetermined?

(iii)  flower figure distinctly configured (e.g. bouquet)?

(iv)   flower figure open/closed?

(v)    flower figure decorative/natural?

(vi)   flower figure in soil/water/cut/scattered?

(vii)  flower figure qualified (e.g. colour term)?

(viii) flower figure real/figurative/artificial/fantasised?

**SYNTHESIS**

Formulation of conclusions based on analyses, where the analyst will determine the textual or private meaning(s) generated by the text's paradigmatic structures. The methodology in its theoretical application is tripartite in that it involves the exploration of the frequency of flower figure occurrences, the study of their semantic contexts and the formulation of evaluative conclusions based on the textual configuration of analogous flower figure paradigms. In practice, however, the three discrete analytical processes fuse as the analyst draws on his knowledge of the texts in a judicious and selective application of the variables which are relevant to each flower figure under scrutiny at each of the stages of the methodology.

The methodology insists in the first instance on the primordial importance of the total number of flower figure references according to *type* (e.g. jasmine) rather than *genus* (e.g. climbing plants), since any analysis of floral genera would be of little interest or value, their very disparate semantic contexts militating against the formulation of coherent signifieds. The first stage of the analytical operation may be carried out with the aid of computer-compiled concordances, where these exist, in conjunction with a meticulously detailed written record of all flower figure contexts. This part of the methodology will focus on flower/context/character configurations. After careful exploration of these, it should be possible to give an overall interpretation of how a particular flower paradigm functions in context. What is interesting is that a general interpretation should vindicate the coherent thematics operative in *Madame Bovary*, since each flower paradigm can be seen to reflect, in metatextual fashion, some aspect of the novel's progressive shift from positive to negative, from a *mirage doré* to *vulgarité*.[24] The methodology, then, underlines the central importance of flower figures as corroborative indices that are grouped by similarity and difference into meaningful clusters to constitute thematic significance. At this stage, it would be helpful to have to hand a list of those meanings ascribed to individual flower types by Latour in her *Le Langage des fleurs* in order to ascertain at a glance how the wider cultural associations chime with textual meaning. Though a detailed account of her work is beyond the scope of this study, suffice it to say that she lists some threeee hundred items, with both value-ascriptions and explanations for them.[25]

The second section of the methodology comprises a series of variables, marshalled only where they are relevant to the specific floral paradigm under critical examination. The first set of eight variables pertain to flowers in the "real" world, to their absolute qualities irrespective of how they might be exploited in the fictional universe. The second set of eight variables focus specifically on the treatment of flower figures in fictional space. The complexity of the operation merely brings into sharp relief the critical role of the reader in the production of meaning. The analyst must recreate the text to interpret it, and interpretations, though broadly similar, will differ in their degrees of subtlety according to the perceptiveness of the reader. For flower paradigms, as for all others, there will never be just one meaning.

Before going on to apply the methodology to two discrete flower paradigms in *Madame Bovary*, a few prefatory comments regarding flower figure ordering and distribution in the novel should be made. *Madame Bovary* is a novel strewn with flowers, fruit-trees and vegetation. All outdoor scenes will notionally contain blooms and trees, even where these are not specifically alluded to in the text. For example, *le jardin* is closely developed in relation to Emma's moods and the reader pictures beeches and poplars every time it is evoked, simply because we know them to be there. Clearly, it is not feasible to use the methodology to evaluate such an unquantifiable referencing-system. Therefore, it might be useful to identify a "trigger" for a particular flower's inclusion in the evaluative process — perhaps analysing only those flowers which are known to produce a *bloom*. This move in itself allows optimum figurative potential to be extracted from flowering plants, where these are associated with Emma, because Emma is seen, on a number of occasions, as a metaphorical flower. She buds, blooms, fades, dies; she grows towards light and heat; and if the flower can be viewed as a sexual organ that is brightly coloured and heavily scented to guarantee its pollination, then Emma, too, is brightly coloured and sweet-smelling as she seeks out sources of stimulation.

The 36 references to the generic term *fleur(s)* in *Madame Bovary* regulate the overall floral tonality of the novel. As the most highly-charged figuratively, and therefore the most emotive, of all flower references, their distribution across the novel is of interest independently of other specific flower types. Distribution analysis reveals the following: in a novel of 352 pages, 36 *fleur(s)* references average out at 1 reference every 10 pages. This, in itself, is not without significance for the tonal qualities with which they invest the text, as outlined above. What is more compelling, however, is how references are distributed by part. Part I, with 66 pages, contains 12 *fleur(s)* notations, or 1 reference per 5.5 pages. Part II, with 165 pages, contains 15 *fleur(s)* references, or 1 per 11 pages. Part III, with 121 pages, contains 9 *fleur(s)* references, or 1 per 13 pages.[26] The implications of this are that the first part of *Madame Bovary* is "overflowered", with 60% more than the average number of references; the second part is "underflowered", with 16% fewer than the average number of references; and the final part is "underflowered", with 25% fewer than the average number of generic floral references. Inferences bearing on the novel's thematic sweep can be made from this data — and this is something one may do even before progressing beyond stage three of the method —, where flowers underpin the shift from illusion to reality from Part I to Part III. If flowers initially contribute to the creation of a chimerical atmosphere where all is promise at the end of the rainbow for Emma, then their frequency of incidence dwindles in Part II as Emma becomes increasingly discontented with her emotional life. Finally, the frenzied merry-go-round of dream and despair gathers momentum, and as repositories of ideality, flowers, with their strong associations with an ideal existence, eventually wither and die. The trend is clear; Emma's journey is from dream to an ironised deflation of that dream as the wished-for ideal is shattered. The progressive diminution of a floral presence in Emma's life underpins this truth.

It would be a happy coincidence if the dwindling of specific flower types from Parts I to III were accompanied by a modulation from positive to negative in the culturally-encoded value-ascriptions of all of the flower types to be found in *Madame Bovary*. Unfortunately, this is not the case. In Part I, 75% of flower references carry a positive value (e.g. *jasmin* = amiability),[27] while 25% carry a negative value (e.g. *rhododendron* = danger).[28] In Part II, 86% are positively charged (e.g. *acacia* = platonic love), while 14% are negatively charged (e.g. *troène* = prohibition); Part III sees 75% of flower types charged positively (e.g. *myositis* = forget-me-not), while 25% carry a negative value (e.g. *géranium* = melancholy spirit). Overall, 70% of flower references in *Madame Bovary* carry positive conventional charges. Is one to see a latent irony even in this? Does the very text of *Madame Bovary*, in its negative thematics, imply a subversion of the powerfully-invested idealisation phenomenon that was *le langage des fleurs* in the 1820s and thereafter? And does Emma's tragic end reiterate the dangers inhering in the pursuit of illusion, in the pursuit of what emerges, in the last analysis, as no more than Romantic cliché? The text, it would seem, can work with, or against, cultural encodings in a variety of engaging ways.

The second stage of the method allows us to establish 16 discrete floral paradigms in *Madame Bovary*.[29] The traditional meanings which will be noted at stage seven of the method are all taken from Latour, where possible. The essence of this work and a shorthand of meanings she ascribes to flowers is now more readily available in Beverly Seaton's *The Language of Flowers*, which includes tables of floral value-ascriptions from French, English and American sources. Excluding all references to the generic term *fleur* and non-specific floral configurations such as *bouquet*, there are some 60 flower references in the novel; 40 of these may be slotted into the following "sets": *iris* (2 instances, "message"); *poiriers* (3 instances, "comfort");[30] *rose* (8 instances, "love"); *églantiers* (2 instances, "pleasure and pain"); *fleurs d'oranger* (3 instances, "chastity"); *géranium* (2 instances, "melancholy spirit"); *marguerite* (3 instances, "innocence"); *ravenelles* (3 instances, "fidelity in adversity"); *seringas* (2 instances, "fraternal love"); *jasmin* (4 instances, "amiability"); *myositis* (2 instances, "forget-me-not"); *troènes* (2 instances, "prohibition"); *nénuphars* (2 instances, "purity of heart");[31] *clématite* (3 instances, "artifice"). Now the analyst is in a position to explore semantic contexts, taking due account of similarities and differences between them, and to decide which of the variables will be operative as each stage of the method is worked through. Once the paradigms have been established, attention should be focused on the eighth of the second set of variables, as the status of a reference, literal or metaphoric, can have wide-reaching implications in terms of the degree of figurative charging with which a flower term may be invested in its paradigm. Scrutiny of the 16 paradigms established reveals that all specific flower references are to *literal* flowers in *Madame Bovary*. The *fleur(s)* paradigm, by contrast, contains 4 figurative references, occurring in extra-diegetic comparisons (pp. 67, 110, 132, 199) and 5 dream references, all fantasised by Emma (pp. 59, 113, 201, 231, 297). There is clearly a marked potential for metaphoric and ironic investment in *fleur(s)*, because the dream-flowers are all cliché, occurring as they do in contexts of sentimentality, luxury and projected elopements with lovers real (p. 201) and imaginary (p. 297). The paradigm carries an extra load of irony when it is noted that only *fleurs* in the plural figure in fantasies. Typically immodest and excessive in her desires, Emma never dreams of single flowers; the sheer *démesure* of her aspirations, then, condemns her to eternal frustration.

All of these pointers and data contribute to a heightened awareness of textual patterning. The methodology will guide analysis on a number of aspects. For example, at stage seven, one should be alert to the fact that a blossom does not always carry the same meaning as the larger plant. For example, cherry tree bears the meaning "good education"; a cherry blossom denotes "insincerity". For reasons of consistency, if nothing else, the bloom must be the focal point of the investigation and analysis. Stage three of the method reveals that in the first two-and-a-half chapters of Part II there are no flower references at all. Metaphorically, this fact connotes the aridity of Emma's existence prior to meeting Léon. One sees the irony in the Bovarys' move to Yonville, for the soil there is evidently not conducive to the growth of flowers and no more conducive to fantasy wherein flowers might figure. Just as a particular soil type is needed for *bonheur* (p. 42), so a particular climate is needed for *amour* (p. 61); proleptically, an absence of flowers suggests that Yonville will be no improvement on Tostes. And there is even a kind of inverse irony at work in the detail of the cherry trees not thriving at La Vaubyessard, the very locus of all of Emma's future dreams, and yet obviously thriving in Tostes, since it is the "cerises superbes" that earn the Bovarys an invitation to the ball (p. 47).[32] Sections of the novel which are "flower-poor" may be compared to those which are "flower-rich"; and it is not surprising that Part I, Chapter viii, covering the episode at La Vaubyessard, is flower-strewn. Indeed, chapters which chart emotional peaks in Emma's life are spangled with flowers (see, for example, Part II, Chapter iii).

By way of a demonstration of the precise manner in which the methodology may be exploited, let us now turn to the analysis of two paradigms in *Madame Bovary* — *iris* and *poirier*. *Iris,* with its two literal references, constitutes a framing floral topos in that it impacts as the first flower reference of the novel and as the antipenultimate, making its second appearance during Emma's funeral procession. The early reference to it is unusual (p. 16) in that its scent (variable I, iv) is perceptible, but the flower itself is not visible. Charles has just set Rouault's broken leg and is now in the downstairs sitting-room, where the *odeur* of *iris* emanates from an oak cupboard, and the fragrance of it is mingled with that of damp linen. Stage four of the method links Emma and Charles metonymically with the flower figure, and stage five reveals how the figure slowly begins to assume an ulterior textual investment. If, at this stage, Emma has written to Charles to mend a broken leg, then the episode where she Rodolphe writes to Emma to break her heart comprises similar semantic elements. Rodolphe takes a tin from a cupboard from which emanates an *odeur* of damp dust and faded roses (p. 206). It is as though this later episode serves to negativise Emma's dream at its inception, for the irises which are set within a magical context of future hope for Emma and Charles are concealed in this cupboard of oak, to be replaced at the moment of Rodolphe's betrayal — which will trigger Emma's suicide attempt — by faded flowers (variable II, vii) which will ultimately be transformed into Emma as a dead flower as she lies in her oak coffin (p. 334) pervading the atmosphere *with senteurs humides* (p. 340). Metaphorically, there is a poetics of concealment, a semantics of dampness and a suggestive paradigm of box-like structures centred around the primacy effect of iris fragrance. It would be inappropriate at this juncture to engage in a discussion of concealment metaphors in *Madame Bovary*, yet one can see how detailed study of a single flower paradigm can open up myriad pathways into other patterns of suggestion that may otherwise have remained concealed.

The perceiving source of that initial *iris* reference is indeterminate, for Flaubert's narrator modulates the narrative into the impersonal "on". *Why* doesn't Charles notice the smell, given that he notices so much else? Perhaps his senses have yet to be awakened? Ironically, not until Emma's death does he come to a full awareness of his physical environment, as the sight of iris-bedecked cottages puts him in mind of happier times with his wife (p. 344). Dare one posit, as a deeper irony, the botanical significance attached to the iris fragrance, implicit in its very nomenclature? The iris produces its scent from a chemical substance called *irone*. Might this not say something about the *irony* inherent in Charles's mistimed responses to his wife's needs, for he only comes to full sensitivity after her death as he assumes the role of Romantic hero, wearing patent leather boots and white ties (p. 349)? And, finally, might not the metapoetical "message" (Latour) of the iris flower be that from the very first flower figure in the novel *irone* will suffuse all other flower topoi in *Madame Bovary*? In this way, the erosion of Emma's illusions is set in motion from the start. Floral irony, then, has both textual and metatextual implications. It bespeaks a truth that Emma refuses to acknowledge; and it constitutes a rhetorical device that shows up how, as Stirling Haig observes, "metonym becomes metaphor through textual determination".[33]

The second figure to be explored uncovers similarly ironic patterns. The *poirier* paradigm, with three elements, may be established as a flower figure since it is in bloom on the three occasions it appears in the text. As a simple mimetic prop, its presence measures the changing seasons. Implementation of the methodology, however, may show the pear tree to be invested with ulterior significance, suggestively embuing the aesthetic infrastructure of *Madame Bovary* with tonal nuances of a latent *désespoir* lurking beneath Emma's *désir*. On its first two appearances, the tree is foregrounded as subject of the verb (variable II, i) "to blossom" and is on both occasions key signifier in a single paragraph (pp. 22 and 64), thereby accentuating its impact. On page 22, the blooms appear in a positive context as Charles begins his courtship of Emma; on page 64, these blooms are the marker of Emma's physical and spiritual degeneration. Its third and final mention occurs on page 72, its impact now thoroughly negativized, as its failure to thrive — appended to it is the adjective *maigre* (variable II, vii) — mirrors Emma's stunted spiritual and affective growth in her "new" surroundings. An immediate irony is to be enjoyed in Léon's vain attempts to *cultiver* a pure love for Emma (p. 109), for she is a blossom that requires *terrains préparés* (p. 61) in order to flourish. As has already been suggested, Yonville soil is arguably less fertile than Tostes terrain and is more than likely of a similar quality to that in the grounds of La Vaubyessard with its ailing fruit trees. What the *poirier* would connote, then, is that neither in the realm of hoped-for *amour* (Yonville), nor in that of fantasised *amour* (la Vaubyessard), do blossoms really thrive. One may posit an extra load of irony when variable I, iii is considered. A pear tree is sturdy. If *it* cannot survive, what hope can there be for Emma's fragile fantasies? The tree, as grimly ironic cultural icon, is clearly *not* a source of "comfort" (Latour).

The final stage of this study is now to concern itself with the wider implications of the generic *fleur* motif and its intimate relationship with Emma.

Because of the many contexts in which the term *fleur(s)* occurs, there is simply not the scope in the present work to detail and investigate it exhaustively. Once again, the elaborated methodology will assist the analyst in his/her work. The following observations, however, may feed into a closer analysis of the paradigm. Emma's "organic" status will render, metonymically, all flower references available for figurative charging, simply because she is herself a metaphorical flower. At the height of her relationship with Rodolphe, Emma is depicted in wholly organic terms: while the sustained floral metaphor masks an ironic subtext, the analysis stresses in "Balzacian" fashion the moral development to be gained in the cultivation of youthful illusions (p. 199). Just as manure, rain, wind and sun are the natural requisites of a healthy flower, so Emma's desires, afflictions, sensuality and youthful ideals contribute to her flowering: "Ses convoitises, ses chagrins, l'expérience du plaisir et ses illusions toujours jeunes, comme font aux fleurs le fumier, la pluie, les vents et le soleil, l'avaient par gradations développée, et elle s'épanouissait enfin dans la plénitude de sa nature" (p. 199). The cynical question one might pose is what is the exact *nature* of this fullness? Is it really as glamorous as the combined details of the image would suggest? Or is her real "nature" somewhat more unidimensional than the capacity for diverse experience and fruitful development translated by the *comparant* of the image would have us believe? Indeed, the remainder of the paragraph proceeds to qualify Emma's *sensuality,* solely, without the merest hint of how the full range of her emotions impact upon her growth. The flower image, rather than conveying notions of uncontaminated beauty and innocence, is stamped with all the hallmarks connotative of a woman who will allow her natural instincts ruinously to dominate her behaviour. Built subliminally into the image is the suggestion that Emma's conduct will lead to her demise, rather than to her fulfilment as an individual, for Emma's pretty development *here* finds its sardonic echo in her egotistical quest for pleasure with Rodolphe at an earlier stage. A now well-manured, well-watered, windswept and well-sunned Emma was *literally* besmirched with mud, if not manure, on her way to satisfy her adulterous desire with Rodolphe: "elle empêtrait ses bottines minces" (p. 168); *literally* windswept: "son foulard s'agitait au vent"

(p. 168); *metaphorically* well-sunned: "les gouttes de rosée [...] faisaient comme une auréole de topaze autour de sa figure" (p. 169) and, albeit earlier, at the very moment of yielding to Rodolphe, was dangerously over-watered: "on distinguait son visage dans une transparence bleuâtre, comme si elle eût nagé sous des flots d'azur" (p. 164). Wind, rain, sun and mud/manure, all the things that make a flower healthy, will undermine, rather than promote, Emma's growth at every turn. With Léon she will be once again brought into close contact with mud, as the *Hirondelle* comes to a halt and Emma steps down onto *muddy* terrain: "Les pierres grinçaient dans la boue, la diligence se balançait, [...] et, vingt pas plus loin, elle sortait de l'*Hirondelle*" (p. 269); well-watered, as she reminisces about the clematis which on three occasions is the cipher for her and Léon's liaison: "emportée dans ses souvenirs comme dans un torrent qui bouillonne" (p. 313); windswept, as the draughty *Hirondelle* adds to the discomfort of her journey into Rouen: "Le vent soufflait par les vasistas fêlés" (p. 267); and metaphorically well-sunned: "Il retrouvait sur ses épaules la couleur ambrée de l'*odalisque au bain*" (p. 271).

The reader is quickly able to sense that Emma's state as beautiful flower is ephemeral. The ideal, for which there is no place in *Madame Bovary*, would be the permanence of beauty. Might one suggest that the very novel into which Emma is written to wither and die is a *mise en abyme* of the cruelly ironic joke that nature has played on all things transient — including flowers? For, just as reality ironises dream in the novel, so reality in extra-fictive space ironizes flowers with their pathetically short life span. Ultimately, Emma's longed-for "terrains préparés" (p. 61) take the form of her grave, a specially prepared location for a "plante particulière" (p. 42); Emma is laid to rest in "une place dans le gazon où la fosse était creusée" (p. 345). Once committed to the earth, Emma's flower status is conferred upon those who find Yonville soil more conducive to growth. Speaking of Homais, the narrator notes the inexorable rise of his progeny set against the inevitable failure of a sickly offshoot, Berthe Bovary: "En face de lui s'étalait, florissante et hilare, la famille du pharmacien, que tout au monde contribuait à satisfaire" (p. 353).

This schematisation of some patterns of suggestion inhering in *fleur(s)* is by no means exhaustive. The methodology can probe areas of the paradigm where flowers are fantasised as a central feature of Emma's most fervent dreams of love and passion. It can assist in the systematic cross-referencing between examples of earth-bound flowers, and the suggestive ways in which these assume greater meaning when considered alongside Emma's moments of supposed bliss which see her as physically proximate to earth, soil or mud. The *bouquet*, too, may be similarly investigated, its complex referencing system equally as rich in symbolic overtones as that of the flower. And, of course, the remaining flower paradigms are still to be subjected to systematic critical scrutiny, their underlying subtleties and ironies teased from subterranean textual depths to send them peeping through the text's fertile surface.

A study of this kind raises a number of technical and aesthetic issues which I have not yet fully addressed. *Le Langage des fleurs*, as a cultural phenomenon of nineteenth-century French life, would have provided a ready-made device for ironic exploitation in a literary work whose very subject is the failure of Romanticism, since the language of flowers was itself a cliché at the time *Madame Bovary* was written. As attractive as it is to read intent into the ironic patterning which the signifieds of the language bring to floral topoi, one is nevertheless forced to question the legitimacy of incorporating it into an essentially text-based analysis. In the light of this uncertainty, it may be preferable to invoke conventional flower values, their colours and fragrances, which may produce greater richness when explored alongside textual floral patterning. For example, on Léon's departure for Paris, Emma strikes a pose at her window, watching "les fleurs roses d'un acacia" being carried away in puddles of water (p. 124). Is Flaubert colouring the bloom of this usually white flower to fit Emma's sentimental mood, the floating petals being seen from her perspective? The detail does, after all, seem to contain an idea of Emma's idealised love being taken away from her. Significantly, the much rarer pink acacia blossom has no perfume. Could this me read as a metaphor for Léon's lack of *amour-passion*? Here, text and extra-text meld to produce greater allusiveness. Other examples are arguably more problematic. One might well expect to find faded flowers as metaphorical backcloth to the adulterous relations between Emma and Rodolphe. Faded waterlilies (p. 165) and faded wallflowers (p. 168) furnish a loaded commentary on the nature of their union; but what of the faded wallflowers that act as backcloth to the liaison between Emma and Léon (p. 97)? Is the flower figure *self*-referentially ironising, rather than referentially ironising? Does irony reside in the problematisation of meaning bearing on flowers, irony seeping out of every textual interstice? Flower figure irony is perhaps, in the last analysis, purely metapoetic. Or should one concede, simply, that maybe sometimes, with supreme irony, a flower *is* just a flower?

## Notes

[1] See, in this connection, Diana Knight's *Flaubert's Characters*.

[2] There are a wealth of French flower books in existence and much writing on them. But see, in particular, Beverly Seaton's work, including "French Flower Books of the early nineteenth Century'" and "A Nineteenth-century Metalanguage: *Le Langage des fleurs*".

[3] See Flaubert's letter of August 26, 1846: "Il t'a fait plaisir, pauvre ange, le bouquet de fête que je t'ai envoyé! Ce n'est pas moi qui ai eu l'idée de mettre dans ma lettre ces fleurs significatives car je n'en connaissais pas le sens symbolique" (*Correspondance*, I, 315). There is little evidence to support the theory that the language of flowers spilled over into the flowers of literature. As Beverly Seaton notes, "there is little or no direct application to most nineteenth-century literature" (*The Language of Flowers: A History*, 162).

[4] All page references will be to the Garnier edition of *Madame Bovary*, ed. Claudine Gothot-Mersch.

[5] Christopher Norris, *Deconstruction: Theory & Practice*, 1.

[6] Cecil Jenkins, *French Literature and its Background: The Late Nineteenth Century*, 55.

[7] See Lilian Furst's *All is True: The Claims & Strategies of Realist Fiction*, 53.

[8] Don Demorest, *L'Expression figurée et symbolique dans l'œuvre de Flaubert*.

[9] Margaret Church, "A Triad of Images: Nature in *Madame Bovary*".

[10] *Flaubert: The Uses of Uncertainty*, 144.

[11] See, in this connection, Phillip Knight's *Flower Poetics in nineteenth-century France*, 1–80.

[12] Charlotte de Latour, *Le Langage des fleurs*. No French edition is available in this country for consultation, but an English translation of this seminal work may be consulted in the Humanities Reading Room of the British Museum. This fourth translated edition was fully

revised by Frederick Shoberl, *The Language of Flowers with Illustrative Poetry*, first published 1834 and revised in 1846 to include "The Calendar of Flowers and the Dial of Flowers" (Saunders & Otley: London, 1834). The number of entries in this dictionary, as in most others in English translation, is, unfortunately, fewer than in the French original. The Victorian reading public's obsession with propriety is the most likely reason for this. See, in this connection, Seaton, *The Language of Flowers*, 80 and 133.

[13] See Seaton, *op. cit.*, 83–4 and 152.

[14] Quoted in Terry Eagleton, *Literary Theory*, 92.

[15] See *supra*, note 3.

[16] *Correspondance*, I, 258.

[17] See Jack Goody, *The Culture of Flowers*, 286.

[18] Seaton mentions this in her articles and *The Language of Flowers*. A satire of the flower book genre had already appeared by this date with the publication of Taxile Delord's *Les Fleurs animées*.

[19] *Correspondance*, I, 464. See, too, the letter of Maxime du Camp, where he berates Louise for overtending Gustave the love-plant in an overheated greenhouse, effectively forcing him to love her at her pace, rather than his and so killing his love (*Correspondance*, I, 827).

[20] See especially two letters of 16 November 1852 and 20 April 1853, *Correspondance*, II, 177 and 310.

[21] See Bernard Boullard: "Présence de la flore française dans l'œuvre et la correspondance de Gustave Flaubert", *Les Amis de Flaubert*, 7. One might be tempted to see *Bouvard et Pécuchet* as a late attempt on Flaubert's part to exorcise a shameful family ghost by turning grandfather's incompetence into novelistic ironic overload. The couple's horticultural failures are legion, so much so that when Pécuchet "se tourna vers les fleurs" the reader knows precisely what to expect. See *Bouvard et Pécuchet, Œuvres Complètes*, II, 211.

[22] Flaubert pronounces on authorial circumspection in many letters, but see in particular the letter of 31 October 1858 (*Correspondance*, II, 839).

[23] Concordances exist for Flaubert's major works, some now out of print. See Carlut et al, *A Concordance to Flaubert's "Madame Bovary"*.

[24] See Pierre Moreau's "L'Art de la Composition dans *Madame Bovary*", 175.

[25] Although the originality of her work is a contentious issue, practically all subsequent language- of-flower books took their cue from her, elaborating similar meanings for flowers to her own. Latour drew directly on the work of Alex Lucot's *Emblèmes de Flore et des végétaux* in the elaboration of her own flower lists (Seaton, *The Language of Flowers*, 73 and Seaton "The Flower Language Books of the Nineteenth Century", 5). Latour lists her flowers, trees, shrubs and herbs according to the season in which they appear; she then appends the meanings she has

ascribed to them (based on myth, metaphor and metonym), together with anecdotes. At the end of the volume, the grammar and syntax of floral schemata are elaborated to demonstrate how flowers and bouquets might be used as a secret language of communication between girl and suitor. The entire work is predicated on the cultural tradition of the Orient, where harem girls used flower arrangements to "talk" to lovers without their masters' knowledge. A full account of her work and the influences which shaped it are given by both Jack Goody in his *The Culture of Flowers* (232–53) and by Beverly Seaton in *The Language of Flowers* (112–49). An English translation of Latour's work (1834) may be consulted in the British Museum, where, for example, *acacia* is given the value-ascription "platonic love" (86). A glut of flower books appeared at the time Latour was writing and it really is difficult to determine whose work was seminal, so fiercely was originality contested (Goody, 236–7; Seaton, 70–1). In addition to the many French publications to appear in the nineteenth century, the vogue for flower lexicons became pan-European. John Henry Ingram's work, *Flora Symbolica*, published in 1869, is largely derivative with meanings taken from Latour and other floral lexicons. It is he, not Latour, who in his lexicon (356) attributes the signified of *insincerity* to the *cherry blossom*. Although Latour started the flower dictionary trend, subsequent floral lexicographers were much more exhaustive in their detailing of flower types (Goody, 240–1).

[26] Even distribution would produce different results. On average, one would expect to find 7 *fleur(s)* references in Part One, with 18 in Part Two and 12 in Part Three.

[27] Latour's signified, reproduced in Seaton, op. cit., 180.

[28] Flower book lexicons are in accord that the rhododendron bears this signified, though Latour does not include it in her own work. See Ingram, 360.

[29] There are twenty "isolated examples" for which it has not been possible to establish paradigmatic divisions. The following occurrences, giving the Part and Chapter of *Madame Bovary* in which the flower is referred to and the conventional value attached to it, have been identified: *digitales* (I,vii = insincerity); *coquelicots* (I,vii = consolation); *rhododendrons* (i,viii = danger); *boules-de-neige* (i,viii = winter/age); *safran* (I,viii = beware excess); *bleuets* (i,viii = delicacy); *véroniques* (II,iii = fidelity); *chèvrefeuille* (II,iii = chains of love); *primevères* (II,vi = first youth); *acacia* (II,vi = platonic love); *bruyères* (II,ix = solitude); *dahlia* (II,xiv = my gratitude surpasses your cares); *œillets* (III,i = strong pure love); *narcisses* (III,i = egoism); *tubéreuses* (III,i = voluptuousness); *mouron pour les oiseaux* (III,i = rendezvous); *juliennes* (III,i = rivalry); *trèfles* (III,i = industry); *colzas* (III,x = no meaning traced); *lis* (III,xi = purity).

[30] The signified "comfort" is taken from Ingram, 360.

[31] The signified "purity of heart" is taken from Ingram, 362.

[32] The cultural signified of "insincerity" attached to cherries adds a further ironic dimension to a recent study of Emma's *bovarysme/mauvaise foi*/self-deception during La

Vaubyessard episode where she eats maraschino ice cream, believing it to be something it is not: "The luxury liqueur flavour is none other than a distillation of the common fruit which has been the very source of the encounter" (Mary Orr, "Reflections on 'bovarysme': the Bovarys at Vaubyessard", 7).

[33] Stirling Haig, "Madame Arnoux's *coffret*: A Monumental Case", 473.

**Works Cited**

Flaubert, Gustave, *Bouvard et Pécuchet*, *Œuvres Complètes II* (Paris: Seuil, 1964)

Flaubert, Gustave, *Correspondance*, ed. Jean Bruneau, 4 vols, (Paris: Gallimard, 1973–98)

Flaubert, Gustave, *Madame Bovary*, ed. Claudine Gothot-Mersch (Paris: Garnier, 1971)

Boullard, Bernard, "Présence de la flore française dans l'œuvre et la correspondance de Gustave Flaubert", *Les Amis de Flaubert*, 56 (1980), 6–36

Camp, Maxime du, *Flaubert, Correspondance I* (Paris: Gallimard, 1973)

Carlut, Charles, Dubé, Pierre & Dugan, Raymond, *A Concordance to Flaubert's "Madame Bovary"*, 2 vols, (New York: Garland Publishing inc., 1978)

Church, Margaret, "A Triad of Images: Nature in *Madame Bovary*", *Mosaic*, 3 (1972), 203–14

Culler, Jonathan, *Flaubert: The Uses of Uncertainty* (Ithaca & London: Cornell University Press, 1985)

Delord, Taxile, *Les Fleurs animées* (Paris: Garnier, 1847).

Demorest, Don, *L'Expression figurée et symbolique dans l'œuvre de Flaubert*, (Paris: Les Presses Modernes, 1931)

Eagleton, Terry, *Literary Theory* (Oxford: Blackwell, 1983)

Furst, Lilian, *All is True: The Claims & Strategies of Realist Fiction* (Durham & London Duke University Press, 1995)

Goody, Jack, *The Culture of Flowers* (Cambridge: CUP, 1993)

Haig, Stirling, "Madame Arnoux's *coffret*: A Monumental Case", *Romanic Review*, 75 (1984), 469–82

Ingram, John Henry, *Flora Symbolica; or, The Language and Sentiment of Flowers* (London: Warne, 1869)

Jenkins, Cecil, *French Literature and its Background: The Late Nineteenth Century*, ed.

John Cruickshank (London, Oxford & New York OUP, 1969)

Knight, Diana, *Flaubert's Characters* (Cambridge: CUP, 1985)

Knight, Phillip, *Flower Poetics in nineteenth-century France* (Oxford: OUP, 1986)

Latour, Charlotte de, *Le langage des fleurs* (Paris: Audot, 1819)

Lucot, Alex. *Emblèmes de Flore et des végétaux* (Paris: Janet, 1819)

Moreau, Pierre, "L'Art de la Composition dans *Madame Bovary*", *Orbis Litterarum*, 12 (1957), 171–8

Norris, Christopher, *Deconstruction: Theory & Practice* (London & New York: Methuen, 1982)

Orr, Mary, "Reflections on 'bovarysme': the Bovarys at Vaubyessard", *French Studies Bulletin*, 61 (1996), 6–8

Seaton, Beverly, "The Flower Language Books of the Nineteenth Century", *Morton Arboretum Quarterly*, 16 (1980), 1-11

Seaton, Beverly, "French Flower Books of the Early Nineteenth Century", *Nineteenth-Century French Studies*, 11 (1982–83), 60–72

Seaton, Beverly, "A Nineteenth-century Metalanguage: *Le langage des fleurs*", *Semiotica*, 57 (1985), 73–86

Seaton, Beverly, *The Language of Flowers: A History* (Charlottesville & London: The University Press of Virginia, 1995)

Shoberl, Frederick, *The Language of Flowers with Illustrative Poetry*, Tenth Edition, (London: Saunders & Otley, 1846)

# GENETICS AND INCOMPLETION
## Peter Michael Wetherill

> "Time present and time past
> Are perhaps both present in time future.
> And time future contained in time past"
> (T.S. Eliot, "Burnt Norton", *Four Quartets*)

Manuscript drafts are an arena of unending conflicts: a whirlpool of reworked versions, hesitations, and contradictions full of floating, throw-away fragments of doubtful character. As a result, many scholars of varied confessions and persuasions have suggested that such drafts, which after all are "only writing", do not know any more than their author what they are up to or where they are going — it is all a matter of chance. These notions, like the critical procedures which they inspire, are based on a theory of textual specificity and distinctiveness which may have been "correct" when structuralism ruled the roost. However, to more modern eyes, they ignore all kinds of history, biography, social conditioning, and even the essential humanity of texts which structuralism set out to destroy, but without which art does not make much sense. If people claim that it is not done to compare one stage of a text's development with the final version and insist that we concentrate on fragmented, formal abstractions and empty linguistic shifts and expression going round in circles, they may well be pointing to things which are truly there, but it is rather perverse to keep everything else out — and they may be rejecting the literature's fundamental complexity.

And yet the approach I am questioning is widespread and unambiguous. Thus Roger Laufer stresses the essential lack of organisation of manuscripts[1] (rather than our inability to spot their organising principles) and says that:

> la génétique textuelle conteste souvent aujourd'hui la perspective finaliste au profit d'un intérêt pour la manière [...]. Elle exprime ainsi la crise actuelle de l'œuvre close au profit d'une écriture polymorphe, proliférante, combinatoire, interactive ou partagée."[2]

Similarly, for Daniel Ferrer, "les documents génétiques sont presque par définition non-linéaires"[3] and Éric Le Calvez, for his part, writes that "chacun sait maintenant que le vecteur téléologique de la production textuelle n'est pas rigidement orienté".[4] Almuth Grésillon seems to offer a résumé of all these points of view when she asserts that "ce n'est pas le résultat final qui compte".[5] Further, if incompletion is the key idea, it is a logical step to claim that "avant-textes" are preferable to the final printed work, which might be considered to be a kind of "avant-texte" itself — for its final state, after all, is arbitrary and provisional.[6] So Michel Espagne writes that:

> Il est bien évident que l'on ne peut réduire les variantes à une sorte de préparation de l'œuvre. [...] Entre l'œuvre éditée par Brod ou Kafka lui-même et l'écrivain s'insère un hiatus qui exclut la téléologie et constitue l'objet même du travail de l'écrivain.[7]

and

> peut-être même [les manuscrits] offrent-ils l'avantage de nous délivrer pour un temps du moins de la double question de l'origine et de la fin.[8]

The threads of the argument are drawn together by Melançon:

> Le texte se dissout dans le maelstrom de l'avant-texte, apparaît comme un moment sans privilège particulier sinon d'être accidentellement le dernier d'une série essentiellement ouverte.[9]

Ferrer and Lebrave take this seriously:

> Les documents génétiques les plus intéressants sont évidemment ceux où la linéarité est mise en défaut.[10]

as does C. Quémar:

> L'intérêt d'étudier les avant-textes du roman proustien n'est pas de retrouver à travers les fragments dispersés dans les brouillons un fil du récit, une histoire racontée. L'attitude génétique restitue un ordre de rédaction, une dynamique de l'écriture quand même les pistes suivies tourneraient court.[11]

while Philippe Lejeune speaks of a Proust's (or anyone else's) final text which "garantit les brouillons plutôt que le contraire".[12]

People have been making this kind of claim for the last 20 years or more.[13] It has allowed them to take the early *cahiers* of *La Recherche* to be novel-writing rather than the writing of a novel[14] and "genetic" analysis to concentrate more or less exclusively on the dynamics of tensions and priorities. Worryingly, priority is given to the idea that the text is going round in circles rather than that it is getting somewhere — and of course all interaction without other kinds of literary criticism is out of the question.[15] When they are referred to, all sorts of distortions take place: for example, we have the psychoanalysis of writing with personality nowhere to be seen. What is more striking still is that this approach does not distinguish between the different kinds of text studied: realist, modernist, open, closed, fragmented, anecdotic, descriptive, narrative — all traditions are bunched together.[16] Char rubs shoulders with Zola, Dürrenmatt with Heine, writers who rewrite obsessively (Hölderlin) with those who forget or neglect what they have written once it has been recopied (Flaubert) — so the continuity of nineteenth-century writing mingles with the parataxes of the twentieth, whilst the latter's wanderings act as a springboard for the inevitable distortion of the former's much more programmatic procedures. Hence it is stressed that "le généticien doit explorer l'avant-texte comme tel".[17] Perhaps it is the dogmatism which especially might be toned down, and we might thus get nearer to reality, which is always a little blurred about the edges.

It would of course be misguided to suggest that "avant-textes" are purely linear, and that all aspects of the writer's work have a precise goal — that all content and a text's whole discursive potential are worked out in advance. The truth is of course that the link between initial project and final version is a loose one, one of potential rather than teleology. Even in the nineteenth century, the "avant-texte" together with the project which is its starting point are subjected to a large number of modifying tensions before the printed version is achieved. This being said, as far as the nineteenth century is concerned — and this is the period which I shall concentrate on here — the constraints of the initial, often clearly formulated, project do indeed seem to determine the content of the "avant-textes", even those which do not have much future, and they lead logically to the final text. The genesis of a text, clearly, is a logical process, or is logically slanted, and manuscript drafts are meaningful only when they are highlighted by other phenomena such as those of the final version with all the complexities of its meanings and explanations.[18] Isolated elements are meaningful (i.e. they are more than an excuse for localised, fragmented critical formulae) only within the broader context of foreseen and foreseeable developments: those which culminate in the text the public finally reads.[19]

This is not to deny the existence for example of Proust's fumbling composition, with its frequent disintegration and reconstruction.[20] Herschberg-Pierrot is quite right to say that Proust takes a long time to work out the way *La Recherche* is to end.[21] However, what needs to be stressed is the fact that these reworkings are invariably a way not only for Proust but also for Balzac, Flaubert and Zola to achieve their already defined ends. So, I think it might be safer to talk about the way an author clears the decks and brings out the meaning he seeks, rather than to concentrate on the more or less theoretical implications of marks, traces, arabesques and motifs in half a page of manuscript. That will get us away from the idea that there is something essentially abstract about literature and help us to take it more seriously than the *Observer* crossword, however subtle this may be, and pay attention to its broadly cultural, and not merely "writerly", voice, which cannot be separated from the rest. The writers who come up most frequently in this kind of work have that voice in good measure: in spite of his claims, Flaubert never wrote anything like a book about nothing, and the meaning of Proust's work is badly distorted if we do not realise that when *La Recherche* fragments from a central core in four different directions[22] ("Balbec", Combray, Paris, literary criticism), the main aim, or result if you prefer, is to reinforce the novel's *argument* (if not its specific formulation), which has already been worked out.[23] Even the early title *Contre Sainte-Beuve* is not a bad choice, for it is a good definition of critical attitudes which *La Recherche* will illustrate. So, even when the narrative substance and focus evolve, the central lesson remains.

Similarly, Flaubert has already put together a huge *dossier* of research notes and detailed scenarios for *L'Éducation sentimentale* when he tells one of his correspondents about the idea which is going to be constantly in his mind as he writes his novel:

> Je veux faire l'histoire morale des hommes de ma génération; "sentimentale" serait plus vrai.[24]

This idea *combines* with the the aesthetic constraints which Flaubert formulated at a very early stage to determine the choice and variety of vocabulary, ironic undercurrents, narrative substance and structure, and authorial stance. The same is true of Zola.[25]

Of course, the point I am making varies historically. However, if more recently we face *La Recherche*'s towering deconstructable pyramid with the endless shuffling of its parts and its ceaseless reformulations, there is no doubt about the way in which these elements *converge* on a final argument worked out between 1908 and 1913 and already in place by 1912.[26] The apparent autonomy of Proust's fragments (whether it is a note or drafted text) cannot resist structural constraints – and these are just as much moral as verbal. This is indeed Claudine Quémar's opinion when she says of the beginning of *La Recherche* that:

> les nombreux brouillons pour cet *incipit* montrent que les différentes reprises de l'ouverture ne sont pas artificielles mais liées au schéma narratif

> de base: les chambres du souvenir nocturne ou diurne, avant la matinée de conversation ou de révélation.[27]

Here the progression if not the progress of the "avant-textes" is stressed: two parallel processes (the construction of the plot and the development of its constituent parts) go forward together (often in different *cahiers*, with all the interaction one may imagine),[28] but even montages, like those which appeared in the *Figaro* of 25 March 1913, give a shorthand version of the work's meaning and directed drive.

How may this confusion about "avant-textes" and their purpose be explained? Firstly, I think it stems from a focus which may not always have much to do with literary analysis, an over-emphasis on "science" and with its tempting implications of clarity and unambiguity. And yet, if the idea of genetic *science* is justified in linguistics, it must be marginal in a field where subjective perception and analysis are a *sine qua non*. It would be a mistake to confuse literary genetics and the perfectly legitimate use to which linguistics put "avant-textes".[29] Indeed, whatever value incompletion may have for linguistics,[30] undertandably linguistics is interested essentially in localised, fragmented and specialised analysis which generally ignores literary matters such as an extract's broader context: its relationship to a more extensive continuity of writing and thought. In addition, literature being a bastard genre draws on a wide variety of approaches and phenomena. So to claim as Grésillon does that genetic readings of literary texts are a distinct genre necessarily distorts the material one is dealing with. Isolated examples which linguists quote without necessarily analysing them[31] produce linguistic *exempla* which are cut off from authorial intention and meaning. Such readings give a highly tendentious and restrictive idea of the genetic processes and ideological complexities of which, in literature, verbal phenomena are only a part.

A way out of all this (to anticipate what I say below) is to suggest that circularity in literature is much rarer than some would have us believe. A useful starting point may perhaps be to suggest that the vast majority of texts are like classical works, namely that they "[s'inscrivent] dans une perspective téléologique. Elle[s] aspire[nt] à s'achever et ce n'est presque jamais que sous une forme achevée du moins provisoirement qu'elle[s] nous [sont] proposée[s]."[32] As we shall see, this is very close to the "mentality" of the nineteenth century. In addition to these specific cases, the anti-teleology group, even when they take a more general approach, make out literature to be what it is not. This is because they tend to concentrate on short-range studies of brief isolated passages. They rarely look at problems of motivation and intention. Description, whatever theory it leads to, can rarely be applied elsewhere — nor indeed is it. More seriously, it is difficult to see how such descriptions, which tend to push problems of meaning to one side, can help one to understand better the novels which they are based on, or even of the broader genetic processes involved. These exercises confirm one critic's impression, that:

> Le feuillet isolé comme espace génétique est un leurre [...] Prélever le fragment singulier du feuillet procède du même geste opératoire que celui qui coupe le manuscrit du texte publié pour tenter de révéler les aspects spécifiques du brouillon [...] et même du balbutiement.[33]

Poetics, when applied to brief concrete examples, is also a source of deceptive clarity, for its analyses suggest an over-optimistic classification of the different categories of manuscript, on the strength of which, like linguistics, it sets about exploring passages which have been torn from their context and their chronology: necessary overlaps are ignored. Plan, scenario, "premier plan détaillé", "résumé", "canevas" etc., are no doubt useful markers, but the clear chronology they imply is a trap which leads to fragments being treated in isolation and therefore hides reality more than it illuminates it: anyone who has worked extensively on manuscripts knows how blurred the progression from one stage to the next can be: for example, documentation may come *after* the writing of much of the narrative text (Flaubert, Zola). The different isolatable "stages", if that is the right term, constantly appear on the same manuscript page. They overlap, and this confirms the manuscript's essential forward drive, rather than conforming to clear-cut categories: Zola, like Proust, "n'enferme pas son manuscrit dans des dossiers clos et déchronologisées (ébauche, personnages, premier plan, deuxième plan etc.)":

> Dans la réalité de la genèse, certains écrits scéniques sont restés en corrélation les uns avec les autres [...] d'une classe à l'autre [...] les étapes sont souvent mêlées dans le temps (par exemple l'ébauche et le premier plan) et [...] les notes documentaires se sont accumulées et distribuées pendant toute la durée de la préparation.[34]

This is true not only of Zola. Some "avant-textes" of *Hérodias* are at one and the same time documents, plans, *scénarios* and drafts,[35] whilst the same folio (See N.A.F. 16652 f° 10) of *La Recherche* may contain drafts of a number of fragments: *clocher, curé, tante Léonie* etc. These parallel activities show how interdependent "avant-textes" are and how with their blurred contours, different kinds of manuscript work contribute to the same end.

This helps one to avoid an over-schematic vision, whilst in the broad overall categories, the prolepses thus set in train ring out a kind of ritualised procedure which is the true dynamic of the creative process. In Zola, this progression is clear. As Mitterand says:

> La genèse du roman [zolien] est *une succession* de calculs, d'hypothèses et d'interférences. Elle fonctionne sur le mode du "si ... alors", du "parce que" et du "pour", selon une constante appréciation et un constant réajustement des corrélations internes.[36]

Mitterand's analyses are exemplary, for they start from the idea that, when Zola submits his plan to Lacroix in the late 1860s, he maps out exactly where he is going for the next 25 years:

> Chaque chapitre, chaque masse doit être une force distincte qui pousse au dénouement.[37]

> Jusqu'à sa dernière ligne, le roman de Zola résulte donc de ce travail, primitif et primordial, d'installation.[38]

Everything is driven by Zola's "besoin de baliser minutieusement ses parcours, la nécessité d'élever ses défenses [...] contre le danger d'inachèvement".[39] This is not far from what Biasi points to in Flaubert:

> Dans la totalité de l'œuvre, on ne distingue pratiquement aucun cas de rédaction qui échappe à l'obsession de la forme maîtrisée, du définitif, de l'achèvement ou du parachèvement.[40]

The huge quantities of manuscripts which have come down to us from the nineteenth century offer massive evidence of the fact that this continuous forward progression is to be found in Zola, Flaubert and Balzac, just as the notes, the jotted marginal instructions and the bits of final text which the manuscripts of *Hérodias* contain show the way for the rest. For this fact to be acceptable, all one needs to do is to overcome one's structuralist fear of time and history. Claims such as the following about Proust's *Cahier 3* (f° 18r.) then become possible:

> Si l'on est certes loin encore de *l'Ouverture* du futur roman, auquel Proust ne songe nullement, semble-t-il, en rédigeant ces ébauches, c'est pourtant, dès lors, *l'incipit* d' *La Recherche* [...] qui commence à se profiler [...] structure temporelle à trois niveaux dont l'auteur ne mesure pas alors toute la portée narrative, mais qui préfigure nettement les trois plans temporels du roman à venir.[41]

Thanks to hindsight, we perhaps quite often know more clearly than the author what is coming: we can read clues which tell us where he is going, so we would be very wrong to "act innocent" and not bear them in mind. At the same time we constantly come across devices in Proust which show how clearly he knew where he was going and how much method and focused development come into play. Hence the significance and the usefulness for example of the author's ritualised digressions, which expand to the point where they cease to be the margin and become the centre, before other digressions make them explode once again. This *technique* cannot be seen as anything but a means to a stylistic and a diegetic end. Even the most dogmatic readers have to make concessions here:

> L'exposé final du *Temps retrouvé* perd de plus en plus de son importance et s'il subsiste après le long déroulement du roman, c'est peut-être grâce à une structure initiale qui tient ensemble les éléments disparates rassemblés dans la genèse.[42]

Proust's text straddles two traditions: it is a revolutionary vision of time and history, and a much more traditional moralising search, which reminds one of *Le Rouge et le noir*, *Middlemarch* or *Buddenbrooks*. So writing as a means to an end is perfectly logical.

There is another idea which deserves scrutiny: the rôle not merely of aimlesness but of chance and the arbitrary. As far as the arbitrary nature of writing is concerned, I frequently feel that all straws are worth grasping if you wish to force textual genetics into an indeterminate and aleatory mould, although, as I have suggested, it is not at all difficult to show that writers' working methods are systematic and culturally (even pedagogically) predetermined.[43] So, for many scholars, the author and his/her text are the impotent victims of involuntary drives, sudden influences and sudden associations of ideas.

In fact, in the tradition under review, there are very few clear examples of wild and unexpected changes of tack, or writers putting down the first thing that comes into their heads — they are very dificult to spot in any case. And one can see why. The line the author is following has nothing vague about it.[44] Zola's massive *dossiers préparatoires*, like Proust's countless *notes de régie* (which are necessarily proleptic) show, especially when they occur on folios which deal with other matters, that a detailed programme has been worked out, even if the edges are blurred, with its documentation, its plans and its scenarios.[45] Even before the drafts get under way,[46] there is a line to be followed and an argument to put across.[47] All levels of the writer's activity confirm this, for each stage is a clear continuation of what comes before and a springboard for what is to come. Thus Zola, in the *dossiers* for *Germinal,* speaks of the need to "préparer l'accident" (N.A.F..10307 f° 139). This is a far cry from Grésillon's idea of "[gestes de la main] qui ne répondent à aucun modèle appris, à aucun programme préconstruit, à aucun vouloir dire".[48] She seems to forget that writing is *always* preconditioned[49] and full of ready-made bits and pieces, like all other human activities.

Intention is a major factor here: far from confirming the idea of a flabby author with no ideas of his own, pushed here and there by all sorts of weird urges, authorial intention invites us to view the final text, like the "avant-textes" which lead up to it most completely, as the expression of sustained aims. They are the culminating point of decisions taken as the work progresses. The final text alone clarifies and confirms the sense, direction and motivation of these decisions. If we sideline the final text as many of the scholars quoted would have us do, we effectively censure a very useful concept (intention) in favour of a slick paradox ("finalité sans fin"), which is apparently relevant to Flaubert's writing.[50] This is a strange idea to attach to an author who knows very precisely how long he will need to finish his text.

Chance (the opposite of intention) is at best a marginal and ephemeral phenomenon.[51] It may on occasion improve the author's aim by suggesting a plot detail or a particular word. But these things can nudge the text along in this way only if they fit logically into structures which have already been worked out. Thus the sudden appearance of the 1848 Revolution in the early plans of *L'Éducation sentimentale* may well be unexpected, but it fits in perfectly with Flaubert's first ideas for the novel.

In the period I am concerned with, "avant-textes" are subjected to long-term considerations — witness Zola's "ébauches". So chance conflicts are worth highlighting; for example the initial tension between discourse and documentation in the "avant-textes" of *Un Amour de Swann,* or *Hérodias,* for the aim here, as we see later, is to write problematically about historical and social experience. So chance often boils down, especially when one is dealing with authors who are less modern than is generally claimed,[52] to the surprise discovery of details which confirm already-established long-term aims. It does not upset original intentions: the new episode or expression or the psychological insight it suggests rather point the author more firmly in the direction of a text whose parameters are fully established. Hence Goldin's remark about the drafts of the "Comices agricoles" episode:

> La nature et place de notre paragraphe 100 se présentent donc comme une *conséquence* à la fois du discours de Lieuvain et de l'intention flaubertienne de mêler des descriptions aux discours.[53]

The way a manuscript progresses depends on the work's possibilities and its established potential.

The teleological idea I am putting forward is quite similar to that of "noyaux et catalyses" in narrative: sequences lead to options whose scope is limited by the continuity and potential of which they are part. So perhaps Quémar is not limiting chance enough when she writes:

> Le point de référence, ce n'est pas l'idée de l'œuvre, mais au contraire les multiples possibilités de ce qui aurait pu être, d'un projet aux différentes étapes de son développement et dont il reste la trace.[54]

If I were to take my argument a little further, I could perhaps say that the only area of uncertainty where chance plays a significant part relates to the ambiguities and the ironies of the *finished* text. In that case, of course, it is not chance creativity which is at stake, but the nature of reader response (which is too easily sidelined in a further reduction of the text's real status). Such ambiguities are the only area of essential meaning which is outside the author's control.[55] Even if, as one frequently has to, one concentrates on shorter extracts (necessarily linked to the whole), it is not difficult to demonstrate that these owe their existence to earlier versions, and that they in turn map out the increasingly powerful constraints which versions to come will have to take into account:

> Quand on écrit [...] une chose *imaginée*, comme tout doit alors découler de la conception, et que la moindre virgule dépend du plan général, l'attention bifurque. Le détail est atroce, surtout lorsqu'on aime le détail comme moi. Les perles composent le collier, mais c'est le fil qui fait le collier.[56]

The author's voice is rarely quoted in this debate — which is perhaps why things have become so distorted.

Yet other factors show what thin ice non-teleological analyses are on, at least as far as the nineteenth century is concerned. I am especially impressed by the fact that no one, even those who are most hostile to the teleological idea can completely ignore the final version and that everyone is in fact prepared quite cheerfully to quote it when it suits their purpose.[57] Thus we read in Grésillon's address to linguists:

> Il s'agit du premier cahier (appelé cahier 3) que Proust remplissait pendant l'hiver 1908–1909 et dont les prolongements devaient aboutir en 1910 au fameux incipit de *RTP*. [58]

Other specialists, meanwhile, refer repeatedly to the final version even though elsewhere they deny its importance.[59] Others even claim that "l'histoire des sources n'est généralement pas assez liée à l'étude des manuscrits et de leur aboutissement".[60] Apparently, everyone is forced sooner or later to explain the dynamic of "avant-textes" by pointing to their final manifestations[61] — like the critic who prints the final version of *Madame Gervaisais* opposite the Goncourts' *carnets*.[62] And, paradoxically, all "geneticists" implicitly subscribe to a finalistic perspective in the need they feel to set up a chronology of composition rather that sticking to the seething, timeless drift which they claim elsewhere to be at the centre of things:[63]

> L'étude de genèse [...] n'est pas seulement descriptive et narrative, elle est aussi explicative. Elle prend conscience de la différence importante qui sépare le document brut, souvent étranger (tel qu'un article de journal ou un livre d'une autre plume) et le texte autographe de préparation (tel que l'Ébauche ou une fiche personnage) qui implique déjà un travail autonome, original de l'imagination et de l'écriture.[64]

There is nother inconsistency which I might mention, which is contained in the idea that there is no "véritable solution de continuité entre une œuvre et une autre".[65] Admittedly, it is useful to accept the idea that authors have preoccupations and working methods which spill over from one work to the next. But there is a real danger in suggesting that all that matters is a text's repetitive circularity, without worrying too much about what a text actually says,[66] even when one is dealing with authors who write "THE END" when that is what they have come to and who then go on to write something else, often with a clear hope that it will be something different: after *L'Assommoir*, Zola publishes *Une Page d'amour*; after *Madame Bovary*, Flaubert writes *Salammbô*; after *Combray*, Proust places *Un Amour de Swann*.

In short, the critical climate seems to allow all imaginable priorities and all conceivable textual links, whether one is dealing with manuscripts or published works — provided of course one does not pay too much attention to what the individual texts contain. For texts, we are assured, are above all *writing*, and if we are to obtain approval we must reduce Félicité's or Marcel's complex living experience ("faire à travers le beau vivant et vrai quand même") to a mass of coagulated words devoid of sequence.[67]

Everything becomes much simpler if it is admitted that it might be useful to put "avant-textes" back into their historical and ideological, as well as their wider verbal, context.[68] For example, one might stress the fact that the nineteenth-century text's direction and meaning are often determined by contemporary production and publishing conventions, to the point that, often, added to the realist novel's essentially programmatic qualities, serialisation forces writers to write at a rate which is out of their control: even the final "message" is worked out in advance, although, of course, some leeway may be possible within strictly defined parameters. So, what has already been written necessarily conditions the rest more or less irreversibly. Zola, Balzac, the Flaubert of the *Trois Contes* (who wrote *Hérodias* so that he could produce a publishable volume) are perfectly aware of what remains to be said, even if they do not know exactly how it is going to be *written*. The way the manuscripts develop clearly shows this, as do long-term projects like *Les Rougon-Macquart* and *Illusions perdues*. Historical specificity and progressive conditioning are not limited to the *feuilleton*, however, for it cannot be stressed enough that teleology, completion and closure are at the heart of the whole ideology of the nineteenth century:[69] teleology relates, not merely to narrative structures but also to the writing which informs them and which gives priority to the chronology and sequence of events.

This is the overarching ideology which defines the stages which "avant-textes" must go through before they come to published form, even if they involve the occasional switch in direction: plan, *plan détaillé, ébauche*, research, drafts, overview, fair copy, copyist's version, proofs, instalment, publication as a book. Even if one bears in mind my earlier remarks, these numerous stages show how sophisticated the planning is. The *scénarios* of *L'Éducation sentimentale*, for example, are a clear indication that the verbal and nominal writing of the drafts is inconceivable as long as the details of the plot have not been worked out. That is what Flaubert really meant when he said that style was "à lui seul une manière absolue de voir les choses".[70]

The points I am making here are not valid merely for the nineteenth century (although this is the period I am concentrating on). Avant-garde writers show too how important it is for them to know where they are going. Kafka's working methods have already been mentioned. Virginia Woolf's notes of intent, as she works on such a revolutionary modernist text as *Mrs Dalloway* are also interesting, for in spite of the undoubted expansion of her original project ("Mrs Dalloway has branched into a book"[71]), her aims are clear, and the centre of gravity will not change:

I adumbrate here a study of insanity and suicide; the world seen by the sane and the insane side by side — something like that.[72]

Even if one discounts autobiographical constraints, it is still possible to say:

From the beginning, Virginia Woolf saw the design of the novel as the converging of everything in the party at the end. This basic design is reinforced and expanded upon in the November 9th notes to include the theme of life and death: "all must bear finally on the party at the end; which expresses life in every variety and full of anticipation; while [Septimus] dies".[73]

To quote further from the same critic:

Every scene will build up the idea of C's (Clarissa's) character. That will give unity as well as add to the final effect.[74]

And Virginia Woolf, with all her modernity, does not seem to think chance is an important factor:

I want to see this book better than the others and get the utmost out of it.[75]

The initial project, like the final text and all the procedures which achieve it, show that modernity in no way sounds the knell of finalistic ideologies; not for writers at least, although their critics may have other ideas. So, if, in contrast to what Virginia Woolf does, the writing of *La Recherche* progresses via "[une] élaboration tâtonnante [...et à une] succession de versions partielles [...]",[76] the result is more or less the same, for parallel and partial versions in the *cahiers* all converge on "deux motifs fondamentaux dont l'écrivain cherche avec une visible difficulté à opérer la fusion au fil des pages".[77] Proust, too, apparently knows where he is going. His drafts are angled in on each other because of this recognised necessity, just as the textual geneticist instinctively grasps the meaning and destination of fragments which he/she comes upon out of context: trial formulation in the margins, "notes de régie" and documentary material. He/she knows that when it comes to the writing nothing unexpected will happen, for the procedures are already in place. So even *La Recherche*'s preparatory fragments are not as "disponibles" as all that, whatever impression one might get from the vague and confusing notes in the *cahiers*: "Je pourrais sans doute [...] dire que"; "Mettre quelque part capitalissime ce que je mets ici faute de place".[78] Such jottngs show that, even after the demise (?) of Realism, writers still subscribe to the clear idea of a goal to work towards according to established procedures. And even the final meaning of *La Recherche* scarcely changes in spite of its permutations: many crucial changes are secondary, for they come after the point when Proust turns away from *Contre Sainte-Beuve*, and the galaxy of ideas, styles and forward-thrusting narrative, fictional behaviour and historical event have already "gelled" and become logical in spite of all polymorphic appearances. When all is said and done, if there is an element of "non finito" in *La Recherche*, it is due to the author's death, and has not much to do with what one normally understands by incompletion.

Such facts, together with my general approach, make it easier to grasp the "isolated" examples found in the "avant-textes", for it soon becomes clear that their permanence or their disappearance confirm and reinforce an overall project which largely predates them, and in the light of which everything needs to be looked at. Thus Zola's plans and "ébauches", as has just been seen, may appear fragmented and hesitant, whereas in fact, the very detail of the plans conflicts with the apparent equal status of the possibilities they envisage. As he considers the mining accident in *Germinal*, Zola attempts to clarify the narrative line he is going to follow:

> L'effet de l'eau qui s'engouffre. Ils [Étienne, Chaval, Catherine] peuvent n'être pas tout à fait au fond [...] où ils se rencontrent [...]. Ils pourraient baiser dans une hallucination, dans la mort [...] Est-ce là que les Grégoire vont porter des souliers au vieux Maheu [...] Étienne doit-il tuer Chaval, là ou même à la fin?

The *dossiers* of *Germinal* contain similar dilemmas:

> Étienne doit il tuer Chaval là ou à la fin? *Son besoin de meurtre satisfait. alors quoi dans *le r[oman]* l'étude sur les chemins de fer?*." [79]

This is a long-term strategy which logic would quickly clarify. It goes beyond *Germinal* and brings in the very different novel which Zola will write four years later. Zola set out his overall and detailed aims as he started work on each novel, so there was no possibility that he could have ended up with a text which was much different from the version we know. The hesitations and dead ends do not point to viable alternatives but rather the only solution possible.

If Zola is unique in the kind of interminable "strategic" inner monologue he indulges in in his manuscripts, he is merely bringing to the surface a widespread, if less generally conscious, process. It fits in very closely, as Grésillon has pointed out, with what Sokolov calls an "inner discourse", and can be viewed as a "composante de l'écriture intervenant *avant* la verbalisation", an *ad hoc*, unstable, private, non-linear and fragmented phenomenon, which is very close to elements which crop up in the drafts.[80] This allows Grésillon to say that "il y a potentiellement un inachèvement chronique dans tout processus d'écriture".[81] And yet, once again, I cannot see how such inner ruminations can be anything other than a fragmented attempt to set out what the text is going to become and define the means of achieving that end, which all the constraints and all the echoes involve. It may be discontinuous, like any long-term undertaking, but it makes room for choices and options in which the outline of the final text is already apparent. Even as a hypertext,[82] it is not a seething aimless mass: far from being what some people have claimed,[83] the basis for a text's growth and development is not linguistic (even if, as we see in Flaubert, some turns of phrase are there from the start) but plans and scenarios. So it might be more profitable to wonder about what writing and structure *are for* and what purpose they serve. We might perhaps examine the constraints and aims which lead to the text's final version. *Hérodias*, for example, recounts an historical event — so it is not essentially mere writing, but rather a tendentious re-writing of lived experience. In the same way, *Germinal* is not just a complex assemblage of words, but especially scenes from mining life.[84] There is nothing exclusive about this (rigid exclusives are not part of real literary study), but is does have the advantage of replacing thematics at the centre of manuscript studies, which opens the way for the eminently nineteenth-century (but strangely neglected) idea of textual cohesion and motivation.[85]

**Notes**

[1] See S. Bourjea et al., "Entretien sur la critique génétique".
[2] R. Laufer et al., "La bibliogénétique: une nouvelle technologie?", 207.
[3] D. Ferrer & J.-L. Lebrave, "Introduction" to *L'Écriture et ses doubles*, 10.
[4] Éric Le Calvez, "Description, stéréotype, intertextualité", 27.
[5] *Éléments de critique génétique*, 206.
[6] See R. Melançon's excellent article, "Le statut de l'œuvre", 53.
[7] M. Espagne, "Les Enjeux de la genèse", 110.
[8] Ibid., 118. We shall see that the starting point is less of a problem than the end point.
[9] "Le statut de l'œuvre", 52. This is not Melançon's view.
[10] D. Ferrer & J.-L. Lebrave, op.cit.
[11] C. Quémar, "Hypothèses sur le classement des premiers cahiers Swann", 23.
[12] P. Lejeune, "Les carafes de la Vivonne", 296.
[13] Hence the droning, oracular dogmaticism we frequently come across. See J. Bellemin-Noel's essay which in spite of its date is still used as a basis for proof ("Reproduire le manuscrit, présenter les brouillons, établir un avant-texte") and R. Debray-Genette's "Esquisse de méthode", which also goes back to 1977 and draws on work which goes back to the early 70s. See also G. Genette, *Palmpsestes*. In English language studies, see G. Falconer, "Genetic criticism", which adopts earlier ideas on teleology without much criticism. Most of these statements have a peremptory ring to them which is rarely contested: see J. Anis, *De la lettre au livre*, 169-91.
[14] C. Quémar, art.cit., 24. Cf. also J. Neefs who considers that *A La Recherche* has "une structure dont la globalité est très tôt concertée." ("Objets intellectuels", 112)
[15] See A. Grésillon (*Eléments de critique génétique*, 147) who claims that "[le] regard privilégié [de la génétique] n'implique pas soumission à un courant de la critique textuelle" but goes on to write: "la critique 'avant-textuelle' doit élaborer sa propre voie."
[16] Once again modern texts, *opera aperta* and finished works, nineteenth and twentieth centuries, Zola, Flaubert, Ponge, Perec, Joyce, Proust, are lumped together (A. Grésillon, op. cit., 17, and *Manuscrits d' écrivains*).
[17] A. Grésillon, *Eléments de critique génétique*, 17. Cf. "[la génétique] ne peut être assimilée aux méthodes de critique textuelle" (146). Why not? I cannot see why the two cannot have very useful things to say to each other.
[18] It is not teleology which is a trap here so much as the ideology which condemns it. See A. Grésillon (op.cit., 18)

[19] Grésillon, however, is anxious for us to "[mettre] le texte aux oubliettes" (*Eléments de critique génétique*, 17)

[20] There are many examples in A. Herschberg-Pierrot, "Les Notes de Proust", for exeample: "Peut-être ce morceau sur les salons pendant la guerre serait-il mieux pendant la guerre quand Cottard vient en major chez les Verdurin [...]"; "quand je parle de Fr le Champi, si j'en parle" (60, 74).

[21] "Les Notes de Proust", 70.

[22] C. Quémar, "Hypothèses sur le classement des premiers cahiers Swann", 17.

[23] *Le Temps retrouvé* was to a great extent already written when Proust came to write the intermediary volumes.

[24] Flaubert, *Correspondance*, III, 409 (Letter of 6 October 1864). See below what Virginia Woolf writes — and the forward dynamic which comes from "definitive" formulations which pepper Flaubert's mansucripts.

[25] See his detailed notes written in 1868–9 for the plan of the Rougon-Macquart.

[26] Thus Herschberg-Pierrot very perceptively points out that "en 1913, quand Swann paraît, il existe une version d'ensemble de l'œuvre finissant par *l'Adoration perpétuelle* et *Le bal des têtes*. Proust confie à A. Beaunier en décembre 1913 'tout est écrit mais tout est à reprendre'" ("Les Notes de Proust", 66). Proust is still unsure of many things, the organisation of the end for example, but many features will remain ("Les Notes de Proust", 70) and he is very clear about his message, whereas throw-of-the-dice genetics gives the impression that he could have written anything.

[27] Quoted by B. Brun, "Les incipit proustiens et la structure profonde du roman", 294.

[28] C. Quémar, "Hypothèses sur le classement des premiers cahiers Swann", 24

[29] See A. Grésillon, *Eléments de critique génétique*, 148–9.

[30] See for example A. Grésillon's collection of essays, *De la génèse du texte. Manuscrit texte, auteur critique.*

[31] This is typical of *Éléments de critique génétique* from beginning to end.

[32] Melançon, art. cit., 63

[33] "Polylogue", *Cahiers de critique génétique*, 4.

[34] H. Mitterand, "Genèse de la *Faute de l'Abbé Mouret*", 184. Mitterand also discusses the dynamics of textual genetics and "[les] origines, [de] sa situation dans 'l'air du temps', [de] la raison de ses étapes, de ses rythmes, de ses stratégies et de ses tactiques, [du] montage des dispositifs, [des] modes d'émergence des composantes romanesques".

[35] See P. M. Wetherill, "L'élaboration des chambres d'*Hérodias*".

[36] Mitterand, art. cit., 202. My italics.

[37] Mitterand, "Le métatexte dans les Ébauches de Zola", 50.

[38] Ibid., 57.

[39] Ibid., 59.

[40] P.-M. de Biasi, "Flaubert et la poétique du *non-finito*", 48. The *non-finito* in question refers to the gaps in the published text which increase its multiple ironies and ambiguities.

[41] C. Quémar, "Autour de trois avant-textes de l'ouverture de la *Recherche*", 9–10.

[42] B. Brun, "Les incipit proustiens", 291.

[43] See my "Aux origines culturelles de la génétique", which suggests links between writing methods and nineteenth-century education.

[44] R. Debray-Genette, "Esquisse de méthode", 31.

[45] Many works demonstrate this. See for example *L'Éducation sentimentale, les scénarios* and the transcriptions of the manuscripts of *Un Cœur simple* and *Hérodias*, in *Corpus Flaubertianum*.. See also K. Matzusawa, *Introduction à l'étude critique et génétique des manuscrits de "L'Éducation sentimentale" de Gustave Flaubert*. Strangely, these publications are not much used. See also C. Becker, *Émile Zola, la Fabrique de Germinal* and H. Marel, *"Germinal", une documentation intégrale*.

[46] See the excellent analysis in R. Pierrot's, *Honoré de Balzac* (243–5), of the first mapping-out of the *Comédie Humaine* and its subsequent development and F. David's analysis (246) of the "Introduction" to the *Études de Mœurs*, ghosted by Balzac himself.

[47] See *La Recherche*, where the "argument" worked out between 1908 and 1913 is then expanded and developed between 1913 and 1922, which is why Proust can say to A. Beaunier in December 1913, that "tout est écrit mais tout est à reprendre" (*Correspondance*, éd., Kolb, XII, 367).

[48] *Eléments de critique génétique*, 19.

[49] This is sometimes called intertextuality.

[50] P.-M. de Biasi, synopsis in *Point de rencontre*.

[51] Even the chance event for Proust of the outbreak of the First World War and its well-documented impact on *La Recherche* only reinforce the novel's basic argument.

[52] Let me stress the risks involved in blocking together texts from different periods and cultures. For one thing, they are much too rich and full of contemporary meaning.

[53] "Les manuscrits flaubertiens ou la recherche de l'absolu", 97. My italics.

[54] "Hypothèses sur le classement des premiers cahiers Swann", 23.

[55] Cf. H. Nyssen, *Du texte au livre: les avatars du sens*, 14: "L'esprit de l'auteur [...] est comme *accordé* sur l'idée qu'il se fait nécessairement de son lecteur" (Valéry) [...] Aucune des étapes qui conduisent du texte au livre ne peut échapper [à cette transaction livre/lecteur] sous peine de fausser le livre tout entier." It would be interesting to explore the emergence of the "ideal" reader in manuscripts — for that too gives meaning to the movement of the "avant-textes".

[56] Flaubert, *Correspondance*, II, 416 (Letter of 26 August 1853).

[57] See R. Debray-Genette, "Genèse d'une description: les écuries d'*Hérodias*", 163.

[58] A. Grésillon, D. L. Lebrave, C. Viollet, *Proust à la lettre*, 69.

[59] See, for instance: "La première [description] est coordonnée, comme dans le texte final, à l'entrée de Frédéric dans ce lieu [...]"; "C'est dans la version publiée, à peu de variantes près, la description du bureau [...]"; "la version finale recèle encore l'analepse 'comme la première fois' [...]"; "le détail du turbot n'est pas absent de la version publiée de *L'Éducation sentimentale* [...]"; "au contraire de ce qu'elle deviendra dans la version finale" (É. Le Calvez, art.cit, 28, 29, 36).

[60] R. Debray-Genette, "Esquisse de méthode", 24.

[61] See B. Brun, "Le dormeur éveillé, genèse d'un roman de la mémoire", 295, note 2.

[62] M. Fumaroli, "Des carnets au roman: l'ironie esthétique des Goncourt dans *Mme Gervaisais*".

[63] I am not suggesting that the manuscripts should be used to explain and clarify the final version. Such readings eliminate ambiguities which might well (as is frequently the case with Flaubert) be a deliberate characteristic of the final version but not of earlier drafts.

[64] R. Debray-Genette, "Esquisse de méthode", 24.

[65] R. Debray-Genette, *Avant texte, texte, après-texte*, 167.

[66] Put simplistically, one is in danger of losing all interest in the differences between *L'Assommoir* and *La Débâcle*.

[67] If you concentrate on the writing and ignores the text, you neglect all questions of value (the final version may be better or worse than earlier versions) in an author's choices and decisions.

[68] I will not repeat what I have written elsewhere. See "Manuscripts and literary history"; "La notion d'avant-texte: perspectives modernes et moyenâgeuses"; "Aux origines culturelles de la génétique".

[69] Grésillon strangely mixes this up with what a masterpiece might be (*Eléments de critique génétique*, 213).

[70] *Correspondance*, II, 31 (Letter of 16 January 1851).

[71] *Diary of Virginia Woolf*, II, 209 (October 14 1922).
[72] Ibid.
[73] C.G.Hoffmann, "From Short Story to Novel", 176.
[74] Ibid, 183.
[75] *Diary of Virginia Woolf*, II, 209 (October 29, 1922).
[76] C.Quémar, "Autour de trois avant-textes de l'ouverture de la *Recherche*", 8.
[77] Ibid.
[78] See H. Bonnet, B. Brun, *Matinée chez la Princesse de Guermantes, cahiers du "Temps retrouvé"*, 292, 343.
[79] N.A.F. 10307, f° 383, in Colette Becker, *Émile Zola. La Fabrique de "Germinal"*, 246–7.
[80] This a paraphrase of a quotation found in Grésillon.
[81] A.Grésillon et al., *Proust à la lettre*, 67.
[82] See J.-L. Lebrave's fascinating analysis: "L'édition génétique".
[83] Ibid., 216.
[84] It must be said that Zola scholars have, in many cases, been much more interested in historical and social matters than, say, some people working on Flaubert's or Proust's manuscript material.
[85] Grésillon in *Éléments de critique génétique* offers a useful analysis of genetic mechanisms but does not seem to be interested in their purpose. Non-finality turns its back on the argumentative, which nevertheless typifies nineteenth-century writing — even Flaubert's.


**Works Cited**

Flaubert, Gustave, *Corpus Flaubertianum, Édition des manuscrits d' "Un Cœur simple"*, ed. Giovanni Bonaccorso et al. (Paris: Les Belles Lettres, 1983)

Flaubert, Gustave, *Corpus Flaubertianum. Édition des manuscrits d' "Hérodias"*, ed. G. Bonaccorso et al. (Vol.1, Paris: Nizet, 1991; Vol. 2, Paris: Sicania, 1995)

Flaubert, Gustave, *Correspondance*, 4 vols, ed. Jean Bruneau (Paris: Gallimard, 1973–98)

Flaubert, Gustave, *L'Éducation sentimentale: Les scénarios*, ed. Tony Williams (Paris: Corti, 1992)

Anis, J., *De la lettre au livre* (Paris: CNRS, 1990)

Becker, C., *Émile Zola. La Fabrique de Germinal* (Lille: SEDES et Presses Universitaires de Lille, 1986)

Bellemin-Noel, J., "Reproduire le manuscrit, présenter les brouillons, établir un avant-texte", *Littérature*, 28 (1977), 3–18

Biasi, P-M de, "Flaubert et la poétique du *non-finito*" in *Le Manuscrit inachevé*, ed. L.Hay et al.

Biasi, P.-M. de, Synopsis in *Point de rencontre*, Colloque de l'Université d'Oslo, 7–10 September 1994

Bonnet, H. & Brun, B., *Matinée chez la Princesse de Guermantes, cahiers du "Temps retrouvé"* (Paris: Gallimard, 1982)

Bourjea, S. et al., "Entretien sur la critique génétique", *Cahiers de critique génétique*, 1 (May 1991)

Brun, B., "Les incipit proustiens et la structure profonde du roman", in *La Naissance du texte*, prepublication text (Paris: CNRS, 1987)

Brun, B., "Le dormeur éveillé, genèse d'un roman de la mémoire", *Cahiers Marcel Proust*, 11 (1982)

Debray-Genette, R., *Avant texte, texte, après-texte* (Paris: CNRS, 1982)

Debray-Genette, R., "Esquisse de méthode", in *Métamorphoses du récit* (Paris: Seuil, 1988)

Debray-Genette, R., "Genèse d'une description: les écuries d'*Hérodias*", in *Les Manuscrits des écrivains*, ed.L.Hay (Paris: Hachette-CNRS, 1993)

Espagne, M., "Les Enjeux de la genèse", *Études Françaises*, 1984

Ferrer, D. & Lebrave, J.-L., "Introduction" to *L'Écriture et ses doubles*

Falconer, G., "Genetic criticism", *Comparative Criticism*, 45 (1993), 1–21

Fumaroli, M., "Des carnets au roman: l'ironie esthétique des Goncourt dans *Mme Gervaisais*", in *Romans d'archives*, ed. J. Neefs & R. Debray-Genette (Lille: Presses Universitaires de Lille, 1987), 79–102

Genette, G., *Palimpsestes* (Paris: Seuil 1982)

Goldin, J., "Les manuscrits flaubertiens ou la recherche de l'absolu", *Urgences* (July 1989), 95-102

Grésillon, A., *De la génèse du texte. Manuscrit texte, auteur critique* (Tusson: Du Lerot, 1988)

Grésillon, A., Lebrave, D.L. & Viollet, C., *Proust à la lettre* (Tusson: Du Lerot, 1990)

Grésillon, A., *Éléments de critique génétique* (Paris: PUF, 1994)

Hay, L. et al., *Le Manuscrit inachevé* (Paris: Éditions du CNRS, 1986)

Hay, L., ed., *Les Manuscrits des écrivains* (Paris: Hachette-CNRS, 1993)

Herschberg-Pierrot, A., "Les Notes de Proust", *Genesis*, 6 (1994)

Hoffmann, C.G., "From Short Story to Novel", *Modern Fiction Studies*, vol. XIV, no. 2 (1968)

Laufer, R, "La bibliogénétique: une nouvelle technologie?", in *La Naissance du texte* (Paris: CNRS, 1980)

Lebrave, J.-L., "L'édition génétique", in L.Hay éd., *Les Manuscrits des écrivains* (Paris: CNRS/Hachette), 208–23

Le Calvez, Éric, "Description, stéréotype, intertextualité", *Romanic Review*, 84 (January 1993)

Lejeune, P., "Les carafes de la Vivonne", *Poétique*, 31 (September 1977)

Marel, H., *"Germinal", une documentation intégrale* (Glasgow: University of Glasgow French and German Publications, 1989)

Matzusawa, K., *Introduction à l'étude critique et génétique des manuscrits de 'L'Éducation sentimentale' de Gustave Flaubert*, 2 vols, (Tokyo: Éditions France Tosho, 1992)

Melançon, R., "Le statut de l'œuvre", *Études françaises*, 28 (Autumn 1992), 49–66

Mitterand, H., "Genèse de la *Faute de l'Abbé Mouret*", in *Les Manuscrits des écrivains*, ed. L.Hay (Paris: Hachette-CNRS, 1993)

Mitterand, H., "Le métatexte dans les Ébauches de Zola", *Genesis*, 6 (1994)

Neefs, J., "Objets intellectuels", in *Les Manuscrits des écrivains*, ed. L. Hay (Paris: CNRS Éditions Hachette, 1993)

Nyssen, H., *Du texte au livre: les avatars du sens* (Paris: Nathan, 1993)

Quémar, C., "Autour de trois avant-textes de l'ouverture de la *Recherche*", *Bulletin d'Informations proustiennes*, 7 (1976)

Quémar, C., "Hypothèses sur le classement des premiers cahiers Swann", *Bulletin d'Informations proustiennes*, 13 (1982)

Pierrot, R., *Honoré de Balzac*, Fayard 1994

"Polylogue", *Cahiers de critique génétique*, 1 (May 1991)

Riffaterre, M., "Sémiologie intertextuelle", *Revue d'esthétique*, 1972

Wetherill, P.M., "Aux origines culturelles de la génétique", in *Sur la génétique textuelle*, eds., D. G. Bevan & P. M. Wetherill (Amsterdam: Rodopi, 1990), 19–32

Wetherill, P. M., "L'élaboration des chambres d'*Hérodias*", *Orbis Litterarum*, 48 (1993), 245–68

Wetherill, P. M., " Manuscripts and literary history", *Dalhousie French Studies*

Wetherill, P. M., "La notion d'avant-texte: perspectives modernes et moyenâgeuses", *Neuphilologische Mitteilungen*, 89 (1988),18–32

*Diary of Virginia Woolf*, vol. II (1920–1924), ed. Ann Olivier Bell, (London: The Hogarth Press, 1978)

# HISTORY IN THE MAKING: A GENETIC APPROACH TO THE TUILERIES EPISODE IN *L'ÉDUCATION SENTIMENTALE*

## Tony Williams

The February Revolution of 1848 represented a major artistic challenge for Flaubert. How was a phenomenon of such complexity to be accommodated, without swamping the novel and without a jarring switch of focus from the apparently minor details of the private life of Frédéric Moreau to the major upheavals in the public sphere? Of the various events that took place during the three days of the February Revolution, which were to be selected for inclusion in the novel?[1] How was the historical significance of the February Revolution to be conveyed, given the technique of impersonality which had been adopted?[2] In grappling with some of these problems, Flaubert would have been conscious of the literary precedent set by Hugo's *Les Misérables*, which contains one of the earliest attempts to integrate a revolutionary upheaval into the novel.[3] Flaubert was critical of Hugo's novel, which had been published in 1862, and adopts a very different view of revolution.[4] The belief expressed in *Les Misérables* that armed insurrection represents "une convulsion vers l'idéal"[5] gives way in *L'Éducation sentimentale* to a vision of revolution as the expression of anarchic, even bestial, drives and energies. In opposition to a substantial body of republican thought which tended to view the successive upheavals of the nineteenth century as so much unfinished business left over by the French Revolution which would finally bring about a fairer and more rational society, Flaubert's view is distinctly anti-teleological.[6] Believing that the February Revolution was essentially backward-looking, rather than forward-looking, he would undoubtedly have agreed with Marx's view that it was "the ghost of the old Revolution which walked in the years from 1848 to 1851".[7] Such a negative view does not necessarily incapacitate Flaubert as a writer or invalidate his depiction of the February Revolution. The reactions provoked by Flaubert's treatment have, however, been extremely varied.

Both historians and critics for a long time held the view that *L'Éducation sentimentale* offers a remarkably accurate depiction of the February Revolution. As recently as 1981 in *Histoire et Langage dans "L'Éducation sentimentale"* Maurice Agulhon claimed that "un historien de 48 peut mettre l'*Éducation* dans son arsenal pédagogique".[8] More recent criticism, however, has tended to stress the problematic status of history in the novel, the refusal of a clear account of events, and the incompleteness of Flaubert's account of the February Revolution.[9] Christopher Prendergast's reading of the storming of the Château d'Eau in *Paris and the Nineteenth Century* persuasively argues that Flaubert refuses "the very idea of a 'history' that could be represented as a coherent and intelligible whole" and offers the reader an account that is so confused, fragmentary, and blurred that it "threatens the conventions of historical and narrative intelligibility".[10] A similar approach is adopted by Priscilla Ferguson, who argues in *Paris as Revolution* that as Flaubert has chosen to filter events through the muddled mind of Frédéric, there is no "artiste-flâneur" to make sense of what happens and "no outsize image, controlling metaphor to subsume the many parts of the city into a powerful unitary definition."[11] What strikes the modern critic is the way in which Flaubert's novel deconstructs the myth of revolution as heroic endeavour. A certain image of revolution as heroic collective purpose as expressed in works such as Hugo's *Les Misérables* or Michelet's *Histoire de la Révolution française* is subverted,[12] just as the component elements of Delacroix's famous painting "Liberty leading the People" are scattered across the pages of Flaubert's novel, leaving the reader with a "Delacroix in bits, disintegrated into devices and degraded fragments".[13]

The outcome of Flaubert's engagement with the problematics of representing revolution is reflected in the final version of *L'Éducation sentimentale* but the full extent and nature of that engagement can be most clearly appreciated by the exploration of the *avant-texte* of the novel, much of which has not been examined so far.[14] A genetic approach, focusing on the way Flaubert grappled with a series of problems relating to the representation of the February Revolution in a prolonged process of planning, documentation and composition, allows a different perspective on Flaubert's treatment of revolution to emerge. Whilst, as has been seen, the insistence of recent criticism, largely based upon the published version of the novel, has been on what might be termed Flaubert's dismantling of history, a genetic approach highlights "history in the making", that is to say the elaborate process of grafting onto the novel historical material drawn from a documentary base which needed to be adapted, expanded, and finally cut back in order to blend with the main fictional element. What is of central interest is the way the "February Revolution", as turning-point in French history, is apprehended, assimilated, demystified and deconstructed in the protracted production process which culminates in the final version of the novel. Preceding what might be called the "unmaking" of history in the final version, lies a "making" of history in the *avant-texte*, that is to say the selection, assemblage and elaboration of historical date destined for inclusion in the novel. Given the amount and complexity of material relating to the February Revolution, I have, therefore, chosen to concentrate here[15] on one particular episode, the ransacking of the Tuileries Palace, which has a particular significance within the mythology of revolution.[16] The discussion that follows is indebted to the pioneering work of Mike Wetherill, whose edition of the novel and analyses of 1848 in the *avant-texte* have done much to draw attention to the complex processes involved in Flaubert's writing of Revolution.[17]

**Scenarios**

Flaubert did not at first envisage that the February Revolution would occupy a particularly important place in the novel. In the very earliest plans[18] it is not mentioned at all and in the *scénarios* he drafted before he began to write the novel in September 1864, its principal significance consists in the effect it has on Frédéric:

> Un bruit de tambour les réveille. 48 éclate. <*Frédéric partage d'abord l'animation générale il se rafraîchit au grand air se retrempe dans l'humanité générale*> [19]

> Un bruit de tambour les réveille. <u>48 éclate</u>.
> Frédéric partage l'animation générale, se [retrempe] <*rafraîchit*> au grand air des Révolutions — veut s'y lancer. <*se compromet [en cela]* <*comme républicain*> *vis-à-vis de Nogent — article lyrique sur le sac des tuileries*>[20]

At this stage, before he embarked upon the composition of the novel, the February Revolution is essentially a backdrop, its main effect being to prompt an enthusiastic response in the generally apolitical protagonist and thereby revive to some extent the narrative momentum of the novel, which might otherwise have appeared to have come to some kind of resolution with the substitution of Rosanette for Madame Arnoux in the rue Tronchet apartment.[21] Referring as he does to the Revolution almost *en passant* means that the difficulties of a full-scale depiction are not envisaged.[22]

It is not until he drafts a detailed scenario for the Chapter, probably in 1868, that the historical element is expanded.[23] In this scenario, Flaubert makes a list in the left-hand margin of the major historical events of 1848 which are loosely co-ordinated with the fictional developments. However, the section relating to the February Revolution is still relatively brief:

> Un bruit de tambour le réveille. il se lève et s'en va.
> <u>Assiste</u> au Château d'Eau. prise des tuileries. homme qui fume sa pipe <*etc*>. <*De dedans le jardin on voit*> laquais déchirant leurs livrées. <*sac du Palais Royal*> promenade du trône. Coup de tonnerre. — Pendant ce

temps-là 4 gouvernements <*provisoires*> simultanés. Frédéric <*rencontre Hussonnet sceptique et blagueur au milieu de l'animation tandis que Frédéric y est pris*> hume l'air de la Révolution [avec délices] [est] <*étant le soir*> éreinté [le soir] et va se coucher chez lui. son domestique. "tout ce peuple!"[24]

Alongside references to major events such as the storming of the Château d'Eau and the ranscking of the Tuileries and the Palais Royal, we find the first indication of the contrasting reactions of Frédéric and Hussonnet, but also details such as the "homme qui fume sa pipe" which suggest that Flaubert has by this stage begun to acquire a documentary base. There is still, however, a striking lack of precise historical information: Flaubert has not yet begun to envisage the historical developments in any detail; surprisingly, there is little indication at this juncture of the importance and prominence which the February Revolution is destined to assume in the final version. History is, as it were, creeping up on Flaubert unawares.

**Documentary Notes**

Flaubert went to considerable lengths to familiarise himself fully with the events of 1848, consulting all the available historical works, newspapers and eye-witness accounts.[25] In addition, he was able to draw upon his own personal recollections, having witnessed both the storming of the Château d'Eau and the ransacking of the Tuileries Palace.[26] Flaubert made well over one hundred sides of detailed notes on the historical events of 1848–51.[27] Notes of this kind fall into the domain of exogenetics, which "designates any writing process devoted to research, selection, and incorporation, focused on information exterior to the writing."[28] Exogenetics cannot, however, be completely divorced from endogenetics, or the writing processes determined by the internal logic of the work. The process of note-taking is teleological; a writer will select those elements which may be of use in the composition of the work and endogenetic considerations infiltrate exogenetics. As Daniel Ferrer has recently argued, "even before the first plans or scenarios, every act of note-taking occurs with the expectation, however vague, that the note will somehow be used."[29] Every part of the *avant-texte* is determined by a projective logic, that is to say by a set of considerations relating to the future work. Paradoxically, as Pierre-Marc de Biasi suggests, since "pre-textual exogenetic elements tend inevitably to be progressively converted into endogenetic material", it follows that "exogenetic procedure contains within itself the principle of its own effacement by writing."[30] What is perhaps most striking is the plasticity of documentary material: pieces of historical information are gathered in order to be reworked subsequently in the fictional mill.

Flaubert's documentary notes on the sacking of the Tuileries are drawn from the accounts of contemporary eye-witnesses and historians.[31] In addition, he made extensive use of Daniel Stern's *Histoire de la Révolution de 1848* and Maxime Du Camp's notes for *Souvenirs de l'année 1848*. Generally speaking, Flaubert seems to have picked out details which serve to promote a negative view of the revolution as pure farce, stressing the way the Parisian mob ironically apes royalty, dressing up in royal garments and sitting on the throne. There is something comical about the man who insists on smoking his pipe in exactly the same place as before: "A la prise des tuileries un homme fume sa pipe sur la balustrade d'une fenêtre 'parce qu'en 1830 j'ai déjà fumé à la même place.'"[32] The figure of the prostitute, in a highly symbolic posture, is also picked out: "Dans l'ancien vestibule du roi, s'établit une Déesse de la Liberté trônant la pique à la main sur les monceaux de vêtements."[33] The selection of this *tableau vivant*, combined with the account of the appropriation and removal of the throne, suggests that what interests Flaubert is not so much the events themselves as the symbolic and mythical significance which is attached to them, revolution being reduced to a kind of symbolic parade.[34] Already in the documentary notes there is evidence of a process of ironic distancing, signalled typically by the use of quotation marks. This can be seen in the notes on Garnier-Pagès's *Histoire de la Révolution*, 1861–2:

> Aux Tuileries, envahissement de la Salle-du-Trône. (un bourgeois mit la robe <*de chambre*> de Louis-Philippe, et harangua le peuple <<c'est toujours avec un nouveau plaisir>> fait vu et rapporté à moi par Edmond de Goncourt) — On s'assoit dessus. Le Peuple est Roi <<fantaisie grotesque. mythe profond>> [35]

The parodic mimicking of royal forms of address is supplemented by the ironising of subsequent attempts by historians to make sense of events in the ultimately reductive commentary on the occupation of the throne offered by Garnier-Pagès.

**Sketches**

The integration of documentary material takes place in a series of sketches, which can be distinguished from the scenarios by virtue of their more detailed presentation and from the rough drafts by the use of the present tense and note-form.[36] There are a total of four sketches[37] in which the documentary material relating to the sacking of the Tuileries undergoes a remarkable process of expansion which transforms the neutral reference of the scenario ("prise des tuileries") into a richly symbolic historical pageant, a revolutionary set piece packed with colourful detail. In the first sketch (17607, f. 161v), which covers the whole of the February Revolution, almost all the details relating to the Tuileries episode correspond to the documentary notes or Du Camp's notes for *Souvenirs de l'année 1848*. Many of the notations involve virtually no change. The reference to the man who sits on the throne is taken from *Histoire de l'Armée*,[38] and the reference to the "Déesse de la liberté" from *La République dans les Carosses du roi*.[39] Other details relating to the portraits in the Chambre des Maréchaux, the rifle fire and the breaking of mirrors correspond to the account subsequently published by Du Camp.[40] The process of fictional adaptation is already apparent, however, in the attribution to Hussonnet of an attitude of mocking cynicism.[41]

In the second sketch (17606, f. 66v) further details are inserted, with the minimum of modification. The reference to "un lampiste", later omitted, corresponds to a note on *La République dans les Carosses du roi*, as does the reference to the portraits.[42] The description of the empty courtyard and the reference to the chess-players are taken directly from Daniel Stern.[43] There are, however, a number of details which suggest that Flaubert wants to go further than his documentary notes in the evocation of the wild and disorderly behaviour of the mob. In particular, the actions of the coachman do not appear to have any documentary basis.

In the much fuller third sketch (17607, ff. 12 and 16) a process of consolidation begins, with the various elements assembled in the first sketch being freely developed, not on the basis of historical actuality but according to fictional requirements and in line with a reactionary view of revolution. The surprise of the servants, the joking about the Reform banquet and the more furtive and animal-like behaviour of the coachman are all plausible rather than historically attested reactions. The participation of fictional characters is specified in a way which is not constrained by any historical account. The facetious comments of Hussonnet, which appear for the first time in the margin, are completely concocted, whilst the strangely precise detail of Frédéric setting his watch corresponds to Du Camp's account.[44] The evocation of the Parisian mob introduces imagery which is frequently found in descriptions of the populace and indicates Flaubert's initial reliance upon the "discours social" of his age.[45] Flaubert's first suggestion, "les fers des souliers comme des ongles", generates the more original image in the margin "comme un animal à plusieurs pieds onglés" (for "ongulés"), whilst the brief "clapotement des voix" and "le flot les repousse" represent the first appearance of the water imagery that will be developed in subsequent versions. The first attempt at determining the collective reaction of the mob on taking possession of the Tuileries Palace is tentative, echoing the account given by Du Camp.[46] At this stage there is a conflict between details which point to the "douceur des vainqueurs" and the incipient orgy of destruction, which leads to actions such as the breaking of the mirrors being relocated to the end of the episode when the mood of the mob has become more frenzied. The appearance of the "figures sinistres", which do not have a documentary basis, is indicative of a determination to develop a negative image of destructiveness designed to discredit the idea of the sovereignty of the people. The account of the removal of the throne is in line with notes made on *La République dans les Carosses du roi*,[47] but is described in emotive terms ("souillé") and the "femme en statue de la liberté" rounds off the episode in a symbolically appropriate way. By this stage the episode has been considerably expanded and is beginning to take on an alarming aspect, one which arguably draws upon a kind of collective paranoia rather than precise documentary sources. The formation of a reactionary view of revolution is clearly apparent; only later does Flaubert cover his ideological traces.

The next version (16707, ff. 7v and 12v) is intermediate between a sketch and a rough draft. Although the present tense is now abandoned for the past tense and although sentences are usually complete, much of the detail and texture found in the rough drafts is still missing. In this version further expansion and adaptation takes place, again with no reference to historical reality in what appears to be a process of free fictionalisation. In expanding the previous version, Flaubert improvises freely, adding to the exchange between Frédéric and Hussonnet. Hussonnet's quip about the throne ("C'est là le cas de le dire le vaisseau de l'Etat balotté sur une mer orageuse") develops the associations of the crowd with water, which had been suggested in the earlier description ("le peuple arrivait — irrésistible comme une marée") and the subsequent comments ("en le voyant tomber <<bon voyage>> — <<pauvre vieux symbole") extend the association further. Descriptive details relating to dress and appearance, such as "Le tricorne d'un général sur celui d'une femme", are multiplied[48] and subjective colouring is added, the bare "souffle chaud" of the previous version being expanded to "Grand souffle tiède le frappa au visage comme l'exhalaison d'un four", for instance. Running counter to this is a move to depersonalise the account which leaves descriptive details hanging loose in such a way as to create a sense of emptiness: when the reference to Frédéric adjusting his watch is deleted, what

is left ("Une pendule marquait une heure vingt minutes") develops a characteristically gratuitous ring. This version also begins the process of orchestration of violence and destruction. The sense of the immense power of the populace is evoked by a new image — the "marée d'équinoxe" — and the first indication of a gradual build-up of savagery is given. Following a brief moment of "douceur" marked by intermittent breakages, a "démolition générale" is ordained, in which there is "plus de frein" and a "joie de carnaval", and the "figures sinistres" multiply. Realising that the references to destructiveness are premature, the added letters indicate how the material will be reordered so that the description of the throne comes before the general ransacking of the palace.

What emerges from this analysis of the sketches is a clear demonstration of the way documentary information functions as a springboard for a much fuller visualisation of the episode, deeply marked by a reactionary view of insurrection prevalent at the time, and benefiting from a considerable degree of fictional licence. At this stage, historical material is still undergoing a slow process of elaboration as Flaubert seeks to establish a relatively clear and coherent, but as yet largely unattributed, image of a revolutionary moment, one which calls into question a received idea of the people as guardian of the nation's future. The status of history in the sketches is consequently very different from the final version: the account refers unproblematically to specific historically attested occurrences, as if it were possible for the fictional account to provide a gangway to the real world, bracketing the whole question of the relationship between narrative account and historical actuality.

**Rough Drafts**

Having integrated, freely adapted and ordered his documentary material in the sketches, Flaubert embarked in the rough drafts on the complex task of full textualisation.[49] The Tuileries episode is covered in three runs each made up of three or four folios.[50] It is in the rough drafts that what is most distinctive about Flaubert's handling of Revolution begins to crystallise and the characteristic densely textured quality of the writing begins to take shape. It is at this stage, too, that the familiar process of rendering descriptions opaque and problematic begins to operate, with the result that the narrative account shimmers with uncertainty.

In the first section of the episode, the account of the coachman stealing sugar is finalised. The reference to the jokes about the "Banquet de la Réforme", (17607, f. 16v), which established a clear historical connection, is deleted, perhaps on account of the monopoly on witticisms Hussonnet is acquiring. In the next section a succession of such witticisms (17607, f. 13v) are attributed to Hussonnet, as Flaubert liberally illustrates the notion of revolution as farce, as well as encoding Frédéric's more earnest response.[51] The description of the portraits in the "Salle des Maréchaux" becomes more detailed, with the historically accurate reference to Bugeaud's lacerated portrait being retained but without any explanation of why he should be made an exception (17607, f. 13). The account hesitates over whether to present the description without reference to who perceives the incongruity of the fierce attitudes depicted in the portraits, the impersonal "ils se tenaient" alternating with an undefined collective "on les voyait" (17607, ff. 13, 14). The depersonalised reference to the time of day is expanded into a curiously precise description — "Une pendule en porcelaine dorée" (17607, f. 13) — which becomes simply "Une grande pendule" (17607, f. 14) in the next version and "Une grosse pendule" (17607, f. 15) in the third. Flaubert also varies the actual time, switching from twenty to half past one and then back to twenty minutes past. Precision combines with inconsequentiality in such a way as to destabilise the account itself, generating a strong sense of insignificance.

The section which describes the mob pouring into the Palace undergoes extensive development. Anne Hershberg-Pierrot has stressed the clichéd nature of the water imagery that is used in connection with the people on the rampage and suggests that it is being deployed ironically.[52] However, it is also possible to detect an attempt to rehabilitate a cliché by expanding it in an unexpected way. Two images are found in the first rough draft — that of the torrent and that of the exceptionally high tide. These are then fused in the second and third rough drafts into the single image "comme un fleuve refoulé par une marée d'equinoxe" (17607, ff. 14, 15), which effectively conveys a sense of one huge group of people being pushed forward by an even greater mass behind them. In a way which anticipates Zola's description of the miners on the rampage in *Germinal*, Flaubert uses water images in an attempt to evoke the almost fluid quality and the immense power of the populace. He also, like Zola, presents the people in aggregate as a single entity, noting how individuals falling make no impression on the overall impression of a "masse grouillante"[53] and reverting to the animal imagery of the sketches when the noise of the voices of the crowd are compared to "les rages d'une bête géante".[54] The power of the crowd, Robert Tombs has pointed out, was an essential image of the revolution, often linked with the forces of nature.[55] It is debatable whether Flaubert is following or ironically contesting the standard way of evoking the behaviour of the mob. In what for the novelist was a new domain, crowd psychology, one senses a struggle to define the collective reactions of the mob in memorable terms: "l'expression d'une gaminerie railleuse" and "l'amusement d'une exhibition" are deleted to be replaced by "le plaisir d'une exhibition" and "l'étonnement joyeux d'une victoire facile".[56] Although this section had begun with a reference to Frédéric and Hussonnet leaning over the stairway, the description of the mob entering the Royal Palace is not focalised: at this point Flaubert wishes to push the account beyond their limited perceptions. Hussonnet's reaction is developed, however, in the comment, "les héros ne sentent pas bon", which is prompted by the newly added detail of the "gens en sueur", found in the margin in the first rough draft (17607, f. 13), integrated in the second version (17607, f. 14), and modified to "les héros ne fleurent pas bon" in the third (17607, f. 15). The description of the "démolition générale", scheduled in the last sketch to begin at this point is postponed. The change is clearly made here not out of a desire for historical accuracy but in order to create a gradual escalation of vandalism and disorder.[57]

The scene in the "salle du trône", now begins with an expanded description of the throne itself and of the "blousier", now a "prolétaire", who sits on it (17607, f. 17). The details, unsupported by documentary evidence, given of his appearance and expression — "l'air jovial et stupide comme un [poussah] <*magot*> chinois" — encode a naked fear of the class which was invariably perceived as "dangereuse". In the first rough draft (17607, f. 17) Hussonnet thinks of taking a turn on the throne but this is deleted in the second[58] and omitted in the third (17607, f. 14v). The expanded description of the way the throne, now demystified as a "fauteuil", is tossed around, thrown out of a window and finally burnt, is accompanied by further witticisms, picking up on the earlier water imagery, from Hussonnet: "<<Ah! saprelotte, comme il chaloupe! [Je comprends la métaphore. le vaisseau] <*le vaisseau de*> l'état <*cette fois*> est balancé sur une mer orageuse. Cancanne-t-il! Cancanne-t-il!>>" and "<<Bon voyage>>" (17607, f. 18). The removal of the throne is the symbolic heart of the February Revolution but is surrounded derisorily by a series of clichés, made faintly amusing by being wrenched out of context. The difference between Hussonnet's cynical wisecracks and the more emotional response that might have been prompted in an earlier period is underlined in a marginal addition in the first rough draft.[59]

The following expanded description of the wanton destruction of the mob, triggered by the removal of the throne, is preceded by an expanded analysis of the delirium produced by the new prospect of unlimited happiness which has just been opened up: "Comme si à la place du trône, une perspective de bonheur illimité se fût découverte" (17607, f.18). The motives for the destructive frenzy of the mob are carefully elaborated ("Moins par vengeance que pour affirmer sa possession, faire à son tour preuve de royauté").[60] The analysis develops a persuasive cogency, suggesting that a coherent overview of events is being sought at points like this. The description of the dressing up, fully documented by Flaubert and part of the popular iconography of Revolution, creates a powerful image of a topsy-turvy, carnavalesque world, bordering in places on the grotesque. Although pejorative terms are not avoided ("la canaille s'affubla, ironiquement [...]", 17607, f. 14v), one suspects that Flaubert himself revelled in the "ivresse de bruit et de couleur" and the inversion of social and gender distinctions as marked by clothing, as examples of cross-dressing and the appropriation of insignia by the crowd proliferate.

There is also an accumulation of what are described in the first rough draft as "épisodes étranges", all pointing to a kind of comical incongruity as members of the "uncivilised" masses engage in civilised activities and a kind of normality prevails in the eye of the revolutionary storm. Although there is documentary evidence to support the presence of some of these figures, they are carefully marshalled to produce a definite effect and Flaubert makes a number of changes. The chess-players become card-players, the man in the mackintosh playing the piano disappears,[61] and the explanation of the presence of the man smoking his pipe "philosophiquement" is deleted,[62] turning him into a somewhat enigmatic figure.

The darker and more alarming side of revolution is strengthened, as the "figures sinistres" first mentioned in the sketches multiply.[63] The account of the frustrated urges to rape and pillage is expanded considerably, without the benefit of a solid documentary base. The whole passage develops a vision of the complete breakdown of the social order, suggesting that, as the historian Furet put it, France was "caught in the trap of its own fantasies of social dissolution".[64] The reference to the "nombreuses intentions de vol reprimés par le trop grand nombre" (17607, f. 17) has a speculative ring, whilst the elaboration of the description of the convicts with their "rires de satyre et de bourreau" cavorting on the beds of princesses owes more to a kind of social paranoia than to historical actuality. Where do the convicts come from? The answer can only be from the foul rag-and-bone shop of the collective social imagination. In the elaboration of the description of the "galériens avec des rires de satyre et de bourreau", Flaubert mobilises a stereotyped image, with references to "des bras tatoués" and "ceux qui couchaient sur la paille enfoncèrent les bras jusqu'à l'aisselle dans les édredons des princesses et se roulaient dessus par consolation de ne pouvoir les violer".[65] The whole passage culminates, as had always been intended, in the magnificent image of the prostitute as statue of Liberty. She is shedding some of her appendages — the "bonnet rouge" and the "pique" — and also loses her earlier ecstatic expression and is made significantly "immobile" (17607, f. 20), turning before our eyes into a frightening symbol. Whilst Daniel Stern, rather heavy-handedly, had insisted on seeing this strange *tableau vivant* as "le signe vivant de la dégradation du pauvre et de la corruption du riche" and "l'ironique symbole de l'honneur populaire outragé",[66] Flaubert turns the prostitute into a monumental figure of profanation, who silently devalues and discredits the whole revolutionary enterprise.

By the time he has completed the third run of rough drafts the episode has taken shape and, as far as the content is concerned, is virtually the same as the final version. In the fair copy and "manuscrit autographe" but few small changes are made, largely designed to make the account more succinct.[67]

**Conclusion**

The genetic approach to the February Revolution inevitably raises the thorny question of the status of the historical element in the novel. As P. M. Wetherill has stressed, examining the *avant-texte* means that "On voit à quel point, au départ, Histoire et fiction sont distinctes — et combien l'Histoire, marginalisée, est manipulée par la fiction déjà en place."[68] Flaubert consistently subordinates history to the requirements of fiction. In the *scénarios,* he uses the Revolution to trigger a change in mood in his protagonist. Although Flaubert was nothing if not industrious in his documentation of the Revolution, it would be a mistake to imagine that he gives us an account which is historically accurate. Note-taking was, as has been seen, a selective process and when integrating documentary material Flaubert grants himself considerable licence, embellishing his material and even concocting happenings for which there is no documentary source. Furthermore, from the outset it is apparent that Flaubert's approach to the sacking of the Palace is shaped by a reactionary ideology which calls into question the idea of the sovereignty of the people and sees "le peuple" not as the guardian of liberty and agent of progress, but as an irresistible force which, once unleashed, is capable of wanton destruction. The extent to which such an alarmist view is questioned is unclear: it is difficult to know whether the stereotyped *topoi* of water and animality in connection with the revolutionary mob are mobilised in a parodic way. Flaubert's characteristic use of an "ironie frappée d'incertitude"[69] is already apparent in the *avant-texte*. The elaboration of the Tuileries episode is also marked by uncertainties over point of view. Initially the various elements are simply listed without any indication of who perceives them. At a certain point perception indicators are inserted, opening up the possibility that the account is focalised. However, such is the weight of detail and the forcefulness of the analysis that the hypothesis that the perspective is switching to that of a more authoritative narrator seems equally plausible. The *avant-texte* allows us to observe how Flaubert's writing constitutes itself in such a way as to make the question "qui voit?" unanswerable. Whilst straightforward historical accounts such as Stern's are characterised by a single perspective, Flaubert's approach involves constant slippage from one viewpoint to another. There is, however, despite the constant shifts of perspective, a strong impetus to ensure that a telling image of revolution is created. The various elements which make up the account are carefully orchestrated in order to make an important point. Flaubert does more than depict the way the behaviour of the mob degenerates. The reactions of Hussonnet and Frédéric, respectively frivolous or uncritical, are an essential part of the problem pinpointed by Flaubert. Likewise, the prostitute in the pose of the statue of Liberty presiding over the spectacle represents not just profanation, but also a fatal paralysis which extends throughout the whole of society, preventing effective restraint. The analysis of the manuscripts reveals that, whilst there is a stage where historical material is assembled by Flaubert, as it might be by a historian, this soon gives way to a stage in which this material is churned around in the *avant-texte* from which it will finally emerge in a solidifed form which is both richer and more uncertain. Although there are clear losses if our expectations are that a totally reliable accurate account is going to be elaborated, there are also significant gains when it comes to developing a more sophisticated, multi-facetted, understanding of what constitutes historical truth.

---

**Notes**

[1] "Et puis, quoi choisir parmi les Faits réels? Je suis perplexe." (*Correspondance*, III, 734)

[2] "Je ne crois même pas que le romancier doive exprimer *son* opinion sur les choses de ce monde. Il peut la communiquer, mais je n'aime pas à ce qu'il la dise. (Cela fait partie de ma poétique, à moi.)" (*Correspondance*, III, 786)

[3] *Les Misérables* contains a long account of the insurrection which took place in Paris in June 1832.

[4] "Décidément ce livre, malgré les beaux morceaux, et ils sont rares, est enfantin. L'observation est une qualité seconde en littérature, mais il n'est pas permis de peindre si faussement la société, quand on est le contemporain de Balzac et de Dickens." (*Correspondance*, III, 236)

[5] *Les Misérables*, 1266.

[6] Pierre-Marc de Biasi has argued that Flaubert rejects "une théorie de l'Histoire illustrée [...] qui permettrait de représenter les événements selon l'ordre d'une causalité téléologique préétablie" (*L'Éducation sentimentale*, 666).

[7] "For it was only the ghost of the old revolution which walked in the years 1848 to 1851, from Marrast, the *républicain en gants jaunes* who disguised himself as old Bailly, right down to Louis Bonaparte" ("The 18 Brumaire of Louis Bonaparte", 148)

[8] "Peut-on lire en historien *L'Éducation sentimentale*", 41.

[9] See in particular the contributions in *Littérature et Révolutions en France*. Graham Falconer, ("Le statut de l'histoire dans *L'Éducation sentimentale*", 116) stresses that Frédéric's reactions to historical events are incoherent and that "face à ce tourbillon d'attitudes différentes, et en l'absence de toute tentative de synthèse de la part du narrateur, on a l'impression que c'est moins Frédéric que l'écriture elle-même qui se met à dérailler". In the view of Marc Girard ("Regard sur la Révolution du regard: à propos de Flaubert", 124), "au terme d'une présentation impersonnelle et lacunaire, les éléments historiques apparaissent donc comme peu objectifs, assez grotesques et fondamentalement inessentiels". P. M. Niang ("L'insertion de l'histoire dans *L'Éducation sentimentale*", 105) claims that "On assiste à une sorte de 'déshistorisation' de l'Histoire, car celle-ci n'est désignée que par des scènes à caractère fictionnel." Gisèle Guillo ("Les Tuileries", in *L'Éducation sentimentale. L'histoire*, 37) makes the point that "La réalité est à peine historique, émiettée, réduite à l'incident, à l'anecdotique et suscite plus de conjectures, de perplexités que de certitude." In addition, P. M. Wetherill ("Flaubert and Revolution", 21–3) observes that "expansion and detail alternate with ellipsis and vague allusion", that "Revolution is a variable and slippery thing in Flaubert" and that the text does not offer a "comprehensive, patterned treatment of revolution".

[10] See Chapter 5, "Insurrection", in *Paris and the Nineteenth Century*, 111, 114.

[11] *Paris as Revolution. Writing the Nineteenth-Century City*, 109.

[12] Prendergast, 111.

[13] Ibid., 120.

[14] See, however, P. M. Wetherill's edition of the novel, Appendice I: "1848 dans les brouillons" and Anne Herschberg-Pierrot, "Le Travail des stéréotypes dans les brouillons de la 'Prise des Tuileries' ", 43–61.

[15] This discussion forms part of a larger study, "History in the Making in *L'Éducation sentimentale*", which has been supported by funding from the University of Hull, the British Academy and the Leverhulme Trust. For an analysis of an earlier episode see Tony Williams, "Comment s'écrit une page d'histoire: 'l'affaire du Château d'Eau' dans *L'Éducation sentimentale*", in *Espace de la page, temps de l'écriture*, ed. Brian Stimpson, "Legenda" series, European Humanities Research Centre (forthcoming).

[16] See Hershberg-Pierrot, 43: "Dans la mémoire de 1848 et des 'journées de février', l'iconographie, les récits et les souvenirs historiques confèrent à l'épisode des Tuileries une place de choix."

[17] See, in addition to the "Préface" to his edition of the novel, "Flaubert and Revolution". Wetherill stresses the way "the idea of revolution, in Flaubert, passes inevitably through language and is defined by language" (29), a point also made by Prendergast: "Questions of language were of paramount importance" (106).

[18] See "Mme Moreau (roman)" in *Carnets de Travail*, 286–96

[19] N.A.F. 17611, f. 91. See Flaubert, *L'Éducation sentimentale: Les Scénarios*, 55. The following conventions are used in the linearised transcription of manuscript material: [...] = Deletions: <...> = Additions (Italics added); [<...>] = Material added then deleted; {...} = Editorial comments. In addition, accents have been restored and abbreviated words given in full but Flaubert's punctuation and underlining have been retained.

[20] N.A.F. 17611, f. 46. (*L'Éducation sentimentale: Les Scénarios*, 164).

[21] Falconer (118) has drawn attention to the way in which, at the beginning of a number of chapters, a historical event functions as an "embrayeur du récit, source d'énergie narrative".

[22] All the evidence suggests that the scenarios covering the three Parts of the novel were written in 1864, before composition began. See *L'Éducation sentimentale: Les Scénarios*, 14–6.

[23] N.A.F. 17611, f. 44 (*L'Éducation sentimentale: Les Scénarios*, 272–5).

[24] Ibid.

[25] Flaubert's documentation of 1848 extended over several years (see *Carnets de Travail*, 371–2). The extent of his reading is suggested in a letter written in June 1867: "Je bûche la

Révolution de 48 avec fureur. Sais-tu combien j'ai lu et annoté de volumes depuis six semaines, Vingt-sept, mon bon" (*Correspondance*, III, 624).

[26] An account of Flaubert's experiences can be found in Du Camp's *Souvenirs de l'année 1848*, 75–110.

[27] These notes were transferred to the Dossier for *Bouvard et Pécuchet* and can be found in the Bibliothèque Municipale in Rouen (MS g 226⁴ ff.125.204). The dossier has been analysed by A. Cento in *Il Realismo documentario nell' "Éducation sentimentale"*.

[28] See Pierre-Marc de Biasi, "What is a literary draft? Towards a functional typology of genetic documentation", 44–5.

[29] "Clementis's cap: Retroaction and Persistence in the genetic process", 227.

[30] "What is a literary draft", 45–6. De Biasi has suggested that we should think of documentation not so much as a way of ensuring that historical reality will somehow make its way into the text, but rather as a strategy which is designed to "give a motivational and heuristic kick-start to the endogenetic process" (*ibid.*, 46).

[31] These notes have been transcribed in Appendix I.

[32] See Appendix I, Notes on *Journées illustrées de la Révolution*.

[33] See Appendix I, Notes on Louis Tirel, *La République dans les Carosses du roi*.

[34] R. Tombs (*France 1814–1914*, 20) has analysed the "revolutionary passion play" (Richard Cobb) as "a rubric of actions, words and symbols which revolutionary events followed and through which they were understood to be revolutionary".

[35] See Appendix I.

[36] The sketches are designated by the terms "esquisse" and "ébauche" by French genetic critics. There is a general consensus that they constitute a distinct type of manuscript and correspond to a distinct stage in the process of literary production.

[37] N.A.F. 17606, f. 161v; 17606, f. 166v; 17607, f. 12; 17607, f. 7v and f. 12v. Diplomatic transcriptions of these sketches can be found in Appendix II. In these transcriptions material is arranged according to its distribution in the original manuscript and Flaubert's spelling, use of accents and diacritical signs are retained. When material from the manuscripts is quoted in the main body of this analysis it is given in linearised form. The transcriptions in Appendix II and III were prepared by Larry Duffy, a research assistant supported by the University of Hull Research Support Fund.

[38] Appendix I, "un homme du peuple s'asseoit sur le trône et proclame la République" (f. 181).

[39] The wording of the sketch is closer to the documentary note (Appendix I) than to the description in Daniel Stern, *Histoire de la Révolution de 1848*, 174: "L'une d'elles, une pique à

la main, le bonnet rouge sur la tête, se place dans le vestibule et y demeure, pendant plusieurs heures, immobiles, les lèvres closes, l'œil fixe, dans l'attitude d'une statue de la Liberté: c'est une fille de joie."

[40] The reference "salle à manger, bocaux de sucre" corresponds to Du Camp, *Souvenirs de l'année 1848*, 94: "Dans une salle à manger prenant jour sur le jardin et située au rez-de-chaussée, nous vîmes une table servie: sur une grande nappe blanche des bols de lait, des cafetières d'argent au chiffre du roi, des petits pains dans des corbeilles." Du Camp's account also refers to the sporadic firing and the breaking of mirrors: "Nous entendîmes quelques détonations; on cassait les glaces à coups de fusil" (96).

[41] Hussonnet's act of writing his name in the visitors book is based upon the note from *Histoire de l'armée*: "sur le registre des visiteurs Étienne Arago s'inscrivit. beaucoup d'autres imitèrent cette plaisanterie" (Appendix I). The sarcastic comment "<<quel mythe>>" is reminiscent of the note from Garnier-Pagès: "Le Peuple est Roi <<fantaisie grotesque. mythe profond>>" (Appendix I).

[42] See Notes on *La République dans les Carosses du roi*: "Un garçon lampiste meurt pour avoir avalé un diamant" and "Les portraits de Soult et de Bugeaud lacérés. [...] On respecta les portraits des Princesses, du duc de Wurtemberg et de Joinville" (Appendix I).

[43] "Pendant que la colonne de Dunoyer sortait d'un côté, une masse considérable de peuple entrait de l'autre dans la cour du château. La place du Carrousel et la cour étaient, depuis dix minutes environ, complètement vides" (171); "On remarque deux individus qui, assis à une table d'échecs, la tête appuyée sur leurs mains, les yeux fixés sur l'échiquier dans l'attitude d'une méditation profonde, donnent, au milieu du plus étourdissant fracas, une muette comédie" (173).

[44] Frédéric sets his watch at the time Du Camp had given for the entry of the mob into the palace: "Nous montâmes au premier étage; je regardai l'heure à une pendule placée sur une très-belle cheminée en marbre vert de mer incrustée de camées; il était une heure dix minutes" (94).

[45] See Herschberg-Pierrot (45): "Les brouillons développent des images, aux trois-quarts effacés de la version définitive, qui sont en fait l'expansion de stéréotypes utilisés, dans un discours social fortement péjoratif, pour désigner la foule populaire, et, en particulier, la foule révolutionnaire: ce sont, d'un côté, la métaphore lexicalisée du 'troupeau', l'image de l'animalité, de l'autre les clichés du 'flot', de la 'marée' et de ses débordements."

[46] "Le sentiment qui dominait était la curiosité; nulle haine, nul ressentiment." (94)

[47] See "Le trône jeté par la fenêtre, porté sur la Bastille et brûlé au pied de la colonne de juillet" (Appendix I). Compare with Stern's account: "Enfin, vers trois heures, le trône,

incessamment foulé aux pieds par les insurgés, qui avaient tous voulu y monter à leur tour, est enlevé à bras et descendu par le grand escalier dans le vestibule du pavillon de l'Horloge" (174).

[48] See also the expanded description of the expression of the portraits: "contenances terribles qui étaient ironie, en la circonstance".

[49] Diplomatic transcriptions of the rough drafts can be found in Appendix III.

[50] The first sequence was NAF 17607, ff. 16v – 13 – 17. The second sequence was 17607, ff. 13v – 14 – 18 – 20. The third sequence was 17607, ff. 15 – 14v – 17.

[51] See "Je constate ma personne" and "Je respire avec orgueil l'air de la corruption" (17607, f. 16v).

[52] "Le travail des clichés, des formules préconstruites du discours social [...] relèverait d'une stratégie concertée de la citation — une forme d'ironie, si l'on entend par là un procédé de reprise déviante, de mention du discours de l'autre, permettant au sujet 'citateur' de s'effacer derrière la citation, derrière l'énonciation d'autrui." (52)

[53] See also the repeated observation "Ceux qui tombaient ne faisaient pas de trou."

[54] This appears in the first rough draft (17607, f. 13) but is omitted in the second (17607, f. 14). The animal parallel can also be found in the references to the "mugissement de cent mille bœufs" (17607, f. 13), the "long mugissement" (17607, ff. 14 and 15) and the "piétinement de tous les souliers" (17607, f. 15).

[55] "The power of the crowd, an essential image of revolution from Delacroix to Eisenstein, impressed contemporaries as a force of nature: a torrent, a flood, an ocean, overwhelming all barriers." (12)

[56] First rough draft (17607, f. 16v). This analysis is retained in the second rough draft (17607, f. 14) but deleted in the third (17607, f. 15).

[57] "Alors de la démolition générale, on brise tout [...] meubles. porcelaine [...]" is deleted in the first rough draft (17607, f. 13) and only the isolated breakages retained in following drafts (17607, ff. 14 and 15).

[58] "Voilà le peuple souverain [j'en fais partie, moi, du peuple! si je m'y mettais?>>] " (17607, f. 18).

[59] See "Ce spectacle qui aurait fait pleurer les gens d'un autre règne <époque> exalta sa joie" (17607, f. 17).

[60] 17607, f. 18. In addition the questionable gloss, "il s'en prend à la matière inerte", is omitted in following drafts (17607, ff. 17 and 18).

[61] "<Un Monsieur en mackintosh jouait une valse sur un piano>", 17607, f. 20; "[Un Monsieur en paletot jouait une valse sur un piano]", 17607, f. 17v.

[62] "[parce qu'il était venu là en 1830]", 17607, f. 17v.

[63] "les figures sinistres sont plus nombreuses", 17607, f. 17.

[64] Quoted in Tombs, 9.

[65] 17607, f. 20. The various descriptions of the second rough draft, one interlinear, one marginal, are resolved into "des galériens enfonçaient leurs bras dans la couche des princesses" in the third ( 17607, f. 17v).

[66] Stern, 174: "L'une d'elles, une pique à la main, le bonnet rouge sur la tête, se place dans le grand vestibule et y demeure, pendant plusieurs heures, immobile, les lèvres closes, l'œil fixe, dans l'attitude d'une statue de la Liberté: c'est une fille de joie. On défile devant elle avec toutes les marques d'un profond respect. Triste image des justices capricieuses du sort: la prostituée est le signe vivant de la dégradation du pauvre et de la corruption du riche. Insultée par lui dans les temps prétendus réguliers, elle a droit à son heure de triomphe dans toutes nos saturnales révolutionnaires. La Maillard travestie en déesse Raison, c'est l'ironique symbole de l'honneur populaire outragé, abruti, qui se réveille en sursaut dans l'ivresse et se venge." For a perceptive comparison of Flaubert's and Stern's presentation of the prostitute, see Jann Matlock, *Scenes of Seduction*, 90–2.

[67] There are two deletions in the one folio of the fair copy that has been found (17607, f. 19): the analysis of the collective reactions of the crowd ("chacun s'excitant de la colère et du tumulte...") and the reference to the urchin who steals brochures. Most of the alterations are purely stylistic, as in the final description of the prostitute: "Dans l'antichambre, <*debout*> sur un tas de vêtements, se tenait une fille publique en, Statue de <*la*> Liberté [et qui ne répondait pas aux interpellations] <*immobile*> – les yeux gds ouverts <2> [immobile] <*1*>, effrayante — ". Here the deletion of "et qui ne répondait pas aux interpellations" is a good illustration of the process of enrichment by subtraction which characterises the stylistic elaboration that takes place in the fair copy, whilst the added numerals reflect a desire to find not just "le mot juste" but also the best possible word order. There are very few changes of significance in the "Manuscrit autographe", which is housed in the Bibliothèque Historique de la Ville de Paris. Apart from the substitution of one word by a near synonym, there are deletions which increase the succinctness of the account, such as "C'était le peuple [qui arrivait]"(f. 336) or the removal of superfluous detail, such as "En bas, dans une petite salle [voûtée]" (f. 336).

[68] See "*1848 dans les brouillons*", 583.

[69] *Roland Barthes*, 146.

## Works Cited

Flaubert, Gustave, *Carnets de Travail*, ed. Pierre-Marc de Biasi (Paris: Balland, 1988)

Flaubert, Gustave, *Correspondance*, ed. J. Bruneau, 4 vols, Bibliothèque de la Pléiade Paris: Gallimard, 1973–98)

Flaubert, Gustave, *L'Éducation sentimentale*, ed. Pierre-Marc de Biasi (Paris: Seuil, 1993)

Flaubert, Gustave, *L'Éducation sentimentale*, ed. P. M. Wetherill (Paris: Garnier,1984)

Flaubert, Gustave, *L'Éducation sentimentale: Les Scénarios*, ed. Tony Williams (Paris: Corti, 1992)

Agulhon, Maurice, "Peut-on lire en historien *L'Éducation sentimentale*", in *Histoire et Langage dans "L'Éducation sentimentale"* (Paris: SEDES, 1981)

Barthes, Roland, *S/Z* (Paris: Seuil, 1970)

Biasi, Pierre-Marc de, "What is a literary draft? Towards a functional typology of genetic documentation", in *Drafts*. Special issue of *Yale French Studies, 89* (1996), 26–58.

Camp, Maxime Du, *Souvenirs de l'année 1848* (Geneva: Slatkine Reprints, 1979)

Cento, Alberto, *Il Realismo documentario nell' "Éducation sentimentale"* (Naples: Liguori, 1967)

Falconer, Graham, "Le statut de l'histoire dans *L'Éducation sentimentale*", in *Littérature et Révolutions en France*, ed. G. Harris and P. M. Wetherill (Amsterdam: Rodopi, 1991)

Ferguson, Priscilla Parkhurst, *Paris as Revolution. Writing the Nineteenth-Century City* (University of California Press, 1994)

Ferrer, Daniel, "Clementis's cap: Retroaction and Persistence in the genetic process", in *Drafts*. Special issue of *Yale French Studies, 89* (1996), 223–36

Girard, Marc, "Regard sur la Révolution du regard: à propos de Flaubert", in *Littérature et Révolutions en France* (Amsterdam: Rodopi, 1991)

Guillo, Gisèle, "Les Tuileries", in *"L'Éducation sentimentale". L'histoire* (Paris: Ellipses Marketing, 1989)

Herschberg-Pierrot, Anne, "Le Travail des stéréotypes dans les brouillons de la 'Prise des Tuileries' ", in *Histoire et Langage dans "L'Éducation sentimentale"*, (Paris: Sedes, 1981)

Hugo, Victor, *Les Misérables* (Paris: Gallimard, 1951)

Marx, Karl, "The 18 Brumaire of Louis Bonaparte", in *Surveys from exile* (Harmondsworth: Penguin, 1973)

Matlock, Jann, *Scenes of Seduction* (New York: Columbia University Press, 1994)

Niang, P. M, "L'Insertion de l'histoire dans *L'Éducation sentimentale*", in *Littérature et Révolutions en France* (Amsterdam: Rodopi, 1991)

Prendergast, Christopher, *Paris and the Nineteenth Century* (Oxford: Blackwell,1992)

Tombs, Richard, *France 1814–1914* (London: Longman, 1996)

Wetherill, P. M., Appendice I: "1848 dans les brouillons", in *L'Éducation sentimentale* (Paris: Garnier, 1984)

Wetherill, P. M., "Flaubert and Revolution", in *Literature and Revolution*, ed. David Bevan, (Amsterdam: Rodopi, 1989)

# APPENDIX I: DOCUMENTARY NOTES

**Notes on Louis Tirel, *La République dans les Carosses du roi*, 1850**
<u>Drame des tuileries après la révolution du 24 février 48</u> — <u>brochure par St Amant</u> <u>négociant en vins, capitaine en 2$^e$ à la I$^{ère}$ légion de la garde nationale</u> rédacteur du Palamide, journal d'échecs. — M$^r$ St Amant s'installa aux tuileries —

pendant la 1$^{ère}$ heure, pas de pillage. <<aux caves>> deux barils de rhum dans l'appartement du Prince de Joinville — les pertes éprouvées par les personnes attachées au service du roi s'élèvent à plus de 500,000 francs.

— dans les combles, des femmes mirent des robes de soie et des dentelles par-dessus leurs haillons. — d'autres remplissent leurs poches de brocarts ou de franges d'or. Dans l'ancien vestibule du roi, s'établit une Déesse de la Liberté trônant la pique à la main sur les monceaux de vêtements.

Les appartemens {*sic*} du duc d'Orléans restés intacts —

Le trône jeté par la fenêtre, porté sur la Bastille et brûlé au pied de la colonne de juillet — lorsque les tapissiers vinrent pour enlever le dais, les <u>blessés</u> se jetèrent dessus et s'en firent des calottes rouges. Les portraits de Soult et de Bugeaud lacérés. 600 fusils déposés près de l'horloge disparurent. On respecta les portraits des Princesses, du duc de Wurtemberg et de Joinville. [...].

Un garçon lampiste meurt pour avoir avalé un diamant. — conduit à St Germain l'Auxerrois avec les honneurs militaires. (g.226$^4$, f. 175 recto and verso)

**Notes on Jules du Camp, *Histoire de l'Armée et de tous les Régiments*, vol. iv (1850)**

sur le registre des visiteurs Étienne Arago s'inscrivit. beaucoup d'autres imitèrent cette plaisanterie.

un homme du peuple s'asseoit {*sic*} sur le trône et proclame la République. (g.226$^4$, f. 181)

**Notes on *Journées illustrées de la Révolution***

A la prise des tuileries un homme fume sa pipe sur la balustrade d'une fenêtre <<parce qu'en 1830 j'ai déjà fumé à la même place. le soir bal. au piano du duc de Nemours. (g.226⁴, f. 185)

**Notes on Garnier-Pagès, *Histoire de la Révolution*, 1861–2**

Aux Tuileries, envahissement de la Salle-du-Trône. (un bourgeois mit la robe <*de chambre*> de Louis-Philippe, et harangua le peuple <<c'est toujours avec un nouveau plaisir>> fait vu et rapporté à moi par Edmond de Goncourt) — On s'asseoit {*sic*} dessus. Le Peuple est Roi <<fantaisie grotesque. mythe profond>>. (g.226⁴, f. 190)

# APPENDIX II: SKETCHES

### Ébauche I: Transcription of 17606, f. 161v (Extract)

Déesse de la liberté
en bonnet rouge
la pique à la main  
sur un monceau de   tetue.   Tuileries. – salle à manger, bocaux de sucre. l'escalier. Chambre des Maréchaux.
       immobile                                  Rencontre Hussonnet qui écrit son nom sur le livre des
    vêtements                    arrivée du peuple. homme qui fume sa pipe.        visiteurs Ils montent
                 Un blousier s'asseoit sur le trône Le Trône souillé et promené – Coups de fusils eclatent     ensemble

           <<quel mythe>> dit Huss.                         bris de glaces  on creve les tableaux

  la chaleur est trop forte    Dans le jardin. – on decharge des fusils. Coup de tonnerre. laquais dechirant
              ils redescendent
                      leur livrées. –


### Ébauche II: Transcription of 17606, f. 166v (Extract)

La Cour des Tuileries vide, car la colonne Dunoyer venait de partir.  αle peuple
n'était pas encore arrivé.
                                   où un dejeuner  servi p' les
          En bas, au rez de chaussée. salle à manger des domestiques. tasses de café
                                         Carrieth.-bocal de sucre
      ?               au lait. bocal de sucre cocher de fiacre. – étonnement α silence
 Frederic xxxxxxxx mains
   . xxxxxxxx
   xxxxxxxx mêlés xxxxxxx.  Au bas de l'escalier, rencontre Hussonnet qui écrit son nom sur le livre des
                          adresses. visiteurs. – un lampiste.
                                                      – portraits – remet sa montre
                                     des Maréchaux
          Montent l'escalier, – salle du trone       – arrivée du peuple. craquemt de
                                                          boiseries,. souffle chaud . Marseillaise
                         sa pipe
          homme qui fume dans l'embrasure d'une fenêtre. – on casse les meubles
               les glaces      puis bruit de pas. – voix   tout à coup crepines rideaux – robes
          etc – bris de porcelaine. Deux joueurs d'echecs. – mascarade. – femmes

               qui se pommadent. un autre qui vole des feuilletons, costumes
              grotesques. – ils sont portés par le flot.
  Fenêtre – Homme qui fume  De là ils
                    de la fenêtre voient, les voitures brûler. – aspect de la Place du
          Carrousel. –

          Un blousier s'asseoit sur le trône – << quel mythe >> dit Hussonnet.

  dans l'antichambre  La foule est trop nombreuse. – ils s'en vont de peur d'être ecrasés.
            Femme en statue de la Liberté –

156

## Ébauche III: Transcription of 17607, f. 12

```
                                      ⌐etait
    et    sur   le seuil  La   cour du  Carrousel  vide. -  car    la colonne Dunoyer qui avait  pris
    les domestiques                       p.t  la chambre
         emus            le chateau venait de   partir. - & le   peuple n'était  pas encore arrivé
    pales d'étonnement   sans rien  demander
                                   que
                                                     voutée   donnant              sur le 1er
  causaient avec ceux    on
         poliment        Entrait  En bas, au rez de chaussée - salle  où dejeuner servi par les
        qui   venaient            bols   xxbxxxx     xxxxxxxxxxxxxxxxxx  xxxxxx
                                  domestiques . tasses de café au  lait - N.Cocher de  fiacre en carrieth.
   qquns s'attablèrent                       - jeta
         en faisant des      prit à deux mains. en poudre   - coup  d'œil   à  la  derobée - croque .
           plaisanteries
         sur le banq    mangeait un bocal de sucre, - etonnement & silence. le nez dans
                                                                                       le goulot
     de la Reforme. - d'autres  debout   M    inquiet         l'orifice ψ
                                Au bas de l'escalier, rencontre Hussonnet, qui ecrit son nom sur
                          le livre des   visiteurs , - un   lampiste .
                                                              Sauf Bugeaud
    que dit Hussonnet?                                                     attributs  guerriers
          maintenant           ils                                              fiers
   <<je fréquente le gd monde α   Montant/arend l'escalier – salle des Marechaux  les portraits - reme/it sa
   je respire l'air des                    ensemble                                       Fr.
   cours                         sur une pendule     à une  pendule de porcelaine
   v'la une farce >> bein ?     montre 1 heure 1/20 minutes.                     bleue
                                Xx  Marseillaise -
                                Arrivée du peuple. - craquement des boiseries . souffle chaud -
                                                       les fers des souliers comme des
    comme un animal                                       mille        ongles
    à plusieurs pieds           Marseillaise. - puis  bruit de pas sur le plancher - α clapotement
    onglés
                          de voix . - Tout à coup un gd fracas = bris d'une glace -  puis
                   bruits partiels de porcelaine
                                  de meubles ...
                          on   casse tout, desordre.      - les  boiseries    craquaient.
                                                                  la chaleur
                                                                  etouffante
                          ψ  douceur des vainqueurs              la foule augmentent
                             ôtent les/a bayonnette
```

## Ébauche III (Continued): Transcription of 17607, f. 16 (Extract)

```
   M  la foule augmente
         le flot  les pousse    d'appartement en appartement - déjà beaucoup de
                                                                      monde
   curiosité                          à part
   l'amusement
   l'entrain d'une exhibition  Deux joueurs d'echecs - mascarades, crepines, rideaux, - - - -
               xxxxx
   l'entrain xx d'une bataille Femmes qui se pommadent – un autre qui vole des feuilletons.
   le sentiment d'une conquête. on  dechire les etoffes - on prend les vêtem
      la joie
   Chacun se sentait        costumes grotesques, - mascarades, crepines, rideaux - figures
   roi. <<vous êtes tous                                                          sinistres
                rois>>                   ouverte  sur le balcon
   des souver            Fenêtre: homme qui fume sa pipe. - De là, ils voient les voitures
   tout à coup un gd fracas brûler.  - aspect de la place -    hotel de Nantes -
   bris d'une glace -                                      brûler. aspect de la place du Carrousel
   puis des/e porcelaine de Un blousier s'assoit sur le trône.<< quel mythe>> dit Hussonnet.
                le trône est boule/s culé, souillé, on l'emmene - jeté par la fenêtre
   meubles.               La foule est trop nombreuse. - ils ont peur d'être ecrasés. α s'en vont.
   les boiseries                                                          bonnet rouge, pique
   craquent M          Dans l'antichambre, femme en statue de la Liberté    immobile. -
```

157

### Ébauche IV: Transcription of 17607, f. 7v

Il prit la rue de Rohan – en regardant à gauche terrain qui monte / hotel de Nantes. – profil des batiments du Louvre – baraques. – doyenneté. ψ

Aspect de la Place — B se tenaient
<del>Dans la cour</del> du Carrousel. des rassemblements d'hommes <del>qui restaient</del>
ça α là M ) devant l'arc de triomphe
ψle Palais vitres  <del>debout</del> – xx restes de bivouac – ⌐un cheval mort <del>sous l'arc de</del>
blanches eclaires                                                          A
entre les <del>le casque d'un dragon</del>       H  sur   des portes⌐
pierres grises – <del>triomphe – toutes les portes etaient ouvertes</del> α⌐le seuil √les domestiques
                          conversaient          venaient
– un gd calme⌐   fort emus <del>pâles causaient</del> poliment avec ceux qui <del>entraient</del>. on entrait

<del>Dans la cour</del>  sans rien demander.
les
                                                du rez de chaussée
              En bas, <del>au rez de chaussée</del>. dans une salle xxxxxxxxxxxxxxxxxx
                                  Des curieux circulaient autour des tables
                                                                s'assirent
       des bols de café au lait etaient servis qques <del>uns des</del> s'<del>attablaient</del>/ en
                                                                èrent
                                                  xxx les     xxxxxxxxxx
          plaisantant , sur le Banquet de la Reforme. <del>et</del> – d'autres restaient
                                       et
           debout. et Parmi ceux-là, un cocher de fiacre <del>en carrieth</del>. Il saisit
                              plein       de droite α de gauche
         à deux mains un bocal⌐de sucre en poudre, jeta <del>autour de lui</del>
                                              <del>voracement, le nez perdu</del>
           un regard inquiet puis se mit à manger<del>,</del>
                  le <del>large</del> goulot                       son nez <del>pl</del>
           dans <del>l'orifice du bocal</del>                             plongeant

                    À l'entrée du vestibule.       <del>crut reconnaître le profil d'en bas</del>
                  <del>Au bas de l'escalier</del>, <del>Frederic</del> rencontra <del>Hussonnet</del>, ecrivant
                                                      un homme
en personne >>  son nom sur le registre des visiteurs.
<del>comme vous</del>                            Mais "tiens Hussonnet." <del>xxxx Fre</del>]
voyez. reprit le bohème <<Maintenant⌐
        - Je frequente <del>maintenant</del> le gd monde. Je respire l'air des cours

      v'là une farce ! hein?>>

                   Et ils montèrent   ensemble l'escalier
                                              ces illustres etaient⌐
                                Les portraits de <del>xxxxx</del>
et arrivèrent La <del>eh</del> Salle des Marechaux. <del>Sauf Bugeaud lacéré</del> – tous etaient
                    ⌐sauf celui de Bugeaud – lacéré. on les voyait
           intacts – <del>attributs guerriers</del>, – ⌐la main sur leur sabre,

              avec des affûts de canon derrière eux…contenance <del>terrible</del>.
                                       qui etaient ironie , vu la
                                <del>sur</del>       circonstance
                   <del>Frederic remonte sa montre</del> Une pendule <del>qui</del> marquait

le frappa au visage    une heure vingt minutes.
comme l'exhalaison
d'un four.                        ⌐ils se penchèrent sur la rampe
                                      un gd souffle tiède –
                                        qui
                 <del>Puis</del> l/La Marseillaise –. ⌐le peuple arrivait – irresistible
                            C'etait l⌐p
                                 d'equinoxe
         comme une marée . Puis le chant s'arrête.
             On n'entendait plus⌐  marchant    le vaste
                    – bruit de mille pas sur le plancher – clapotement de
                            ⌐frappant
                            ⌐contre les murs⌐
                         voix.  ⌐Cependant douceur. – on avait retiré les
                                            bayonnettes des fusils –

**Ebauche IV (Continued): Transcription of 17607, f. 12v**

On se promenait   il entrait. l'amusement
   rien que de la Curiosité où se melait le pe d'une exhibition, l'entrain d'une
               bataille,   la   joie d'une conquête. chacun se sentait roi.
   cependant
   de temps à autres une tombait
   vitre. un meuble qui ⌠tout a coup un  gd frac. la  une glace est brisée – une
                              meubles.
            demolition      generale.    vases de porcelaine. . . . . . . . .

                                        les boiseries craquaient,
            La foule augmentait. ¶le flot les poussait d'appartement
                         plus de  frein . - c'est le signe de la possession -joie de  carnaval (2)
                         N choses singulieres         sur  un gueridon
   en appartement. A -      deux joueurs d'echec, à part - des femmes qui

   se pommadent.      Un autre me/it des feuilletons sous son tablier.
       un homme  fume  sa pipe - philosophiquement - Puis
   ⌠Ça s'aigrit. On dechire les rideaux –  (I) crepines d'or – chapeaux
               Là  plumes
   de femme – sur la d'un forgeron – Le tricorne d'un general
                                       puis. . . .
   sur celui d'une femme –  . . . figures sinistres sont plus
             mechanceté.
   nombreuses. C

                                                     accoudé
               Fenetre ouverte. un  homme   fume   sa pipe  sur le
   balcon.
                  terrain un peu montueux -
       ⌈De là – aspect de la Place  –  hôtel de Nantes  –  profil   des

   bâtiments du d/Doyenneté. – barraques du Louvre.⌉
             où tombait du plafond un
   ⌡B salle du trône  –  dais de velours rouge.
                          dessus         un autre lui succède
       ⌠Un blousier s'asseoit sur le trône – <<quel mythe>>
   dit Hussonnet. –  on  fit plus que de s'y asseoir. –
                                au dessus des têtes.
       puis soulevé, – balancé xxxxxxxxxxx

   – C'est là le cas de  dire  le Vaisseau de l'Etat balotté sur
                                  Pauvre
   une mer orageuse. ce vieux symbole!>>

                 puis jeté par la fenêtre - en bas où il fut
                   en le voyant tomber << bon voyage –  << pauvre vieux
                                                     symbole – M
   repris . α promené  jusqu'à  la  Bastille, où on le brûla

                                   compacte. – chaleur.
           Mais la foule devint trop nombreuse. Ils ont peur

   d'etre ecrasés α s'en vont.⌡Dans l'antichambre – une

   fille en Statue de la Liberté, bonnet rouge, pique –

   ouvrant de gds yeux – immobile – eff ne repondait pas

                   aux interpellations – effrayante, extatique.

# APPENDIX III: ROUGH DRAFTS

## Brouillons I: 17607, Transcription of f. 16v (Extract)

En bas, dans une salle du rez de chaussée, des bols de
          et
café au lait etaient servis. Des curieux circulaient autour des tables.
        en
Qques uns s'attablèrent, ~~se faisant des~~ plaisanteries/ant ~~sur le banquet~~
~~de~~

~~la Reforme~~ – les autres restaient debout; α parmi ceux-là un
      prit   gd plein
cocher de fiacre. Il saisit à deux mains un bocal ~~plein~~ de sucre
         un regard
en poudre, jeta de droite α de gauche inquiet, puis se mit
   voracement
   ~~les xxxxxxx~~
à manger, son nez plongeant dans le goulot.

 à l'entrée du vestibule, un homme ecrivait son nom sur
       Fr. le reconnut par derrière
le registre des visiteurs α ~~croyant le reconnaître~~

         Je m'introduis à la Cour.
– tiens! Hussonnet.     ~~Je constate ma personne~~
         ~~Comme vous voyez~~
– en personne!>> reprit le Bohème. << ~~Maintenant je frequente~~
     avec orgueil  { Maintenant je frequente
le ~~gd monde~~! Je respire L'air ~~des Cours~~. Voilà une farce, hein?
       de la corruption
    avec orgueil  ~~le grand~~
  Et Et ils montèrent ensemble l'escalier α arrivèrent
dans la salle des Marechaux.

## Brouillons I (Continued): Transcription of 17607, f. 13

percé, au ventre et à la tête
sauf celui de Bugeaud lacéré
lacéré
Les portraits de ces illustres etaient tous intacts - sauf celui de
α ces illustres ils se tenaient    leur
Bugeaud lacéré... On les voyait / la main sur le sabre, - avec des
On voyait ces illustres
                                                 attitudes
unaffûts de canon derrière eux    dans des contenances terribles
                                        jurant
        contrastaient xxxxxxxx   avec            en porcelaine dorée
        qui etaient xxxxxxxxxxxx) les circonstances Une pendule marquait
                                  la situation
une heure, vingt minutes.
                        Hussonnet xxx α Frederic
        sous le Pavillon de l'horloge, tout à coup
Mais tout à coup              Huss. Fr.
plus fort        La Marseillaise - ... Ils se penchèrent sur la rampe. -
eclata comme le          monta d'en bas
rugissement      un gd souffle, tiède comme l'exhalaison d'un four les frappa au visage.
mugissement de cent                    B  Un impulsion le chassait d'en bas
mille            C'etait le peuple qui arrivait ... ..irresistible, tassé .... comme
boeufs                        α se roulait en montant
bizarrerie des costumes.  un torrent qui montait les marches, comme un marée d'equinoxe
resserré etroitement              palier
          deux        elargissement au premier-.. s'etala - se dispersa -.    tous les
entre les murs de l'escalier  Puis α le chant s'arrêta. I On n'entendait plus que le bruit de mille pas
        les deux pans  abrupts         parquet  comme      humaines    etourdissant comme
comme des precipices à pre.  s'arrêtant sur le planche. le vaste clapotement des voix contre le xxxx/plafond
- un fusil sur le xxx         comme les rages d'une bête geante,    p' ne rien abimer
glissait sur le poxx    Cependant xxxxxx. on avait retiré les bayonnettes des fusils.
tombait sans même           contentait d'avancer  toujours
faire un trou      on se  pxxxxait, jusqu'à xxxxxxxxx,  à/en regardant.. rien que
             sur            avec curiosité α etonnement
compacte xxxxxxx
la foule se xxxxxxxxxxx  l'expression d'une gaminerie railleuse. - plaisir où il y avait
se precipitait de bas en haut                          l'entrain d'un combat
montant/t en tourbillonant
d'une xxxxxxx    d'un mouvement qui agitait l'amusement d'une exhibition, / la joie d'une conquête. Chacun se
sans pouvoir s'arrêter                    comme
- tetes. xxxxxxx, piques, fusils.         le plaisir d'une exhibition  α l'etonnement joyeux d'une
qqfois une main sur la     Sans que ceux
muraille p' se retenir. - Ceux sentait roi.                       victoire facile -
qui tombaient ne faisaient  fissent
     de            Cependant, de temps à autres un coude casse une vitre,  un objet
même pas de trou. A          - Un gd fracas, une glace c'est
    dxxxxant       tombe d'une console. - tout a coup un gd fracas. une  glace
en roulant à
on s'agitait         se brise) - Alors de la demolition generale, on brise tout ..
  flots pressés         bruits de
  des tetes .. des       meubles. porcelaine ....
  bonnets rouges,
  des fusils, ψ         Là foule augmente. les boiseries craquent. - gens en
                              à grotes grouttes
remarques sur le
mobilier poncif.
                sueur, - les flot les poussait de chambre en chambre
les heros
l'heroisme ne sent pas bon>>
- xxxx - Vous etes agaçant. d'appartement en appartement.

        ψ poussée par un x/impulsion d'en bas, avec un mouvement si fort que
                les mains touchant le mur  p' se retenir
                    glissaient, que ceux qui tombaient
                                sans     de
                    par terre  ne fai/re/saient pas de
                            dans la masse
                        trou . - tassée
                                irresistible

161

## Brouillons I (Continued): Transcription of 17607, f. 17

dont les maintenus,
à gdes draperies relevés par
des cordielles d'or
pendait du plafond, xxxxxxxxxxxxxx assis
un rouge sur le qu'il abritait neirs ras à cheveux
poussah chinois Salle du trone – dais de velours qui tombait du plafond – trone. un proletaire
bleue noire ebouriffée l'air stupide
chemise bottes.. α jovial, etait
laissant voir la poitrine à barbe, en petite chemise bleue comme s'il est assis dessus d'autres lui
comme un poussah chinois
gravissaient l'estrade α se mettent là à tour de rôle
p' prendre succèdent, comme en procession. xxxxxxxx par'.
sa place.
<<definitivement>
– quel mythe>> dit Hussonnet. le peuple souverain – si je m'y mettais
est. aussi.>> mais n'a
spectacle Car le fauteuil fut enlevé, pas le temps de realiser son desir
Ce spectacle qui Puis, soulevé, balancé au bout des bras – traversait la salle en se balançant.
aurait pleuré porté
com un album sacrilège est
les gens d'une C'est là le cas de dire, le vaisseau de l'Etat balotté sur une mer orageuse!
epoque bien comme il chaloupe! il cancane-t-il ? xxxxxxx
autre regne La metaphore
excita sa joie. Je comprends maintenant la metaphore
(2) où, ramassé, α couvert
le boheme approche d'une fenetre xxxxxxxx d'emeutiers
il le suivait Puis jeté par la fenêtre en bas où il fut repris α promene,
de l'oeil p' y
où on le brûla triomph. jusqu'à la Bastille etre le/bruler/é
jusqu'à la Bastille pour être brûlé derisoirement
" au milieu de hués, α de sifflets
Ah! saprelotte le peuple en le voyant tomber. <<Bon voyage>>
comme il chaloupe." et Hussonnet dit H. le voyant tomber dans le jardin(1)
– Pauvre vieux symbole,.. dit Hussonnet.(2)
va!
(x)Mais une bien feroce
à partir de ce moment, plus frein. La Une gaieté se dechaîna -
moins par vengeance que p' affirmer sa pour affirmer
On etait en possession α comme le droit de la propriété est d'abord
possession, faire à son tour acte de maître α preuve de royauté. il s'en prend
un xxxxx. xxxx tout à la fois.- vengeance sur à la matière
glaces, lustres, les xxxxxxxxxxxxxxxx xxxxxxxxx. mascades enroulés autour
Statues et meubles. inerte/ vêtements roy des princesses – crepines d'or – galons +
tintamarre d'or
objets porcelaines, les α marabouts les ceinturons militaires
les flambeaux chapeaux de femme sur la tête des forgerons, – le tricorne d'un général
meubles, portraits, taille chacun assouvissait sa fantaisie
les bustes, les albums, sur la tete des prostituées. – episodes etranges. deux
pianos dechirés – faisaient une partie
– une ivresse de bruit joueurs d'echec, à part sur un gueridon – femmes qui se
α de couleur. vivent des bandeaux met un paquet de
ψ robes de princesse – pommadent – un autre qui xxxx de feuilletons sous son tablier
y mettant le nez – d'un air rêveur
– se vautra dans – un homme qui fume sa pipe, philosophiquement.
les lits. curiosité obscène. - fouillant tous les cabinets, tous les recoins
par consolation ouvrant les armoires , soulevant les doublures des robes ψ
de ne pouvoir les nombreuses
violer. Mais ça s'aigrit , les figures sinistres sont plus xxxx
nombreuses intentions de vol reprimés par M
le trop gd nombre – les ivresse decuplé
mechantes, ivresses du mal.
B suffocante,
Par le linteau des portes La foule devient trop compacte.. chaleur –/ils ont peur d'etre etouffés
à l'infini, masse de et s'en vont.
peuple noir entre debout sur un tas de vêtements
les dorures. A Dans l'antichambre. une fille – en statue de la Statue de la Liberté - bonnet
publique en
rouge. pique. les yeux gds ouverts. – ne repondant pas aux
interpellations – extatique – effrayante –

**Brouillons II: 17607, f. 13v (Extract)**

En bas, dans une salle ~~xxxxxx rez-de-chaussée~~ petite voutée, des bols de café au lait etaient
servis. ~~Les curieux circulaient autour des tables.~~ qques uns s'attablèrent
~~qques-uns~~ s'y assirent
en plaisantant ~~sur le banquet de la Reforme~~ le gouvern qui avait empeché. les autres restaient
debout, α parmi ceux-là, un cocher de fiacre. Il saisit à ~~deux~~
~~mains~~ plein un bocal ~~plein~~ de sucre en poudre, jeta de droite α de
gauche un regard inquiet, – puis se mit à manger voracement
son nez plongeant dans le goulot.

au bas du gd escalier ~~en paletot~~
~~à l'entrée du vestibule~~, un homme ecrivait son nom sur le registre
– – xxxxxxxxxxx
des visiteurs. Frederic le reconnut, par ~~derr~~ derrière
en passant

tiens Hussonnet! ~~Main~~
comme vous voyez!>> ~~Je frequente le gd monde~~
~~en personne~~, reprit le Bohème. << Je m'introduis à la Cour. ~~Je~~
Mais oui –
~~respire avec orgeuil l'air de la corruption.~~ Voilà une farce, hein?
Si nous montions?>>
~~Ils montèrent ensemble l'escalier~~/α ils arrivèrent

~~dans la salle des Marechaux –~~ dans la salle des
Mare chaux –

## Brouillons II (Continued): 17607, f. 14

sauf celui de Bugeaud percé au ventre  on les voyait appuyés
Les portraits de ces illustres étaient tous intacts –.  et  ils se tenaient ~~debout~~
~~xxxxx~~         α
sur leur sabre, un affût de    canon derrière eux, et dans les attitudes

~~freces~~  ~~qui jurant~~                              gde
terribles   contrastant avec la situation . Une pendule xxx marquait une
               vingt minutes
heure   ~~et demie~~        tout à coup     retentit
Mais sous le pavillon de l'Horloge, la Marseillaise ~~eclata dans~~ ~~un long rugissement~~.
                                                      pr voir
Hussonnet α Frederic se penchèrent sur la rampe.– un gd souffle, tiède les
resseré etroitement                   frappa au visage. C'etait le peuple qui arrivait
    resseré
    ~~xxxxxxxx~~
    ~~Pris~~      ~~Pris~~   ~~Pris~~   ~~resseré~~    parois ~~de marches~~           bords
         ~~tesserré~~ e/E/troitement entre les deux murs de l'escalier, comme entre les pans abrupts
                                   pris  il  rua ruait  de bas      d'en
comme un fleuve    d'un   precipice  la foule se precipitait  ~~de haut en bas bas~~ de bas ~~en haut~~
que ~~refoulé~~                                xx      frenetique
refoulé par une              ~~dans une confusion vertigineuse xxxx~~  des casques, bonnets rouges des xxxx
marée d'equinoxe  en                                               les bayonnettes
          en  secouant  à  flots pressés, ~~des tetes~~  ~~des epaules~~ nues  ~~xxxxxxxx~~
                                                         d'une xxx frenetique
     α epaules  et si   impetueusement                                     mur
toujours         ~~avec~~ ~~une telle fureur~~ que les mains touchant les ~~mu~~ pr se retenir
~~xxxxxxxxxx~~          ~~xxxxxxxx~~
                 ~~xxxxxxxx~~        hom              sans faire de
qui montait ~~toujours~~ glissant/aient α que l/d/es gens tombaient/ant ~~sous les autres~~ ne faisaient pas de trou dans
comme un  fleuve    ~~grouillante~~  ~~impulsion~~    sous les autres ne faisaient pas
~~refoulé par une~~  la masse . . . tassée . irresistible .
~~vaste~~             xx    grouillante
~~marée d'equinoxe~~   Puis
~~avec un mouvement~~  ~~xxxx~~ – en haut sur le  ~~ayant plus d'espace~~ ,  elle se repandit α
d'une confusion       Puis parvenue (au palier   ~~à cause de la plus gde dispersion~~  α le
~~xxxx vertigin~~                      au
avec une impulsion    chant tomba.
continue                                   pas   battant.
formidable α                                ~~leurs~~   parquet
irresistible          On n'entendait plus que le bruit de tous les ~~pas sur le plancher~~ . avec le ~~vaste~~
fin                                           se repercutant                   jusqu'à
long                                          ~~humaines~~                    ~~jusqu'à ce point~~ inoffensive
~~rugissement~~        clapotement des voix ~~humaines~~ contre le plafond. – La foule ~~etait~~ ~~douce~~
                                                   même                            elle
sous une impulsion    ~~on avait retiré les bayonnettes et les fusils pr ne rien abimer~~ . elle se contentait
formidable α irresistible                                    en savourant
~~continue~~          se xxxxxxxxxxxait    tant  ~~elle~~  ~~etait~~
d'~~xxxxxxxxx~~       de ~~xxxxxxxxx~~ de regarder  et en goutant comme   le plaisir d'une
objet xxxxxx                  circuler   α                              joyeux
                      exhibition ,  ~~xxxxxxxxxxx~~ l'etonnement ~~joyeux~~ d'une victoire facile
                                           avec    α    joyeux    un    se briser
                                                              sous le heurt    les carreaux
                      Cependant de temps à autres d'un coude ~~casse une vitre~~ –  ~~un~~
un vase, une statuette                           console    par terre.
La foule augmentant   ~~objet tombé d'une meuble~~ – xxxxxxxxxxxxxxxxxxxxxxxxxx des fronts
toujours          les boiseries ; craquaient – ~~la foule augmente~~ ~~gens qui~~  la sueur   coulait à
                                                        toutes     les visages etaient  etaient
                 larges
                 grosses gouttes. Hussonnet          rouges.
                – Les heros ne sentent pas bon!»
       Par les linteaux – Ah Vous etes agaçant." reprit Frederic
       ils apercevaient  des portes
       entre les  ~~dondres~~  tout au loin et     d'appartement en appartement
       le peuple noir.                 Poussés ~~de chambre en chambre~~, ils arrivèrent ~~à la~~
                                                                                  dans
                                                                                  l'une
                       salle du trône.  ~~et cedant au flot qui les poussait~~    rsalle.

164

## Brouillons II (Continued): 17607, f. 18

Et poussés d'appartement en appartement, ils arrivèrent dans une salle
semblent
maintenus
relevés de droite α de        s'etendait au        gd        avec
relevés des deux        gauche où pendait du plafond un dais de velours rouge – dont les draperies maintenues
cotés                câbles d'or. sur                pareilles
Maintenues        par des cordelières d'or. Le trône qu'il abritait, etait assis un proletaire à
des deux côtés     cheveux courts        entr'ouverte
cheveux courts, à barbe noire herissée, sa chemise bleue laissant voir
et stupide
                et stupide        magot
sa poitrine, α l'air jovial comme un poussah chinois. D'autres gravissaient
        un à un prendre        et        à
l'estrade,   p'    sa place s'y mettaient tour à tour de rôle.
        s'asseoir à        et        se mirent.
                        Voilà
– quel mythe >> dit Hussonnet. << definitivement le peuple est souverain." j'en
fais partie, moi, du peuple! si je m'y mettais? >>
                                et        α        toutes
Mais le fauteuil fut enlevé, porté à bout de bras traversa la salle
                                                toute –
entière en se balançant.
                le vaisseau de
"– ah! saprelotte, comme il chaloupe! Je comprends la metaphore. le vaisseau de
l'état est, balancé sur une mer orageuse. Cancanne t-il ! Cancanne t-il ! >>
        cette fois    l'avait    pr        Puis        xxxxxxxxxxxxxxxxx
                Puis on l'approcha/é d'une fenêtre        au milieu des huées α des sifflets
on le lança,                                α                degringoler
        <<–Pauvre vieux symbole, va!>> dit Hussonnet, en le voyant tomber dans le
Comme si à la place                des patriotes        couvert d'un monde
du trone, une persp.    jardin . d' où il fut ramassé    puis promené, derisoirement jusqu'à
infini                        où il fut repris vivement α        en le        ensuite
de bonh illimité se                où il fut
fut decouverte – A        la Bastille, p' y être brûlé.
        tout à coup                p' y être brûlé.
à la place du trone                        joie    frenetique
disparu        dans    Alors    Mais à partir de ce moment une gaieté feroce se dechaina    et à la
alors    Comme si le vide fait par le trône    xxxxxxx la place
la perspective                du trône    B    α le peuple moins
Un avenir de bonheur    place vide c'était la Liberté, α la Populace moins par vengeance
illimité eût apparu .                        est apparu .
                        son droit
        delire de    que p' affirmer sa possession, faire à son tour, acte de maitre et
                                son droit
Ce fut une xxxx                preuve de royauté dechargea sa colère sur la matière inerte .
triomphe                                gds    à    coups de sabre    en les attaquant
                                        à coups de pied    avec les crosses des
                        en brisa                                fusils
                les        les tables    les lustres . . .    les glaces . . . les lustres . . .    les meubles
et les cristaux        pianos    les chaises, les tabourets tous    tintamarre
les porcelaines    les flambeaux ,    les meubles . . .    les portraits . . .    les plus
les flambeaux
                                la rage    prit    plus        cureux
par    La canaille s'affubla.    des porcelaines.    delire s'en prend aux petits objets on
                ironiquement    jusqu'aux        jusqu'à des paniers à ouvrage.        toutes
– Ironie On se xxxx dans,            de dessin    α des palettes
        fourrures                rechire des albums.    une ivresse de bruit α de couleur. qui – –
cachemires                chacun s'enivrant de la /à la colère des autres tourbillonne
les    baptistes            immense s'ensuivit crepines    arracheés des        aux
toile fine            et une Mascades    Des galons d'or    s'enroulèrent autour des
de dentelles.                                    bonnets de dentelles .
                manches des    bleues                        plumes d'autruches
                /blouses bleues .    – cha chapeaux de femmes, à marabout
                        peaux de femme .    rubans
        coiffèrent                gds    cordons    dela legion d'Honneur
        sur la tête    des    forgerons    Ceinturons militaires à la
        sur la tete?            firent    des ceintures aux
                        taille des        prostituées.

165

## Brouillons II (Continued): 17607, f. 20

~~Dans la confusion –~~
~~le tumulte general.~~
  remarquèrent   ~~des choses etranges.~~ les uns   trinquaient. Les/D'autres dansaient
   satisfaisait         sur un piano, Un   M⁵ en mackintosh
Chacun ~~assouvissait~~    ~~cependant~~   H. le fit remarquer à Fr.   jouait une valse sur un
 son caprice                        piano
 ~~sa fantaisie~~
   ~~Chacun assouvissait sa fantaisie~~ : Deux joueurs d'echec faisaien/an/t une partie
          derrière   un paravent
              ~~un coin~~   Dans la chambre de la   devant    une ψ
ψ morceau de miroir \\ sur une gueridon, ~~dans~~ l'embrasure d'une fenêtre   une ~~femme~~/fille qui
            ⸌reine
       lustrait     avec de la pommade    un paquet de    sous
      se pommade   l/ses bandeaux. ~~un autre~~ me/it des feuilletons ~~son~~
                          gamin
      continuait   son tablier. ~~Dans une autre chambre les sons d'un piano~~
 delire redoublait   son tablier. ~~Un Monsieur en paletot jouait une~~ (valse/ait sur
et ~~aussi pendant ce temps~~       Ils causèrent un peu avec     ⌐<< 1830 >>
  tumulte     ~~un piano.~~ un homme qui fume/ait sa pipe, philosophe.⌐
 là ~~le tapage continuait~~
 augmentait – tintamarre
 ~~etiquetis~~(incessant ⸌     xxxxxxxxxxxxxxxxxxxxxxxxxxxxxxxxψ
 des tintamarres de      ~~Mais ça s'aigrit.~~   une curiosité obscène fouiller tous les
 qui brisés α les morceaux       tous        fit
 porcelaines, ~~notes~~      tous ~~les recoins~~ ouvrir ~~tout à la fois~~ les tiroirs
 de cristal d'harmonica.   cabinets, ~~tous les recoins ouvrant~~ les armoires relever les jupes des
                           leurs couches
           de dentelles    N   roulaient sur ~~des princesses~~
          princesses – se ~~vautrant~~/aient dans les lits /par consolation de ne pouvoir
          flairer xxxxxxxx la baptiste.     sombres circulaient
Des galeriens avec       xxxxxxx
des rites de satyres         les violer.   les ~~fines~~ figures ~~sinistres sont plus nombreuses~~
et de bourreau et la         baptiste       que
~~Des bras tatoués~~      intentions   contenait trop     des xxxxxxx/assistants
        Dans les   regards des   de vol, reprimés par le gd nombre la foule devient/enait
                               on s'apper
           de plus en plus compacte. α Par le linteau des portes, il s'apercevaient
            à l'infini   la succession          que
               dans ~~l'enfilade~~ des appartements à l'infini, la masse noire du
                    sous un nuage
ψ quand tout fut brisé    peuple, entre les dorures ~~chaleur~~ xxxxxxxxxxxxxxxx xxxxxxxxx de la poussière –
on voulut voir.               les deux amis   suffocante – ~~ils ont~~ peur
en voir la coulisse.           ~~ils~~ se retirèrent   L'atmosph devenait       α craignant
             d'etre etouffés, ~~et s'en vont~~.

                           |se tenait|
            Dans l'antichambre   debout – sur un tas de vêtements   une fille publique
                    α qui
           en Statue de la Liberté. – ~~bonnet rouge, pique~~ les yeux   ne repondent
   Des galeriens           ni aux plaisanteries
~~Ceux qui couchaient~~    pas aux interpellations    les yeux gds ouverts,   effrayante
~~par la paille~~ enfoncèrent                        immobile
xxxxxxxx
les/urs bras, ~~jusqu'à l'aisselle~~   effrayante –
   la couche
dans ~~les edredons~~
des princesses α se M
roulaient dessus,
par consolation
de ne pouvoir les violer

**Brouillons III: 17607, f. 15**

Les portraits de ces illustres, sauf celui de Bugeaud percé au ventre, etaient tous
intacts. ~~On les~~ Ils se tenaient appuyés sur leur sabre, un affût de Canon
derrière eux - α dans des attitudes ~~terribles~~ ~~contredisant~~ avec la ~~situation~~.
       jurant       circonstance
       grosse    formidables jurant
Une ~~gde~~ pendule marquait une heure vingt minutes.
      tout à coup, en bas
    Mais ~~sous le pavillon de l'horloge~~, La Marseillaise retentit. Hussonnet α
         p' voir     chaude exhalaison
Frederic se penchèrent ~~sur~~ la rampe pr voir Un ~~gd souffle tiede~~
     sur la rampe    gd souffle tiede
~~les frappa au visage~~. C'etait le peuple qui arrivait.
        abrupts
 Pris    abrupts      dans l'espace
~~Resserré etroitement entre les deux parois de l'escalier~~, i/Il se precipita en
     des xxxxxxxxx vertigineux
secouant à flots ~~pressés~~ des tetes ~~nues~~, des casques, des bonnets rouges, des
       nues
bayonnettes α des epaules, si impetueusement que les mains touchant les
           gens ~~tombaient~~
           hommes
murs pr se retenir glissaient, α que des ~~gens~~ ~~tombaient~~ ~~sous~~
           sans faire de trou.
~~les~~ ~~autres~~ disparaissaient dans cette masse grouillante qui montait
toujours ] comme un fleuve refoulé par une marée d'equinoxe ]
avec un long mugissement – sous une impulsion ~~formidable~~
          l'espace etant plus large
et irresistible. Puis en haut, ~~sur le~~ palier elle se repandit
        l'espace etant plus large
et le chant tomba.

      les pietinements
      ~~battements~~   pas
      infini  les souliers
On n'entendait plus que le bruit de tous les pas ~~battant le parquet~~
      xxxxxxx xxxxxxxxxxx
avec le clapotement des voix ~~contre le plafond~~.
         xxxxxxxx
   inoffensive ~~jusqu'à present~~
La foule, ~~jusqu'à present, etait inoffensive. Elle~~ se contentait de
     regarder xxxx
    ~~circuler de~~ de regarder.- ~~goûtant comme le plaisir d'une exhibition α~~
 aussi     xxxxx la joie
où se melait la xxxxxxxxxx
    l'etonnement joyeux ~~d'une victoire facile~~
        joyeux
     Mais    trop et à l'etroit, enfonçait
~~Cependant~~, de temps à autre, ~~sous le heurt d'un coude~~, un ~~carreau~~ de vitre se
         xxxxxxxxxx
~~brisait~~, ou bien un vase, une statuette, ~~tombait~~ d'un console par
         roulait
terre. ~~La foule~~ augmentait ~~toujours~~; ~~les boiseries~~) craquaient.
        peu à peu. trop pressées
Les haleines des poitrines
haleta/ie/ntes ~~echauffaient~~ toutes les visages etaient rouges. M la sueur coulait des ~~fronts~~ à
un grand souffle tiede        en  en  fronts
fait par toutes les larges gouttes. -~~Hus~~
haleines poitrines  fit cette remarque.
 fais    Hussonnet : «les heros ne fleurent pas bon"! ~~decidement~~
echauffaient l'air    à voix basse decidement
     et - Ah! vous ~~etes agaçant~~ » reprit Frederic. ~~qui~~...
       ... m'agacez

**Brouillons III (Continued): 17607, f. 14v**

Et poussés d'appartement en appartement, ils arrivèrent dans une salle où s'etendait au plafond, un dais de velours rouge – avec des draperies ~~semblables~~ pendantes ↳relevées ~~semblables~~) maintenues ~~de droite et de gauche~~ symmetriquement par des câbles d'or. – Sur le trone ~~qu'il abritait~~, etait assis un proletaire en dessous ~~à xxx à cheveux courts~~ noire hilare α stupide à barbe noire ~~herissée~~ la chemise entr'ouverte, l'air ~~jovial~~ comme un magot. D'autres gravissaient l'estrade, ~~un à un~~ un à un p[r] s'asseoir à sa place.

– "quel mythe" dit Hussonnet. <<Voilà le peuple souverain!>>

Mais le fauteuil fut enlevé ~~xx~~ à bout de bras, α traversa ~~toute~~ la salle, en se balançant.

– ~~Ah!~~ saprelotte, comme il chaloupe. Le vaisseau del'Etat, cette fois, est baloté sur une mer orageuse! Cancane-t-il! Cancane-t-il!>>

On l'avait approché d'une fenêtre. α aumilieu des sifflets on le lança.

– Pauvre vieux," ~~symbole~~ >> dit Hussonnet, en le voyant tomber vivement↳relevé dans le jardin, où il fut repris, ~~et~~ promené ensuite jusqu'à p[r] ~~la xx~~ et xxx la Bastille, ~~pour y~~ être brulé.

Cont | ~~Mais~~ tout à coup ~~xxxxxxxx~~ tout à coup
 | Alors une joie frenetique eclata, comme si à la place du trône, une
 un | avenir illimité avait surgi
~~triomphait~~ | ~~perspective~~ de bonheur ~~infini~~ se fût decouverte – α le peuple,
Puisqu'on ~~etait victorieux~~ | xxxxxxxxxxxx
etait victorieux | moins par vengeance que p[r] affirmer sa possession, ~~xxxxxxx~~
nefallait pas s'amuser? | p[r] α faire à son tour preuve de royauté lacera les meubles ~~et tous~~
 | ~~et faire à son tour preuve de royauté~~, brisa les glaces ~~à gds~~
 | les rideaux
 | ~~coups de pied, à coups de sabre~~ les lustres) ~~avec~~ ~~la crosse des~~
 | ~~fxxxxxx. fusils, et les cristaux~~ les flambeaux, les tables, les
 | xxxxxxxxxxxxxxxxxxxxx
~~on etait vainqueur~~ | chaises, les tabourets, tous les meubles. ~~La rage~~ s'en prit
~~il fallait rire~~ | jusqu'aux des albums ~~en dechirxxxxxxxxxxxxxxxxx~~
 | ~~jusqu'aux~~ ~~jusqu'à~~ des albums de dessin jusqu'à des
 | des xxx à la colère des autres vibrations
 | jusqu'à corbeilles de tapisserie ~~dans~~ ~~le bruit~~
 | paniers à ouvrages. Chacun s'excitant etourdi par du tapage
Ce fut un paroxysme d'orgeuil ~~xxxxxxxx~~ ~~par le tumulte~~ ~~qui~~ ~~tourbillonnaient~~
une gaieté monstrueuse ~~qu'on faisait dans~~ les couleurs. ~~qui etaient xxxoussantes~~
 | qu'on faisait ~~xxxxxx~~
revanche – triomphe.

La Canaille s'affubla, ironiquement, de dentelles α de cachemires. – Des crepines d'or s'enroulèrent aux manches bleues des blouses ~~bleues~~ – des chapeaux ~~de femme~~ à plumes ornaient la tête d'autruche ~~coiffèrent~~ des forgerons. Des rubans de la ~~legion~~ legion d'honneur firent des ceintures aux prostituées –

## Brouillons III (Continued): 17607, f. 17v

~~cependant~~
Chacun satisfaisait ~~sa fant~~ son caprice. les uns trinquaient. d'autres dansaient
~~un monsieur en mackintosh jouait un valse sur un piano.~~ ~~Hussonnet fit remarquer à Frédéric deux joueurs d'echec faisant une partie derrière un paravent.~~ Dans la chambre de la reine, une
femme
~~fille~~ lustrait ses bandeaux avec de la pommade. Un gamin
 fourra
derrière un paravent ~~mit~~ un paquet de feuilletons sous ~~un~~ son tablier. - ils
 montra
deux amateurs. H. fit remarquer à Frederic / son brule gueule en reg. le ciel
jouaient aux Cartes. ~~causèrent~~ avec un omme qui fumait ~~sa pipe~~ en philosophe
 accoudé au bord
 et redoublait
~~parce qu'il etait venu là en 1830.~~ - ~~Ma~~ le delire ~~continuait~~
 Cependant ~~la joie~~
 continu
au tintamarre ~~incessant~~ des porcelaines brisées. α des morceaux
 sonnaient
 cristal ~~xxxxxx~~ des sons
de ~~verre~~ qui rebondissant, ~~faisaient comme des notes~~ d'harmonica
 comme des notes

~~Puis~~
~~Mais~~ La fureur s'assombrit. une curiosité obscène fit fouiller
tous les cabinets, tous les recoins, ouvrir tous les tiroirs – des
galeriens enfonçaient~~erent~~ leurs bras dans la couche des princesses
et se roulaient dessus, par consolation de ne pouvoir les violer.
 D'autres ~~D'autres hommes~~ plus
 ~~Des hommes~~ à figure sinistre, ~~calmes au milieu des autres,~~
 errai ent silencieusement avec des manifeste
 circulaient, ~~ayant dans leur regard dans des~~ l'intention/s de voler.
 Mais la multitude etait trop nombreuse - ~~et trop~~
~~que contenait le trop gd nombre d'assistants.~~ ~~La foule devenait~~
 xx
~~de plus en plus compacte.~~ – Par le linteau des portes on n'apercevait
 qu'une
~~tout à la fois~~, dans la succession des appartements, ~~que la~~ masse
 ~~qui qui enfilait~~ ~~que la sombre~~
 ~~masse~~ du peuple ~~ventre~~ les dorures –. sous un nuage de
toutes les poitrines sombre du ~~du~~ peuple.
haletaient
 de plus en plus devenait ~~xxxxxxxxxx~~
poussière. La chaleur ~~était~~ suffocante – α les deux amis

craignant d'etre etouffés, se retirèrent.

Dans l'antichambre, debout sur un tas devêtements, se tenait
une fille publique, en statue ~~de la Liberté; – et qui ne~~ repondait
pas aux interpellations, ~~ni aux plaisanteries les gds~~ les yeux
 xxxxxxxxxxxxxx
gds ouverts – immobile – effrayante –

169

# WHATEVER HAPPENED TO BOUVARD AND PÉCUCHET?

## Diana Knight

"Peu d'œuvres aujourd'hui sollicitent plus la recherche que celle de Flaubert." So wrote René Pomeau in his preface to the published *actes* of the centenary conference held in Paris in 1980. My impression, approaching the first conference on Flaubert that I had personally attended since this event, was that this was no longer the case. Moreover, reflecting upon "new" critical directions, I was not sure that there had been any significant renewal of Flaubert Studies in recent years. Was it simply that Flaubert had ceased to be central to my own research? To some extent, perhaps, yet I had maintained contact through reviews, readers' reports and editorial responsibilities, and whenever in a bookshop would still gravitate to the Flaubert section in search of anything new. The fact that the most recent book I had purchased, Marc Girard's study of *Madame Bovary*, was ironically dismissive of many of the former objects of my intellectual admiration — from the incisive and lucid structuralist approach of a Jonathan Culler, to the interpretative panache of a Jean-Paul Sartre — contributed to my vaguely defined unease.

For me, the 1970s were the Golden Age of Flaubert Studies: inaugurated by the publication of *L'Idiot de la famille* in 1971 and 1972, accompanied by the *Uses of Uncertainty* (1974) and *La Production du sens chez Flaubert* (1975), culminating in 1980 with an avalanche of conference papers and the stimulating (re)birth of genetic criticism celebrated in *Flaubert à l'œuvre*. This was not merely an especially rich period for Flaubert criticism *per se*. Always the writer's writer, always a source of fascination for critics of every persuasion, Flaubert in the 1970s had colonised the field to become a central figure in the discussions of language and representation that underpinned intellectual debate across a whole range of disciplines. No surprise, then, that a Parisian *table ronde* on Flaubert in November 1980 should bring together the likes of Robbe-Grillet and Tournier, of Genette and Derrida. Only the recent deaths of Barthes and Sartre, one felt, could have kept them too from the platform, and in any case they were there in spirit.

To claim, twenty-four years on, that 1972 was a privileged moment to embark on research on Flaubert, was to find myself curiously positioned at a 1996 *table ronde* on new critical approaches. A fairly general resistance to "theory" took the specific form of rejection of the very Golden Age I have just described. Indeed, this was seen as an age of lamentable critical orthodoxy, with Jonathan Culler, "language" and "undecidability" as the chief culprits. My timid attempts to defend the conceptual excitement of Flaubert Studies of the time, or more generally to suggest the critical leverage of the grand interpreters from Freud to Sartre and Bourdieu, were more or less tactfully dismissed through allusions to the intellectual posturing and name-dropping that were felt to characterise passing critical fashions. Meanwhile, *L'Idiot de la famille* seemed still not to have been read, on the grounds that, as Flaubert himself so aptly put it: "LIVRE. Quel qu'il soit, toujours trop long".

That Flaubert is no longer the height of critical fashion, that 1970s frameworks for thinking about him no longer inspire reverence, that *Bouvard et Pécuchet* is no longer *the* emblematic Flaubertian text, may well be a normal and healthy state of affairs. It is true that the relative reluctance to think in terms of new interpretative frameworks, or at least to think through what is at stake in their disappearance, made it hard at times to focus, as the *table ronde* had been billed to do, on the "broader theoretical issues" pertaining to Flaubert Studies today. Yet it is easy to see why broader pragmatic issues both inflected the discussion and are currently inflecting the content and direction of research, be it the equation of PhD topics with gaps in the market, the promotion of IT-related projects as good funding bets, or the evaluation of the merits of IT and genetic criticism through considerations of time (completion rates, CVs and Research Assessment

Exercises). These institutional pressures currently affect all of us, postgraduates and professors alike. Retrospectively, I am struck by a more curious and paradoxical resistance to the theme of the conference. For alongside the reluctance to engage with theoretical approaches, a relative unease emerged with the very phrase "Flaubert Studies".

My own failure to anticipate this as an issue is certainly symptomatic. I am probably a good example of someone who could well have chosen to work on Balzac or Proust instead of Flaubert, but who instinctively wanted to invest their critical desire in a rich but single *œuvre*. To begin research on Flaubert in the 1970s was still to promise oneself the luxury of three or four years of engagement with the body of writing by which one was most seduced at the time. Put another way, one could read, reread, think about and write on one's favorite author for years on end. Today's research students, it was suggested, pick a "problem" rather than an author, even if they often restrict themselves to a single author, arbitrarily chosen, to some extent, so as to keep their PhD thesis under control. Were this generally the case, such a shift might itself be viewed as a legacy of poststructuralist approaches. Nevertheless, thinking this through, it strikes me that two things were missing from the declared motivations for beginning research on either Flaubert or a particular topic relating to his *œuvre*. One was an absence of the traditional fascination with the personality, obsessions and ambivalent ideological positions of the man himself, all of which have exercised commentators from the Goncourt brothers to Sartre. If this accounts to some extent for a lack of interest in the latter's attempt to get to the bottom of Flaubert, it was also used to justify the general repudiation of psychoanalysis. To quote Anne Green: "As Tim Unwin was saying earlier, trying to get into Flaubert's psyche is not something I'd want to attempt." My point is not that we should all be adopting psychoanalytical models to explain Flaubert. Rather, I am genuinely surprised that so many participants should appear indifferent to the intriguing mind that created the slippery texts with which they have engaged for so many years. Secondly, and perhaps more strangely, no one confessed to any particular passion (or even enthusiasm) for Flaubert's writing, for reading the texts themselves. Several of the day's papers, of course, belied this later silence, in that we were treated to a series of fine close readings which can only have resulted from intense engagement with the texts, and which admirably demonstrated the capacity of those texts for ever renewed readings according to context. Yet, at the *table ronde*, close reading and interpretation appeared to have few defenders, and those entities called *Madame Bovary* or *L'Éducation sentimentale* seemed to have disappeared somewhere between the *avant-* and the *hyper-*text.

I leave it to the editors of this volume to analyse the lively debate around the impact of IT, and to develop the interesting theoretical considerations underlying the current hegemony of a genetic approach to Flaubert. Interestingly, though we all paid lip-service to the latter, few participants were actually working with it, others suggesting apologetically that they were hampered by lack of time. Of course, once we have found time to master and harness the powers of the computer, we may gain enough time to get to grips with the ever-expanding demands of the *avant-texte*. A truly Flaubertian paradox, worthy (as ever) of the *Dictionnaire des idées reçues*: "ARTS. Sont bien inutiles, puisqu'on les remplace par des machines, qui fabriquent même plus promptement". All of which conjures up the reassuring fantasy of Bouvard and Pécuchet *ébahis* by the wonders of the Internet, or taking notes from *Drafts* (the recent special issue of *Yale French Studies*), before reaching the inevitable conclusion on the status of the *avant-texte*: "Après tout, c'est peut-être une blague!" For me, at least, the image is a positive one, and encapsulates the past, present and future of Flaubert Studies. The mythical declaration of Bouvard and Pécuchet is of course a ruse, a false closure which keeps everything open, just as the false naivety of the ex-clerks propels author, readers and critics along an unending chain of enthusiasms.

**Works Cited**

Contat, Michel, Hollier, Denis & Neefs, Jacques (eds), *Drafts*, special issue of *Yale French Studies*, 89 (1996)

Culler, Jonathan, *Flaubert: The Uses of Uncertainty* (London: Elek, 1974)

Debray-Genette, Raymonde (ed.), *Flaubert à l'œuvre* (Paris: Flammarion, 1980)

Girard, Marc, *La Passion de Charles Bovary* (Paris: Éditions Imago, 1995)

Gothot-Mersch, Claudine (ed.), *La Production du sens chez Flaubert,* Colloque de Cerisy (Paris: Union générale d'éditions, 1975)

Pomeau, René, "Avant-propos" to special issue on Flaubert, *Revue d'histoire littéraire de la France*, 81 (1981)

Sartre, Jean-Paul, *L'Idiot de la famille. Gustave Flaubert de 1821 à 1857*, 3 vols (Paris: Gallimard, 1971–2)

# GENDER ROLES IN THE NOVELS OF FLAUBERT
## Steven Beigbeder

Apparently, around two hundred critical studies are written every year on Flaubert. It seems indeed presumptuous to assume one may add anything new to such an output of academic research. Yet, an in-depth investigation of a particular angle may, one hopes, uncover new material. One of Flaubert's intentions was to bring to light any received idea and overturn it with his use of irony, but in doing so he also managed to draw attention to the complex and subtle nuances of human nature (e.g. the possible co-existence of conflicting qualities in one person). For instance, Emma possesses both what are commonly regarded as masculine qualities and feminine ones: she is a dreamer *and* a woman of action. This study will also examine whether Flaubert's variations on gender roles represent a successful attack on patriarchy, as Roger Huss asked himself about *Madame Bovary*.[1] As far as other lines of enquiry are concerned, I shall refer to and contest a number of approaches when they are relevant to my subject. For instance, without rejecting Freudian readings altogether, I am not always entirely convinced by some of the psychoanalytical findings (e.g. phallic symbols and substitutes, or symbolic emasculation). Some critics seem to get carried away and endow any object with symbolic significance or interpret any erect monument or cutting instrument as part of a pattern which in reality should reveal the writer's unconscious fears of castration. For instance, Tony Williams, in his otherwise excellent article, writes: "Male characters undergo a symbolic emasculation – Emma's father breaks his leg, Hippolyte has his amputated." [2]

I understand this is to support the idea that in *Madame Bovary* masculinity is somewhat weakened and does not necessarily coincide with control, influence or authority. Indeed, M. Rouault will end up completely paralysed. However, is the sexualised Freudian phrase absolutely relevant? Furthermore, one could, in contrast, mention at least three "successful" male characters who end up in more favourable circumstances financially or as far as their reputation is concerned: Lheureux, Dr. Canivet and Homais. Let us take a close look at another passage loaded with symbolism from the text itself: "Le curé en tricorne qui lisait son bréviaire avait perdu le pied droit et même le plâtre, s'écaillant à la gelée, avait fait des gâles blanches sur sa figure." [3] On one level, the statue in the Bovary's abandoned garden, with its broken foot and its disfigured face covered with scabs, conveys a sense of decay and neglect. On another, the deteriorating figure also announces the inefficiency and powerlessness of religion as far as Emma is concerned. Later in the novel (Part II, Chapter 6), Bournisien's lack of perspicacity is evident when all he can offer a confused Emma is inept banalities instead of the spiritual guidance she needs. I do not think that in this case it would add anything to speak of symbolic emasculation. In other words, a Freudian reading may insist too much on the centrality of sexuality in all aspects of human existence. Frédéric's "softness" in *L'Éducation sentimentale* is a case in point. It does not necessarily suggest sexual ambiguity and can be interpreted in different terms.

In my view, to examine gender roles in a literary context is doubly interesting. In literature, the concepts of masculinity and femininity are indeed the results of a double construction. Firstly, they may reflect the writer's values which themselves belong to a social and historical background (e.g. Flaubert as a nineteenth-century French writer). Secondly, a character is a literary construct set in a context where gender roles may reflect another scale of values (e.g. Mâtho in *Salammbô*). Critics such as Bart, Czyba, Orr and Williams[4] have touched upon or explored thoroughly the representation of femininity and masculinity in Flaubert's works.

My thesis will focus on the way, in Alison Fairlie's words, "Flaubert deliberately plays on generally accepted ideas about the contrast between the nature of man and the nature of woman."[5] Although my study will concentrate on the six mature published works, I shall also refer to the earlier works to see if there is any consistency in Flaubert's presentation of gender. I shall examine the ways Flaubert challenged conventional gender roles in non-sexualised relationships (unattainable love, friendship) and sexualised ones (love, marriage, adultery, prostitution) and discuss their implications. For instance, the "softness" found in characters such as Frédéric and Léon will be contextualized (comparisons will be drawn with other key contemporary works by Balzac, Sand and Stendhal) to show how it is essentially a romantic character's trait. In the light of the works of Bart and Heath,[6] I shall also study the effect of male and female hysteria on gender roles. Flaubert's use of irony as a powerful undermining device, his misogyny and his pessimistic vision of life, which come across in his presentation of characters, will be examined as well..

Today, gender roles are much discussed and questioned by the media and in universities. Gender studies are indeed not any more restricted to feminist, gay or lesbian issues. As Elisabeth Badinter points out, there are more than two hundred departments of Men's Studies in the United States.[7] Definitions of manliness and unmanliness are less clear-cut than before. Similarly, what is considered as acceptable behaviour on the part of women has shifted. Therefore, the study of male and female attitudes in the public and private domain, whether in a literary context or not, appears as relevant as ever. Although cultural studies merge such lines of enquiry, Flaubert's work exhibits modernist complexities *avant la lettre* and possesses a relevance for an understanding of identity formation which other approaches seem only to limit.

---

**Notes**

[1]    Roger Huss, "Masculinité et féminité dans *Madame Bovary* et *Ulysses*".

[2]    Tony Williams, "Gender Stereotypes in *Madame Bovary*", 137.

[3]    *Gustave Flaubert, "Madame Bovary"*, 102.

[4]    Benjamin F. Bart, "Male Hysteria in *Salammbô*"; Lucette Czyba, *Mythes et Idéologies de la Femme dans les romans de Flaubert*; Mary Orr, "Flaubert's *L' Éducation sentimentale*

Revisited".

[5] Alison Fairlie, *Flaubert: "Madame Bovary"*, 56.
[6] Stephen Heath, *Gustave Flaubert: "Madame Bovary"*.
[7] Elizabeth Badinter, *XY, de l'identité masculine*, 18.

**Works Cited**

Flaubert, Gustave, *Madame Bovary* (Paris: Le Seuil, 1992)

Badinter, *Elizabeth, XY, de l'identité masculine* (Paris: Éditions Odile Jacob, 1992)

Fairlie, Alison, *Flaubert: "Madame Bovary"* (London: Edward Arnold, 1962)

Heath, Stephen, *Gustave Flaubert: "Madame Bovary"* (Cambridge: Cambridge University Press, 1992)

Huss, Roger, "Masculinité et féminité dans *Madame Bovary* et *Ulysses*", *James Joyce 2. Scribble 2, Joyce et Flaubert, Revue des Lettres Modernes*, 1990, 100–22

Bart, B. F., "Male Hysteria in *Salammbô*", *Nineteenth-Century French Studies* (1984), 313–21

Czyba, Lucette., *Mythes et Idéologies de la Femme dans les romans de Flaubert* (Lyon: Presses Universitaires de Lyon, 1983)

Orr, Mary, "Flaubert's *L' Éducation sentimentale* Revisited", *French Studies*, 46 (1992), 412–23

Williams, Tony, "Gender Stereotypes in *Madame Bovary*", *Forum for Modern Language Studies*, 28 (1992), 130–9

# MOBILITY IN FLAUBERT'S FICTION: DYNAMICS, DISORDER, DISCONTINUITY
## Larry Duffy

Late nineteenth-century French fiction is rich in representations of the changing patterns of mobility engendered by rapid technological and social change. My PhD thesis, with the working title "Mobility in late nineteenth-century French fiction: dynamics, disorder, discontinuity", will examine and evaluate literary responses to various aspects of what might be termed the "transport revolution" and its aftermath. A basic premise of the study will be that mobility provides a useful index of nineteenth-century perceptions of and attitudes to a whole range of issues, including science and technology, social relations, modernity, psychology and indeed literature itself. Accordingly, a broad range of primary texts, chosen for their representation in specific contexts of movement by specific forms of transport, will be examined. The principal authors studied will be Flaubert, Zola, Maupassant and Huysmans, on the grounds that their work spans a period during which new forms of mechanised transport, initially perceived in terms of their novelty, became entrenched gradually in the French landscape, both physically and culturally. Rather than examining each of these authors in chronological order, the thesis will identify some major nineteenth-century preoccupations and consider them in the light of certain key "texts of mobility". Other authors will be incorporated as and when appropriate, as will manuscript material. My principal aim will be to apprehend mobility as a key motif in the evolution of an organic Naturalist canon from Flaubert to Huysmans, considering it variously in the contexts of technology, psychology (in particular the "phenomenology of movement"), changing social and spatial relationships, and of the metaphor of the "circulus".

One important element of the study will be a consideration of mobility in its most explicitly technological representations. I hope to examine in particular, in its scientific specificity, the notion of entropy within the context of the wider development of Naturalism in literature. "Running-down", disintegration and disorder are crucial to Naturalist fiction, and the area of mobility, specifically in relation to transport technology, is particularly privileged in this respect, in that many of the technological processes which engender new subject matter for literature function according to the laws of thermodynamics. That is, the fictional representation of certain forms of mobility actually constitutes representation of entropic processes in the fullness of their meaning. Much criticism (notably Michel Serres's *Feux et signaux de brume*) has dealt in detail with the entropic processes functioning in Zola's work, placing them in the context of nineteenth-century views of the social significance and potential of science. It is to be hoped that this type of analysis can be applied to works which are less technologically explicit than Zola's (or at least where narrative reliance on technological detail or metaphor is not immediately as apparent), in particular Flaubert's *L'Éducation sentimentale*.

Flaubert's fiction has often been overlooked in works dealing with the literary exploitation of movement and transport technology (such as Baroli's *Le Train dans la littérature française* and Noiray's *Le Romancier et la machine*) due to its apparent lack of explicit technological information. The point to be made here, as elsewhere in Flaubert studies, is that the few details which are present can be examined in order to reveal a highly complex authorial awareness of the technological specificity of transport, leading textually to what might be termed an implicit "rhetoric of entropy". It is perhaps in this context that examination of the genetic process will be particularly enlightening, since it may provide a fruitful approach to the question of just how much scientific knowledge (implied) authors actually possess, and how much technological awareness their narrators are granted. Relevant also in terms of nineteenth-century perceptions of science and technology will be *Bouvard et Pécuchet*, but the key Flaubert text will be *L'Éducation sentimentale*.

This novel's importance to a changing "phenomenology of movement" is central. The various journeys depicted in it reflect many aspects of the nineteenth century's transformation of the subject's position in movement, from total organic immersion in the immediate travel environment to detached "panoramic" observation. From the moment where "les deux berges filèrent" and the material processes by which movement occurs begin to disrupt Frédéric's vaporous dreams, to the idealisation of Mme Arnoux's imagined train journey towards the end of Part III, the novel is rich in suggestions of an awareness on the part of the implied author of correlations between psychological processes (whether these be motivational, perceptual or otherwise) and the functioning of the new forms of movement which emerge from mid-century onwards.

The study will not be limited to mechanised means of transport alone. Flaubert's descriptions of horse- and even human-powered forms of movement can be seen to be as important in reflecting disorder and degradation as his descriptions of steamboats and trains, especially when recognised as appearing at a time when steam-powered travel had become normalised, and are very interesting in terms of their recreation of forms of perception of space which are known to be no longer the only ones. Furthermore, they succeed no less in representing modernity, particularly in terms of changing social and spatial relations. One episode which comes to mind is the description of the *encombrement* on the Champs-Élysées in Part II, which provides a static tableau of late July Monarchy society written from a late Second Empire perspective, and which, it will be argued, is a model for descriptions of social relations in later, more explicitly "naturalist" texts such as Zola's *La Curée*. The thesis will, finally, examine mobility in quite an abstract context: that of the "circulus" and of its sociological, psychological and physiological implications. The circulation of germs and disease, as well as that of people and goods within specific closed social parameters, will be central. An example of the type of mobility to be analysed here is that of the "contagion" of ironised revolutionary fervour and the carnivalised motion of frenetic individuals in Flaubert's depiction of the February Revolution. What is as common to the representation of this type of mobility as to the description of vehicles, in Flaubert and elsewhere, is a maximum of disorder and discontinuity often concealed under an apparently seamless order. It is hoped that the thesis will go some way towards establishing a unified and organic conception of the significance of mobility as a representational *leitmotiv* common to apparently disparate areas of what is arguably a literature of disintegration and disorder.

**Works Cited**

Baroli, Marc, *Le Train dans la littérature française* (Paris: Éditions N.M., 1969)

Noiray, Jacques, *Le Romancier et la machine*: *l'image de la machine dans le roman français (1850–1900)*, 2 vols (Paris: Corti, 1981)

Serres, Michel, *Feux et signaux de brume* (Paris: Grasset, 1975)

# FLAUBERT: THE CLASSICAL DIMENSION
## Stephen Goddard

The thesis upon which I am currently working, entitled "Flaubert and the literature of classical antiquity", which I hope to complete in 1998, is a new investigation of a question upon which many *Flaubertistes* have touched, but which few have explored in detail. A number of well-known studies have investigated the influence of Greek and Latin classics upon individual works in Flaubert's *œuvre* (Jean Seznec's investigations of *La Tentation de Saint Antoine*, for example) or specific aspects of that influence (for instance, Margaret Lowe's work on Flaubert's use of myth in *Towards the Real Flaubert*). Equally, a good many articles have been published which touch on the subject, many of which have been useful "pointers" for my work.

One thing which is clear is that Flaubert has been regarded as an unusually accomplished classical scholar both by those who knew him and by later critics. It seems that he was introduced to Louise Colet as something of a master of the classics, a reputation of which he attempted to rid himself: in a letter of October 1846, he tells her that "Ce bon Toirac [...] est trop indulgent ou trop illusionné quand il dit que je connais les anciens à fond [...]. C'est-à-dire que je les épelle, voilà tout."[1] During the "querelle de *Salammbô*", Flaubert was able to engage upon a learned discussion on a more or less equal basis not only with Sainte-Beuve, but also with the archaeologist Frœhner, using his extensive knowledge of, among others, classical historians such as Polybius and Procopius. His "disciple", Guy de Maupassant, writing in 1876, maintained that, "[Flaubert] a fouillé toutes les littératures, prenant des notes dans beaucoup de livres inconnus, les uns parce qu'ils sont rares, les autres parce qu'on ne les lit point."[2] And Flaubert himself considered his knowledge a rarity among his contemporaries, despite the vast preponderance of Latin and Greek in the school curriculum; in a speech in 1862 in honour of Louis Bouilhet, he called Bouilhet's comprehensive knowledge of Latin, "chose rare aujourd'hui et indispensable cependant à la connaissance de notre langue et de notre littérature".[3]

A number of critics have placed great emphasis upon Flaubert's interest in the classics. Édouard Maynial, writing barely three decades after Flaubert's death, states that,

> C'est une vérité banale aujourd'hui que la passion de Flaubert pour l'antiquité. Elle emplit sa vie, elle déborde de son œuvre. L'amour, la hantise des peuples disparus et des civilisations écroulées forment le fond de son inspiration, malgré la variété des thèmes.[4]

A more recent critic has claimed that, specifically, Flaubert was "intimately absorbed, even obsessed, by the writings of Virgil",[5] and this writer has indeed been named by a number of scholars as a key *point de repère* in Flaubert's work. However, as far as I am aware, no scholar has yet attempted to investigate the question of a range of Latin and Greek influences upon the whole of Flaubert's work.

My approach has been quite traditional in its main features: I have sought to establish the extent of Flaubert's acquaintance with the classics, both as a result of his school career and later voluntarily. Using the information thereby gleaned as a guide, I have considered possible references to classical texts in his works more or less chronologically, finding some degree of classical influence in almost all of them. This is unsurprising in works such as *La Tentation de Saint Antoine*, *Salammbô* and "Hérodias", which are set in what can more or less be described as classical antiquity; there exist extensive studies of Flaubert's sources, many of which are classical, for each of these works (although even here I have found a certain amount of new material to add to what is already known). However, I believe that Flaubert can be demonstrated to have used a variety of classical texts and myths in practically all his adult works. Some of these are quite well-known, although the extent and complexity of Flaubert's borrowing from them has not always been appreciated; others are less apparent, but many reappear from text to text with almost obsessive persistence. I have engaged little with the question of the precise nature of Flaubert's intertextual imitation; it seems in many cases that the degree of borrowing from classical texts is such that Flaubert must have been consciously imitating the texts in question, instead of being unwittingly influenced. Although the conclusion of my thesis remains to be written, I hope to be in a position to demonstrate the importance of classical antiquity and its literature through the whole spectrum of Flaubert's works.

**Notes**

[1] Letter 208, *Correspondance, Œuvres Complètes de Gustave Flaubert*, Vol.12 (Paris: Club de l'Honnête Homme, 1974), 544.

[2] Guy de Maupassant, *Chroniques I* (Paris: Union Générale d'Éditions, 1980), 22.

[3] *Œuvres Complètes de Gustave Flaubert*, Vol.12, 33.

[4] Édouard Maynial, *La Jeunesse de Flaubert* (Paris: Mercure de France, 1913), 258–9.

[5] Frederick Busi, "Flaubert's use of saints' names in *Madame Bovary*", *Nineteenth-Century French Studies*, vol. 10, no. 2 (Fall, 1990), 103.

## *LA TENTATION DE SAINT ANTOINE* AND THE WORKS OF FLAUBERT: AN INTERTEXTUAL STUDY
## Mary Neiland

The starting point of this thesis was my interest in the evolution of *La Tentation* and in the striking resonances of this work that are to be found throughout Flaubert's fiction. My approach has always been focused first and foremost on the texts themselves rather than being centred on any particular branch of literary theory. Although my study makes extensive use of manuscript material and examines the relationship between the different texts, it does not ascribe rigidly to either a genetic or an intertextual school of thought. Instead I sought a more "mixed" approach to enable me to work on the dense material which is *La Tentation*.

*La Tentation* was a work with which Flaubert was obsessed and which he reworked on three occasions. His correspondence bears witness to the freedom of expression he experienced in the writing of these texts: to Louise Colet he remarks that it was "un sujet où j'étais entièrement libre comme lyrisme, mouvements, désordonnements, je me trouvais alors bien dans ma nature et je n'avais qu'à aller".[1] *La Tentation* has received considerably less critical attention than Flaubert's other writings: it is often regarded as inaccessible and set apart from the rest of his works. Much work thus remains to be done on it.

The most recent extensive critical works that have been published on *La Tentation* come from very different perspectives. Jeanne Bem sees the three versions as one and gives a Freudian reading of this work.[2] Yong-Eun Kim's analysis of the scenarios of the 1849 version traces the developing conception of this text "pour observer enfin la manière dont sous le vêtement de l'Histoire, peuvent s'articuler l'examen du Moi et l'élaboration d'un monde où ce Moi parvient à se situer".[3] Finally, Gisèle Séginger has recently published a detailed genetic study of *La Tentation* and traces the evolution of the three versions, analysing the transformation of the author's approach to artistic representation.[4] Reference has frequently been made to the relationship between the author's early works and *La Tentation* and Gisèle Séginger explores some parallels between *Salammbô* and the 1874 text but no research has been done on the interplay of the three versions of *La Tentation* and Flaubert's other texts.

My thesis takes up this rich and neglected area and examines the "intertextual" relationship between *La Tentation* and the rest of the author's fiction. I have used the term "intertextual" to describe my study. This term was created by Julia Kristeva who defined it as "cette transposition d'un (ou de plusieurs) système(s) de signes en un autre".[5] Many theories of intertextuality have been advanced by critics, but rather than selecting as the basis of my thesis any one of the nuanced definitions of intertextuality, I have preferred to keep it as an umbrella term with which to describe the relationship between the texts that I have examined. The questions raised by the particular instances of "intertextual" echoes that are revealed are the starting point of my study.

Traces of what Flaubert refers to as this "déversoir" are to be found throughout his other works which at first seem far removed from "la Thébaïde".[6] My thesis analyses the interplay between *La Tentation* and the rest of his fiction and exposes a web of recurring and obsessive images. This study of intertextual relationships sets out to shed new light on Flaubert's changing techniques and to give new insights into the particular significance of *La Tentation* within his creative processes. The structure of my project comprises the exploration of a series of themes and scenes in *La Tentation*; their analysis across the three different versions of this work; and the study of the ways in which those same themes and scenes recur in the remainder of Flaubert's work. I have selected the banquet scene, the description of the town, the portrait of the seductive woman, the role of the Devil, the description of the crowd, the description of death, and the structure of endings as they present the most striking parallels between the different works.

My study of the finished texts was considerably enriched by working on the original manuscripts. During a year of research in Paris, I was able to examine the manuscript versions of the scenes and themes selected. Genetic criticism was an invaluable tool with which to analyse the relationship between the texts but my study does not try to establish a genetic classification of each relevant scene in each work. Instead I present the specific details that are of interest, transcribing whole folios or sections of folios as necessary. Access to the manuscripts allowed a far more detailed examination of the interplay between Flaubert's texts. His manuscripts confirm my hypothesis of direct and important links between *La Tentation* and the other works: what is felt as an echo in the final texts very often exists in a much more developed form in the drafts.[7]

Three important strands are revealed by my thesis. My study exposes the developing technique of the author: for instance the crude allegories of the Deadly Sins in the 1849 version of *La Tentation* are reworked throughout Flaubert's other texts with increasing sophistication. Emma Bovary, for example, is prey to the temptation of different "sins" and Lheureux takes on the stooping and whistling form of "Envie". The texts of *La Tentation* also vividly highlight networks of recurring, obsessive images and metaphors which form a fundamental underlying structure for each of the parallel scenes that are examined. For example banquet scenes throughout Flaubert's works emerge as visions giving access to a world the protagonists had only dreamed of: they are places of multiplicity and confusion, of violence and bestiality. Finally, it also becomes apparent that *La Tentation* allows the author to reflect, at the heart of his texts and in an implicit manner, on the role of the artist: for instance, the description of the laden table with its creative inventiveness is a "mise en abyme" of the work of the artist as he transforms the material world.

My work combines genetic analysis with an examination of the "intertextual" in Flaubert to produce an original perspective on the composition, construction and meaning of Flaubert's works generally. Furthermore, with its central focus on *La Tentation* in its changing forms, this thesis also brings back to the centre of Flaubert studies the much neglected text that has not yet been properly recognised as "l'œuvre de toute ma vie".[8]

**Notes**

[1] Flaubert, *Correspondance,* ed. Jean Bruneau, 4 vols Bibliothèque de la Pléiade (Paris: Gallimard, 1973–98), II (1980), 31 (to Louise Colet, January 1852).

[2] Jeanne Bem, *Désir et savoir dans l'œuvre de Flaubert: Étude de "La Tentation de saint Antoine".*

[3] Yong-Eun Kim, *"La Tentation de saint Antoine", version de 1849, genèse et structure,* 281.

[4] Gisèle Séginger, *Naissance et métamorphoses d'un écrivain: Flaubert et les "Tentations de saint Antoine".* The thesis on which this work is based contains a substantial annex of transcriptions: Gisèle Séginger, *"La Tentation et ses métamorphoses. Étude génétique et textuelle de La Tentation de saint Antoine de Gustave Flaubert (1849–1874)"* (Doctoral thesis, University of Paris VIII, 1991).

[5] Julia Kristeva, *La Révolution du langage poétique,* 59.

[6] Flaubert remarks with reference to the writing of *La Tentation* that "c'était un déversoir". *Corr.*, II, 297 (to Louise Colet, 6 April 1853). The opening line of the 1874 version of *La Tentation* reads "c'est dans la Thébaïde". Flaubert, *Œuvres Complètes*, I, 523.

[7] "Il est deux domaines, connexes, où la critique génétique, sans innover théoriquement, apporte des dossiers solides et enrichissants. Il s'agit de l'intertextualité et de l'autotextualité." Raymonde Debray-Genette, "Hapax et paradigmes. Aux frontières de la critique génétique", 80.

[8] *Corr.*, IV (1998), 531 (to Madame Leroyer de Chantepie, 5 June 1872).

**Works Cited**

Flaubert, Gustave, *Œuvres complètes*, 2 vols (Paris: Seuil, 1964)

Flaubert, Gustave, *Correspondance*, 4 vols, ed. Jean Bruneau (Paris: Gallimard, Bibliothèque de la Pléiade, 1973–98)

Bem, Jeanne, *Désir et savoir dans l'œuvre de Flaubert: Étude de "La Tentation de saint Antoine"* (Neuchâtel: Les Éditions de la Baconnière, 1979)

Debray-Genette, Raymonde, "Hapax et paradigmes. Aux frontières de la critique génétique", *Genesis. Manuscrits, recherche, invention. Revue internationale de critique génétique*, 6 (1994), 79–92

Kim, Yong-Eun, *"La Tentation de saint Antoine", version de 1849, genèse et structure* (Chuncheon, Korea: Kangweon University Press, 1990)

Kristeva, Julia, *La Révolution du langage poétique* (Paris: Seuil, 1974)

Séginger, Gisèle, *"La Tentation et ses métamorphoses. Étude génétique et textuelle de La Tentation de saint Antoine de Gustave Flaubert (1849–1874)"* (Doctoral thesis, University of Paris VIII, 1991)

Séginger, Gisèle, *Naissance et métamorphoses d'un écrivain: Flaubert et les "Tentations de saint Antoine"* (Paris: Honoré Champion, 1997)

# PROCESSES OF LITERARY CREATION: FLAUBERT AND PROUST
## Marion A. Schmid

My PhD dissertation (completed 1994; revised version forthcoming with "Legenda", European Humanities Research Centre, Oxford) is part of a flourishing tradition of Flaubert studies commonly referred to as "genetic" studies, which have gained prominence over the past thirty years. In contrast to earlier "genetic" works, however, such as Claudine Gothot-Mersch's seminal study *La Genèse de Madame Bovary*, I did not concentrate on one single author or text, but, instead, examined the genetic processes that shaped two of the great masterpieces of Modernity: Flaubert's *L'Éducation sentimentale* and Proust's *A La Recherche du temps perdu*.

Flaubert and Proust, each in turn, have been classified under two basic modes of literary production. Together with most nineteenth-century Realist and Naturalist writers, Flaubert's work is usually placed in the category of "programmatic writing".[1] Flaubert produced a prodigious quantity of planning documents (a first sketch, plans, scenarios) in the early phases of the genesis in order to ensure maximal control over the evolution of his text. Proust, on the contrary, is generally catalogued under "immanent" writing or "écriture à processus" as it is also called. Proust allowed his work to develop far more freely and spontaneously. The macro-genesis of *A La Recherche* has often been described as an open-ended and potentially infinite process of transformations and expansions, which was only brought to an end by Proust's untimely death in 1922.[2]

The aim of my comparative genetic study was to evaluate how the two almost diametrically opposed practices of the two authors shaped a first narrative and thematic framework, for both *L'Éducation sentimentale* and *A La Recherche du temps perdu*. The documents under investigation were Flaubert's notebooks and scenarios, from the period 1864 to 1869, which had recently been published by Pierre-Marc de Biasi and Tony Williams, and Proust's *Cahiers*, from the period 1908 to 1911. Methodologically, my work falls under a branch of genetic criticism known as "génétique scénarique" or "génétique structurale".[3] This genesis of structures, a diachronic approach *par excellence*, focuses on the narratological and thematic components of a literary work. It examines the evolution of narrative strands, the creation of themes and motifs, as well as the diegetic organisation and actantial distribution of the emerging text. Its objective is to illustrate the logic and dynamism of the compositional process, its necessities and hazards.[4]

The Flaubert part of my dissertation addresses a number of issues that are crucial for the macro-structural elaboration of *L'Éducation sentimentale*: the interaction between notes and scenarios in the early genesis of the novel, the textual and linguistic status of the scenarios, and, finally, the architectonic and narrative organisation of the *avant-texte*. Although my enquiry is concerned first and foremost with the textual and formal elaboration of *L'Éducation sentimentale*, its critical bearings are not exclusively philological. Rather, I look at ways in which our knowledge of the author's writing practice and of the creative process at large can change our reading of the published text. With regard to Flaubert, I argue for instance that specific features of his texts which are commonly considered as "modern" (narrative complexity, decreased readability, gaps and blanks) are not necessarily the result of a conscious strategy of subversion and obfuscation on Flaubert's part, as is claimed by many modern and postmodern critics.[5] A genetic examination of the scenarios for *L'Education sentimentale* shows, on the contrary, that it was often purely textual processes, such as textual dislocation, at work in the transition from *avant-texte* to published text that made certain passages more difficult to evaluate for the reader.[6]

Up to now, immanent and genetic studies of Flaubert have developed almost separately from each other (mostly owing to the fact that most critics today still consider any textual, and, by extension, any genetic investigation as taking place prior to and independently of interpretation proper). Critics in the future will need to bridge the gap between the two disciplines and engage in a new dialogue between philological (or, more specifically, genetic) and interpretative methods. Genetic studies merit the important place in the canon of literary methods they claim at present because they are able to elucidate and, indeed, to change our reading of published texts. They are not only complementary to, but crucial and cogent for interpretation. One powerful new direction for Flaubert studies (and for literary studies in general), I would thus argue, lies in a fruitful exchange between textual and interpretative criticism, and, ultimately, between *avant-texte* and text.

### Notes

[1] For more detail on the two modes of writing see Louis Hay, "Die dritte Dimension der Literatur", 311–14.

[2] See for instance Rainer Warning & Jean Milly, eds., *Marcel Proust. Écrire sans fin*.

[3] For a definition see Henri Mitterand, "Avant-Propos", vi.

[4] Cf. Mitterand, *Zola. L'Histoire et la fiction*, 134.

[5] For modernist readings of Flaubert, see for instance Jonathan Culler, *Flaubert. The Uses of Uncertainty*; Nathalie Sarraute, "Flaubert", and the articles collected in *Littérature* 15 (1974), "Modernité de Flaubert". For a postmodernist interpretation see Naomi Schor & Henry F. Majewski, eds, *Flaubert and Postmodernism*.

[6] For more detail see Marion A. Schmid "Reading it Right".

### Works Cited

Flaubert, Gustave, *Carnets de travail*, ed. Pierre-Marc de Biasi (Paris: Balland, 1988)

Flaubert, Gustave, *L'Éducation sentimentale. Les Scénarios*, ed. Tony Williams (Paris: Corti, 1992)

Culler, Jonathan, *Flaubert. The Uses of Uncertainty* (London: Elek, 1974)

Gothot-Mersch, Claudine, *La Genèse de "Madame Bovary"* (Paris: Corti, 1966)

Hay, Louis, "Die dritte Dimension der Literatur: Notizen zu einer 'critique génétique'", *Poetica*, 16 (1984), 307–23

Mitterand, Henri, "Avant-Propos", in *Leçons d'écriture, ce que disent les manuscrits*, eds. Almuth Grésillon & Michael Werner (Paris: Les Lettres Modernes, 1985), i–xiv

Mitterand, Henri, *Zola. L'Histoire et la fiction* (Paris: Presses universitaires de France, 1990)

"Modernité de Flaubert", special issue of *Littérature*, 15 (1974)

Sarraute, Nathalie, "Flaubert", *Partisan Review*, 33 (1966), 193–208

Schmid, Marion A., "Reading it Right: Transparency and Opacity in the *Avant-Texte* and the Published Text of *L'Éducation sentimentale*", *Nineteenth-Century French Studies*, 26 (1997–8), 119–32

Schor, Naomi & Henry F. Majewski, eds, *Flaubert and Postmodernism* (Lincoln: University of Nebraska Press, 1984)

Warning, Rainer & Jean Milly, eds, *Marcel Proust. Écrire sans fin* (Paris: Éditions CNRS, "Textes et Manuscrits", 1996)

# NEW LAMPS FOR OLD?
## Mary Orr

When the idea first came to hold a day conference to gather together scholars in a field which combines a major canonical author of central importance to nineteenth-century French Literature and syllabuses teaching the period in British University French courses, we were already unsure what shape a "Flaubert Day" might take. Even though many of the participants were known to one another, and not all those working on Flaubert could be invited because of the one-day format, one thing was certain. There would not be homogeneity or clear division of Flaubert scholars into camps by critical approach. While there is the seeming division between those who work principally on manuscript material and those whose research focuses on the final version of the major works, their methodologies and approaches immediately cause such categorisations to blur and converge. A number of the papers presented in this volume, and several of the current theses being written, demonstrate this overlap. As far as approaches to Flaubert in Britain are concerned, diversity is immediately apparent, replicated both by British contributions to Flaubert Studies, as assessed by Tony Williams in the Introduction to this volume, by the variety and range of the papers in this volume itself, and by the necessarily abridged bibliographical survey by Flaubert's most dedicated bibliographer, David Colwell. It seems that in monographs and articles devoted solely to Flaubert or to thematic studies where he is a major player, his centrality comes not because he is part of the Great Tradition, but because the richness of the *œuvre* itself guarantees the future as it has sustained a past. Michel

Foucault's designation of *La Tentation de Saint Antoine* as "La Bibliothèque fantastique" of reading applies equally to the eclectic diversity of the responses by Flaubert's critics.

But does this "richness" of the *œuvre* speak for itself? The day conference was an attempt to assess it from a specific context to see if any new critical fashions were predominant in ways in which Sartre or Culler dominated in past decades. Were there any radically new approaches or optics or did this richness stem from the way Flaubert's texts lend themselves to various kinds of scrutiny and analysis? Diana Knight's opening remarks to the *table ronde*, that there were perhaps no new approaches, were picked up and qualified by the other speakers and participants. Tim Unwin described the situation as one in which there were no "paradigm shifts" in the field, words echoed by Mike Wetherill's assessment that there were no new frameworks to rethink Flaubert. This could, however, be said of any author-specific research field. What did emerge, particularly from the contributions from current research students, was that there were specific approaches which were largely being avoided, namely psychoanalytical theories, deconstruction, and Sartrean. Flaubert's psyche, or biographical approaches, are not current research interests amongst postgraduates.

The question then is "Why Flaubert"? Why does Flaubert rather than Balzac, Zola, Maupassant, Huysmans or Proust remain continually central to the "champ de travail" of so many scholars and research students? Indeed, can one begin to gauge literary, aesthetic, cultural, even interdisciplinary or international research by mapping an author's research popularity? Do literary tradition, cultural and educational heritage, pedagogical exposure or censorship temper, or determine, authorial circulation, research, and critical responses?

The influence of Sartre and Culler is a particularly interesting one given the several generations of researchers on Flaubert at the conference and represented by the essays in this volume. Both figures represent two national critical identities without replicating the inherent stereotypes. Culler's Flaubert of uncertainty and Sartre's adoption of Flaubert as alter ego of the intellectual and marginal writer were both integrated into British Flaubert Studies a decade or so ago. The tremendous excitement generated by these critics, however, was possibly more a shift in critical thinking *per se* than specifically concentrated on Flaubert. To talk of Flaubert's "modernity" was no more or no less than to repackage the debates in critical reception. Instead of the Romanticism versus Realism debate one talked of the undecidabilities of deconstruction or of the psychocritical dimensions of the text. Critical reception obviously plays a strategic role, especially if it is also given a national focus. Can we then talk of a British Flaubert Studies? Is it in the setting of what is "foreign" or "other" to the writer and the language and context of his writing that new approaches are stimulated?

In organising a conference to survey what has happened in research in Flaubert Studies since the early eighties in Britain, there was no attempt to privilege any one movement or approach over the others. The main contributors were not necessarily to be taken as representative of key developments. Rather they were to represent the divergences and variety of research method, critical approach and focus. The similarities were, first, that the person of Flaubert and his intentionality were treated with caution or ignored; second, Flaubert's texts rather than a critic's approach were the point of reference; and third, reference was made where appropriate to other critics, both positively and negatively with a distinct deconstruction of particular critical *idées reçues*. The marked individuality of the six papers was also underpinned by a very similar empirical and pragmatic method, often made visible by a criss-crossing of several strands of approach. Lemot's famous cartoon of Flaubert "dissecting" Madame Bovary, her heart on his "stylo-scalpel", might be one way of illustrating this common aim: to get to the heart of the matter.

One of the key questions we had set out to investigate was whether there is a definable "British" Flaubert Studies in which we could then examine "new approaches". The six main contributions do not represent "British" Flaubert Studies but some marker pegs. Others would be Adrianne Tooke's investigations of Flaubert's use of painting or Alan Raitt's study of Flaubert and the theatre. One is also fully aware of the implications in an international context of "British" involvement alongside American, French, Italian or Japanese studies of any author or *œuvre*. Flaubert, I think, would have heartily enjoyed the futility of our question and the decision nonetheless to undertake the task of investigating it, especially given his delight in *idées reçues*, clichés of all kinds and stereotypes.

The interest in the day conference shown by scholars working in the field and in related ones of the nineteenth-century French novel, gender theory, manuscript studies, clearly affirmed that Flaubert Studies are very much alive in the British context. While some researchers who were Flaubertistes a decade ago have moved on to other areas, they have nonetheless carried with them into their new fields of interest what they learned through working on him. Others have joined the field because of primary research in related areas, or as the research student contributions in particular have demonstrated, because no other author seemed more interesting. Cynics could argue that new researchers are inspired because reading the *œuvre* of Flaubert, instead of that of Zola for example, to complete a PhD thesis according to British Academy guidelines seems slightly more feasible. The diversity of new interest from the postgraduates is a clear rebuttal to cynics or sociologists of the higher education climate in Britain. One undertakes no project on Flaubert lightly, whether this is a study of the works or the study of a problem where Flaubert is one of the key players. In either case, the secondary critical reading presents a daunting task.

So whither Flaubert Studies in Britain? Close reading, whether of manuscript, the final version, the *Correspondance* or all three, is certain to continue, regardless of the theoretical approach which is then applied. The publication of the new Pléiade, edited by Claudine Gothot-Mersch and Guy Sagnes, as well as fourth volume of the Jean Bruneau's edition of the *Correspondance* will be, as Mike Wetherill suggested, the moment of reevaluation *par excellence* in Flaubert Studies not just in Britain, perhaps even the moment to hold another day conference. The *table ronde* discussions after the papers also elicited much excited debate about the other major resource to be exploited now and in the future — Information Technology. In future textual study, it will provide a tool whereby comparison could be made about style and language in the works of Flaubert or the means by which wordfields in various nineteenth-century novels might be compared and contrasted. The Chicago-based ARTFL allows access to exciting searches in the socio-cultural as well as literary contexts and points to increasingly cross-contextualised study possibilities. Much is still waiting to be uncovered through further study of intertextuality in Flaubert. The other largely uncharted territory is philosophical influence. Seeing Flaubert as metaphysician opens up the medico-spiritual dimensions of his work as well as a wider understanding of his philosophical erudition and engagement with many other philosophers than Spinoza. Such studies would be much facilitated by CD-ROM as too would be research in linguistics. The revival, for example, of stylistic studies of Flaubert will not focus simply on image or linguistic occurrence or "nœuds de significations". Alan Raitt made the point that no real attempt has been made to understand the stylistic developments in Flaubert's prose. These IT resources could raise questions of image usage and recurrence of motif, foreign words or loaded terms, which might previously, as Tony Williams signalled, have been of more interest to the translator. Tim Unwin, however, challenged the notion of the computer as but a grandiose concordance, a tool, and suggested that it is a resource whereby mindsets in the user can be cracked open as searching inevitably leads into forking paths. Both Tony Williams and Mike Wetherill underlined the importance of the CD-ROM for the wider dissemination of the manuscripts beyond the research group in the archive. The textual encoding of the major works as hypertexts presents other, more multi-media, approaches whereby the visual in Flaubert, his descriptions as cinematographic, could be investigated in ways which take further Adrianne Tooke's work on Flaubert and the Visual Arts or film studies. All the main contributors were in agreement that no IT resource or new technologies, however sophisticated, would ultimately devalue individual response, intuitions or the formulation of such ideas once searches and research had been done.

At the end of the conference and *table ronde*, there were no obvious "new" approaches. What emerged was a consensus that New Approaches in Flaubert Studies, in the British context of French Studies, means at the very least two things. First, his *œuvre* and his erudition provide a portmanteau resource for future British scholarship which will continue its eclectic, at times self-mocking and ironic, mix of pedantry and passion, often hinging on "le petit détail qui fait vrai" and Flaubert's own love of the bizarre. Flaubert attracts the scholar and ferret researcher who spots a gap, a theme or motif, and then follows it up, assiduously. Paul Tipper would see these as the different rhetorics which criss-cross Flaubert's writing; Alan Raitt calls them "langages"; Anne Green adopts the word "motif"; Mary Orr sees them as discourses. The range and depth of expertise in British Flaubert Studies is in no small part due to its academic heritage and lives devoted to it. Alan Raitt must be thanked for his lifelong contribution to both Flaubert in print and to people he has mentored into the discipline. Modestly, he sees himself in Flaubert Studies as coming "at the tail end" with the quiet, and British, wit of the remark. This wit, if anything, is where I would pinpoint the hallmark of the British Flaubertiste. Where else but in the *French Studies Bulletin* could a series, an academic soap opera of unlikely but exuberantly empassioned academics, run on the subject of literary parrots? And this nerve end of activity in British French Studies spills over to the second, particularly British, response to Flaubert. This is to Flaubert as Le Garçon, the trickster and humorist, doyen of the deadpan and player with the erudite intertext. The appreciation of him as the virtuoso of fiction's fiction, but in the deadly humorous tradition of Swift and Sterne, finds its contemporary response in fiction itself. Julian Barnes's *Flaubert's Parrot* not only voices a Flaubertian narrator à la britannique, but combines careful research and fiction which imitates Flaubert to create a fictional genre of the creative ventriloquist: free indirect speech with Bull instead of Bovary ("Quand on ne sait pas le nom d'un Anglais, on l'appelle John Bull").

Flaubert's supreme distaste for the embourgeoisification of the culture machine (of which colloquia, publications, research ratings and assessments are all a part) must make dedicated Flaubert scholars fill with self-doubt as regards the validity of holding such a conference let alone of participating in or publishing it. In the unenviable task of trying to write this conclusion, I was speculating how Flaubert might have appeared today as "Talking Head", and how he would have played it in different cultural contexts. How would he have responded to an

*Apostrophes* interview? Would he have turned it down? Would he have reverted to being Le Garçon and mocked the whole show? Or would he have been camera shy, a very unsuitable media presence, mopping his brow under the lights? And what of a big, US, media interview? Can one imagine him answering questions on deconstruction or gender theory without comment, later, to his correspondents on its jargon? And the Institute of Romance Studies, which so generously enabled us to host the conference and speculate on such matters as Flaubert's Art, how would it have brought out a "British" Flaubert if we had been able to invite him as our guest of honour? I suspect we would have witnessed an older Flaubert, of *Bouvard et Pécuchet*; more relaxed, more erudite, and the more eccentric our group, the more at home he would feel in the gentlemanly setting of the University of London's Institute of Romance Studies.

Knowing the folly of daring to end, this coda is the best place to acknowledge that there will be ongoing work on Flaubert in British French Studies in multifarious ways. An approach like that of Sartre in *L'Idiot de la Famille,* "literary criticism as conceptual adventure" to quote Diana Knight, with its misquotations, erroneous "facts" and all, has been eschewed, but needs reconsideration in itself and as a mindset, perhaps, as Tim Unwin suggested, to provide new models to renegotiate "L'homme et l'œuvre", but in un-British style. The other new approach to research is the creative as undertaken by Julian Barnes or, less successfully because less humorously in my opinion, in France, by Jean Améry in his rewriting of *Madame Bovary* from Charles's perspective. Our conference resolved none of our questions, nor converted us, but nonethess it renewed our enthusiasms for Flaubert. This "tailpiece" is thus *en guise de conclusion* and is dedicated to Alan Raitt and to all who will pursue Flaubert Studies in Britain.

JB: Well, it is a rare honour to have this opportunity to interview you at the end of this conference on "New Approaches in Flaubert Studies", M. Flaubert, on virtual link, and to have you back in London with us. The organisers chose November both as a tribute to one of your early works

and of course because they were then more guaranteed to have fog which they knew would make you feel at home here again. [Lettre à Louise Colet, 30 sept. 1851: "Adieu, nous partons pour l'exposition. Quel atroce brouillard!"]
Some things don't really change in London, you know, with our exhibitions to mark our place in Empire, rather like France's mania for landmarks. "Érection — Ne se dit qu'en parlant des monuments", n'est-ce pas? And before I get on to those questions on art and writing which our viewers and readers are eagerly awaiting your responses to, I'd like just to ask you about our recent national érections! First, France, and La Pyramide.

GF: Ouvrage inutile! [Pause]

JB : And what about our controversial Dome?

GF: On s'étonne de ce que cela puisse tenir seul. En citer trois maintenant: celui des Invalides et celui de Saint-Pierre de Rome et ensuite celui de Pierre Mandelstamm...

JB: Mandelson.

GF: lui-même, ministre sans portefeuille en Angleterre, si je comprends bien, mais selon moi, avec portefeuille! En avoir un sous le bras donne l'air d'un ministre. Notre époque — il faut tonner contre elle. Et se plaindre de ce qu'elle n'est pas poétique. L'appeler époque de transition, de décadence...

JB: So you do see art not just for itself, as "la manière absolue de voir les choses"?

GF: L'art est plus utile que l'industrie, le beau est plus utile que le bon. S'il en était autrement, pourquoi les premiers peuples, les premiers gouvernements ne seraient-ils pas industrieux, commerçants. Ils sont artistes, poètes, ils bâtissent des choses inutiles (comme des pyramides, des cathédrales pour l'an deux mille), ils font des poèmes avant de faire le drap[eau]. L'esprit est plus gourmand que l'estomac. J'aime mieux l'inspiration que la réflexion — le sentiment que la raison, la clémence que la justice, la religion que la philosophie — le beau que l'utile, la poésie avant tout...

J'ai [...] beaucoup écrit, et peut-être aurais-je bien écrit si au lieu de forcer mes sentiments pour les porter à l'idéal et de monter mes pensées sur les tréteaux, je les avais laissé courir dans les champs comme elles sont, fraîches, roses...

JB: So you see the writing profession as a hierarchy, on a scale of utility at the bottom and art and the ideal at the pinnacle?

GF: Les folliculaires — ce sont les journalistes. Quand on ajoute de bas étage, c'est le comble du mépris. Et des idéologues. Tous les journalistes le sont. Dans ce sens, écrire, *currente calamo*, c'est l'excuse pour les fautes de style ou d'orthographe.

JB: It happens in our Press too.

GF: L'imprimerie — quelle découverte merveilleuse. Mais sur le plan orthographe, elle a fait plus de mal que de bien. Et ce qui est donc "bien écrit", mots de portier, désigne les romans-feuilletons qui les amusent. L'écriture, surtout si elle est belle, mène à tout ... comme illustrent bien d'ailleurs mes copistes, Bouvard et Pécuchet...
En ce qui concerne l'auteur — surtout s'il est mort — on doit "connaître des auteurs"; inutile de savoir leurs noms.

JB: So you would see yourself as an Author?

GF: Mais pas du tout de nationalité anglaise! Les Anglais sont tous riches! Oui, peut-être, ou plutôt auteur que dentiste — ils sont tous menteurs.

JB: M. Flaubert, you do have this reputation for being a bit of a recluse, the hermit of Croisset, you refuse to give interviews and be a celeb.

GF: Les célébrités: on s'inquiète du moindre détail de leur vie privée, afin de pourvoir les dénigrer... Enid Starkie, Jean-Paul Sartre et plus récemment Mary Orr ont tous parlé de mes proclivités personnelles et strictement privées. Je leur répondrai que tous les gens de lettres sont constipés.

JB: So paparazzi *and* literati are to be distinguished from serious critics?

GF: Le critique est toujours éminent... est censé tout connaître, avoir tout lu, tout vu. Quand il vous déplaît, l'appeler Aristarque, ou eunuque, Culler ou Derrida. La philosophie a le gosier séché par la poussière du néant de tous ses systèmes.

JB: Your own work methods of course are well-known, your meticulous corrections to the manuscripts, the search for the "mot juste". How do you decide when the page is finished when you have also avowed that conclusions are the height of stupidity?

GF: La Méthode ne sert à rien! Quand on écrit on sent ce qui doit être, on comprend qu'à tel endroit il faut ceci, à tel autre cela. On se compose des tableaux qu'on voit, et on a la sensation que l'on va en quelque sorte les faire éclore. On se sent dans le cœur comme l'écho lointain de toutes les passions qu'on va mettre au jour — et cette impuissance à rendre tout cela est le désespoir éternel de ceux qui écrivent, la misère des langues qui ont à peine un mot pour cent pensées — les malheurs de la France viennent de ce qu'on n'en sait pas assez — la faiblesse de l'homme qui ne sait pas trouver l'approchant et à moi particulièrement mon éternelle angoisse.

JB: Well that brings me to one of the hottest debates of this conference, whether work on your manuscripts and documents — largely the direction taken by your French critics — is more important than interpretations of the works in print which is where most American critics are involved. Or both? as the British contingent have exemplified today. Can you clarify this for us?

GF: Le document – c'est toujours de la plus haute importance. Et on doit croire tout ce qui est imprimé. J'ajouterai aussi l'illisible! Une ordonnance de médecin doit l'être — je suis fils de médecin — et toute signature *ITEM*. Cela indique qu'on est accablé de correspondance, comme Bruneau le sait très bien!

JB: But can I press you a bit further on the British approach?

GF: Moi, je dirai que le flegme c'est toujours bon genre, et puis ça donne l'air anglais!
Toujours suivi de l'imperturbable!

JB: I thought of writing books myself once. I had the ideas; I even made notes. You know I made many pilgrimages to Rouen to see where you worked, how you were inspired by parrots, and to understand how you created Art. Now I have the opportunity I didn't have when my jottings were published so aptly by Picador in the early eighties to ask you at last: For you, what is Art?

GF:   Ça mène à l'hôpital, mon ami, mon lecteur, mon frère et cher docteur! A quoi ça sert, puisqu'on le remplace par la mécanique qui fait mieux et plus vite. Le rôle des ordinateurs, des CD-ROM pour les recherches, font éclater tout Club du Livre. C'est le sujet d'exaspération pour les conservateurs! Et mon dernier mot, en tant que L'Auteur impersonnel – E-MAIL: Le secret est perdu. C'est tout. On peut éteindre.

JB:   M. Flaubert! M. Flotbear!

(Turning to the audience)

Flaubert's Dictionary offers a course in irony: from entry to entry, you can see him applying it in various thicknesses, like a cross-Channel painter darkening the sky with another wash. It tempts me to write a Dictionary of Accepted Ideas about Gustave himself. Just a short one: a booby-trapped pocket guide; something straight-faced yet misleading. The received wisdom in pellet form, with some of the pellets poisoned. This is the attraction, and also the danger, of irony: the way it permits a writer to be seemingly absent from his work, yet in fact hintingly present. You *can* have your cake and eat it; the only trouble is, you get fat.

FIN

FOOTNOTE: Flaubert's words are more or less faithfully copied by a contemporary amanuensis from his *Souvenirs, Notes et Pensées Intimes* and the *Dictionnaire des Idées Reçues*. "JB" bears only initial ressemblance to Julian Barnes, but his final remark and the line, "I thought of writing books myself once. I had the ideas; I even made notes." are quotations from Geoffrey Braithwaite © Pan Books by kind permission.

# BIBLIOGRAPHY: FLAUBERT STUDIES, 1989–97

## D. J. Colwell

## Part One: Selected Books

**Editions of Flaubert's works**

**Correspondance**

*La Bêtise, l'art et la vie.* En écrivant *Madame Bovary.* Présentation et établissement du texte par André Versaille. Bruxelles: Complexe, 1991. 121p. (Correspondance between Flaubert and Louise Colet, 1851–55.)

*Correspondance,* Tome III. Janvier 1859–décembre 1868. Édition établie, présentée et annotée par Jean Bruneau. Paris: Gallimard, 1991. xii + 1727p. (Bibliothèque de la Pléiade.)

*Correspondance,* Tome IV. Janvier 1869–décembre 1875. Édition établie, présentée et annotée par Jean Bruneau. Paris: Gallimard, 1998. x + 1484p. (Bibliothèque de la Pléiade.)

*Flaubert – Guy de Maupassant. Correspondance.* Présentée et annotée par Yvan Leclerc. Paris: Flammarion, 1993. 520p.

*Flaubert – Ivan Tourguéniev. Correspondance.* Texte édité, préfacé et annoté par Alexandre Zviguilsky. Paris: Flammarion, 1989. 362p.

Bouilhet, Louis: *Lettres à Flaubert.* Texte établi, présenté et annoté par Maria Luisa Cappello. Paris: CNRS, 1996. 780p.

*Lettres d'Orient.* Avant-propos de Pierre Bergounioux. Bordeaux: Horizon chimérique, 1990. 336p.

**Dictionnaire des idées reçues**

*Dictionnaire des idées reçues.* Édition de Jean-Yves Clément. Paris: Cherche-Midi, 1993. 228p. (Les Pensées.)

*Dictionnaire des idées reçues. Le catalogue des idées chic.* Édition d'Anne Herschberg-Pierrot. Paris: LGF, 1997. 250p. (Le Livre de Poche classique.)

**L'Éducation sentimentale**

*L'Éducation sentimentale. Histoire d'un jeune homme.* Postface et notes de Pierre-Marc de Biasi. Paris: Seuil, 1993. 691p. (L'École des lettres.)

*L'Éducation sentimentale. Histoire d'un jeune homme.* Parcours rapide, résumé et commentaires de Véronique Anglard. Alleur: Marabout, 1996. 540p. (Collection Lecture fléchée.)

*L'Éducation sentimentale: Les Scénarios.* Édition préparée par Tony Williams. Paris: Corti, 1992. 378p.

**Madame Bovary**

*Madame Bovary.* Avec une introduction, des notes et un dossier sur l'œuvre par Marie-Anne Barbéris. Paris: Larousse, 1989. 399p.

*Madame Bovary.* Extraits avec une notice biographique, une notice historique et littéraire, des notes explicatives, une documentation thématique, des jugements, un questionnaire et des sujets de devoirs. Édition de Paul Jolas. Paris: Larousse, 1990. 176p.

*Madame Bovary.* Postface et notes de Pierre-Marc de Biasi. Paris: Seuil, 1992. 531p. (L'École des Lettres.)

*Madame Bovary. Mœurs de province.* Présentation, notes et transcriptions de Pierre-Marc de Biasi. Paris: Éditions de l'Imprimerie Nationale, 1994. 635p. (La Salamandre.)

*Plans, notes et scénarios de "Madame Bovary".* Présentation, transcription et notes par Yvan Leclerc. Paris: CNRS; Cadheihan: Zulma, 1995. 198p. (Manuscrits.)

**Œuvres de jeunesse**

*"Mémoires d'un fou", "Novembre" et autres textes de jeunesse.* Édition critique établie par Yvan Leclerc. Paris: Flammarion, 1991. 340p. (Contains: Mémoires d'un fou; Novembre; Un Parfum à sentir; La Peste à Florence; Bibliomanie; Rage et impuissance; Une Leçon d'histoire naturelle; Quidquid volueris; Passion et vertu; Agonies; Angoisses; Les Funérailles du Docteur Mathurin; Souvenirs, notes et pensées intimes.)

*La Première "Éducation sentimentale".* Préface et dossier critique de Martine Bercot. Paris: LGF, 1993. 445p. (Le Livre de Poche Classique.)

**Pour Louis Bouilhet**

*Pour Louis Bouilhet.* Textes édités et annotés par Alain Raitt. Exeter: University of Exeter Press, 1994. liv + 85p. (Textes littéraires, 87.)

**Salammbô**

*Salammbô.* Préface de Pascaline Mourier-Casile; dossier historique et littéraire par Claude Aziza. Paris: Presses Pocket, 1995. 499p. (Presses Pocket, 6088.)

**Trois Contes**

*Un Cœur simple.* Conte. Édition présentée, annotée et expliquée par Edouard Bessière. Paris: Larousse, 1992. 160p. (Classiques Larousse.)

*Corpus Flaubertianum. II. Hérodias.* Édition diplomatique et génétique des manuscrits. Édition de Giovanni Bonaccorso et al. Vol. I, Paris: Nizet, 1991. cxi + 333p + xxxii pl; Vol. II, Messina: Sicania, 1995. 550p.

*Hérodias.* Conte. Édition présentée, annotée et expliquée par Daniel Couty. Paris: Larousse, 1990. 144p. (Classiques Larousse.)

*Trois contes.* Texte intégral. Postface et notes de Pierre-Marc de Biasi. Paris: Seuil, 1993. 283p. (L'École des Lettres.)

**Voyages**

*Voyage en Bretagne. Par les champs et par les grèves.* Préface de Maxime Du Camp et Maurice Nadeau. Bruxelles: Complexe, 1989. 368p. (Le Regard littéraire.)

*Voyage en Egypte.* Édition intégrale du manuscrit original établie et présentée par Pierre-Marc de Biasi. Paris: Grasset, 1991. 464p.

**Exhibition**

Catalogue d'Exposition. "C'è chi dice Madame Bovary. Certains disent *Madame Bovary*. Some say *Madame Bovary*". Una esposizione a cura di Marina Giaveri, Aosta, 1991. Fabbri editore, 1991. 82p.

**Critical Studies**

**Collections of Articles and Special Issues of Journals**

*Approaches to Teaching Flaubert's "Madame Bovary"*. Edited by Laurence M. Porter & Eugene F. Gray. New York: MLA, 1995. xvi + 167p. (Approaches to Teaching World Literature). (Contains the following articles: Bart, Benjamin F.: Teaching *Madame Bovary* in a Humanities Course, 13–20; Furst, Lilian R: Emma Bovary: The Angel Gone Astray, 21–27; Ahearn, Edward J.: A Marxist Approach to *Madame Bovary*, 28–33; Wolf, Susan L.: The Same or (M)other: A Feminist Reading, 34–41; Pinzka, Lauren: A Psychoanalytic Approach to *Madame Bovary*, 42–8; Motte, Dean de la: Will the Real Emma Bovary Stand Up, 49–54; Nelles, William: Myth and Symbol in *Madame Bovary*, 55–60; Ginsburg, Michal Peled: Vision and Language: Teaching *Madame Bovary*, 61–8; Schlossman, Beryl: Flaubert's Moving Sidewalk, 69–76; Issacharoff, Michael: Unwrapping the Comic, 77–83; Prince, Gerald: A Narratological Approach to *Madame Bovary*, 84–90; Kelly, Dorothy: Teaching *Madame Bovary* through the Lens of Poststructuralism, 90–7; Winchell, James: Reading (in) *Madame Bovary*, 98–105; McKenna, Andrew: Desire, Difference, and Deconstruction in *Madame Bovary*, 106–13; Donaldson-Evans, Mary: Teaching *Madame Bovary* through Film, 114–121; Brown, Monika: Reading Realist Literature: *Madame Bovary* in a Great Books or World Literature Course, 122–9; Rifelj, Carol de Robay: Teaching *Madame Bovary* through Writing, 130–6; Berg William J. & Martin Laurey K.: Teaching Reading Tactics in *Madame Bovary*, 137–43; Chambers, Ross: Relevance, Reading, and Meaning, 144–52.)

*Emma Bovary*. Edited and with an introduction by Harold Bloom. New York: Chelsea House, 1994. xiv + 222p. (Major Literary Characters). (Contains a variety of short critical extracts, and the following articles: McConnell, Frank D.: The lexicography of *Madame Bovary*, 59–71; Smalley, Barbara: Illusion, counterpoint and the darkened universe, 72–80; Bernheimer, Charles: The psychogenesis of Flaubert's style, 81–90; Lowe, Margaret: "Madame Bovary, c'est moi", 91–101; Goodwin, Sarah Webster: Emma Bovary's dance of death, 102–120; Peterson, Carla L.: *Madame Bovary*, Dionysian rituals, 121–32; Wing, Nathaniel: Emma's stories. Narrative, repetition and desire in *Madame Bovary*, 133–64; Fleming, Bruce E.: An essay in seduction, or the trouble with Bovary, 165–73; VanderWolk, William: Memory and the transformative art in *Madame Bovary*, 174–88; Danahy, Michael: *Madame Bovary*: a tongue of one's own, 189–210.)

*Emma Bovary.* Dirigé par Alain Buisine. Paris: Éditions Autrement, 1997. 154p. (Contains the following articles: Leclerc, Yvan: Comment une petite femme devient mythique, 8–25; Buisine, Alain: Emma, c'est l'autre, 26–51; Bellemin-Noël, Jean: Le sexe d'Emma, 52–78; Marder, Elissa: Madame Bovary en Amérique, 79–99; Pedraza, George: Le Shopping d'Emma, 100–21; Fonyi, Antonia: Sa "vie nombreuse", sa "haine nombreuse", 122–44.)

*Flaubert, l'autre. Pour Jean Bruneau.* Textes réunis par F. Leclerc et S. Messina. Lyon: Presses universitaires de Lyon, 1989. 186p. (Contains the following articles: Leclerc, F. et Messina, S.: Avant-propos, 5–6; Mouchard, Claude: Limbes (On Louise Colet and Flaubert's *Correspondance*), 9–16; Biasi, Pierre-Marc de: L'esthétique référentielle. Remarques sur les carnets de travail de Flaubert, 17–33; Herschberg-Pierrot, Anne: Sur les notes de lecture de Flaubert. (On Flaubert and Voltaire's *Dictionnaire philosophique*), 34–9; Sagnes, Guy: Flaubert lecteur des *Psaumes* d'après des notes inédites, 40–54; Neefs, Jacques: L'écriture des confins. (On Flaubert's *Notes de voyage*), 55–72; Gothot-Mersch, Claudine: Notes sur l'invention dans *Salammbô*, 75–84; Bonaccorso, Giovanni: Science et fiction. Le traitement des notes d' "Hérodias", 85–94; Kim, Yong-Eun: La philosophie de la nature, source de l'épisode des animaux de *La Tentation de saint Antoine* (1849), 95–103; Oehler, Dolf: La répudiation de la photographie. Flaubert et Melville, 105–15; Czyba, Lucette: Les silences de Justin, 119–26; Cigada, Sergio: Le chapitre des "Comices" et la structure de la double opposition dans *Madame Bovary*, 127–37; Bart, Benjamin F.: Le style indirect libre chez Flaubert. *Madame Bovary* et les richesses de l'indéterminé, 138–44; Leclerc, Yvan: Ponctuation de Flaubert, 145–51; Gaillard, Françoise: *Bouvard et Pécuchet*. Un conte sur la folie ordinaire, 152–60; Burgelin, Claude: Graal-Flaubert, ou la leçon de méthode de Julian Barnes, 163–72; Douchin, Jacques-Louis: Petit supplément au *Dictionnaire des idées reçues*, 173–75; Bibliographie: les publications de Jean Bruneau, 177–9.)

*Flaubert. "L'Éducation sentimentale". L'histoire.* Paris: Ellipses-Marketing, 1989. 125p. ("Analyses et réflexions sur..".) (Contains the following articles: Fenaux, Jean-Paul: Flaubert ou l'éducation d'un écrivain, 5–25; Fenaux, Jean-Paul: Un jeune homme sur un bateau, 27–9; Adam, Colette-Chantal: Le rendez-vous manqué, 30–5; Guillo, Gisèle: "Les Tuileries", 36–40; Bartoli-Anglard, Véronique: *L'Éducation sentimentale* comme texte critique, 41–4; Aurégan, Pierre: Temps historique, temps narratif dans *L'Éducation sentimentale*, 45–52; Collet, Paule: Discours et vision politique dans *L'Éducation sentimentale*, 53–60; Jaunet, Jean-Luc: L'histoire et l' "Histoire" dans *L'Éducation sentimentale*. De la difficulté et de l'art d'introduire la réalité historique dans la fiction romanesque, 70–7; Borrut, Michel: Les détournements de l'histoire, 78–82; Borrut, Michel: Les lieux de l'histoire, 83–92; Aurégan, Pierre: Réalisme et naturalisme au XIX$^e$ siècle. Flaubert au milieu du siècle, 109–17; Fricaud, Solange: Regards sur *L'Éducation sentimentale*, 118–21.)

*Flaubert – Maupassant.* Numéro spécial préparé sous la direction de Yvan Leclerc, *Études normandes,* XXXIX, 2 (1990) 144p.

*Gustave Flaubert 4. Intersections.* Textes réunis par Raymonde Debray-Genette, Claude Duchet, Bernard Masson et Jacques Neefs. Paris: Les Les Lettres Modernes, 1994. 203p. (*Revue des Les Lettres Modernes*, 1165–72.) (Contains the following articles: Bellemin-Noël, Jean: Gustave, Poulou, Julien et nous autres, 3–20; Ginsburg, Michal Peled: La tentation du biographique, 21–42; Ogura, Kosei: Le discours socialiste dans l'avant-texte de *L'Éducation sentimentale*, 43–76; Mertès-Gleize, Joëlle: Le livre, gris banal. Livres et lecture dans les deux *Éducation sentimentale*, 77–97; Pliskin, Fabrice: La norme et l'exception, 99–113; Backès, Jean-Louis: Le divin dans *Salammbô*, 115–34; Luoni, Flavio: *Saint Antoine* et les deux voies vers la matière, 135–53; Thomas, Yves: La tentation du désert chez Flaubert, 155–67; Jameson, Maureen: De Villequier à Pont-l'Évêque, un palimpseste flaubertien?, 169–86; Séginger, Gisèle: Une version apocryphe de *La Tentation de saint Antoine*, 187–203.)

*James Joyce 2. Scribble 2, Joyce et Flaubert.* Textes réunis par Claude Jacquet et André Topia. Paris: Les Lettres Modernes, 1990. 189p. (*Revue des Lettres Modernes*, 953–958.) (Contains the following articles: Jacquet, Claude: Joyce et Flaubert, 5–11; Hayman, David: Towards a Postflaubertian Joyce, 13–63; Brown, Richard: Shifting sexual centres. Joyce and Flaubert, 45–84; Neefs, Jacques: Écrits de formation. *L'Éducation sentimentale* de 1845 et le *Portrait*, 85–99; Huss, Roger: Masculinité et féminité dans *Madame Bovary* et 'Ulysses', 102–122; Brunazzi, E.: La narration de l'autogenèse dans *La Tentation de saint Antoine* et dans *Ulysses*, 123–31; Schlossman, B.: "Che vuoi?", *"Don Giovanni"* and the seductions of Art, 133–53; Mayoux, Jean-Jacques: Du côté de chez Circé, 155–64; Rabaté, Jean-Michel et Biasi, Pierre-Marc de: Joyce, Flaubert et *Exiles*, 165–72; Senn, Fritz: Intellectual Nodality of the "Lisible": "Genus omne", 173–88.)

*La Méthode à l'œuvre. "Un Cœur simple" de Flaubert.* Edición de Alicia Piquer y Alain Verjat. Actas i Simposio Internacional. Barcelona: Universitat de Barcelona, 1992. 217p. (Contains the following articles: Vierne, Simone: La Sainte et le perroquet ou le travail du mythique dans "Un Cœur simple", 13–30; Prado, Javier del: "Un Cœur simple": un proceso destructivo, 31–59; González, Salvador Ana: Un cœur complexe, 61–78; Gutiérrez, Fátima: Tiempo entrópico y neguentropía en "Un Cœur simple" de Flaubert, 79–93; Segarra Montaner, Marta: La représentation de l'espace dans "Un Cœur simple", 95–105; Huici, Adrián: "Un Cœur simple", o la salvación por el imaginario, 107–31; Real, Elena: Le pouvoir de l'image, 133–47; Piquer-Desvaux, Alicia: Pour une lecture "ironique" d' "Un Cœur simple", 149–59; Borot, Marie-France: Agnus Dei. Taureau. Perroquet. La vierge et les bêtes, 161–74; Ma Todó, Lluís: La mujer de madera, o la confusión de todos los órdenes, 175–86; Caamaño, María Ángeles: Félicité ou l'histoire d'un nom, 187–98; Jou, Maite: Hacia una geometría de las imágines, 199–216.)

*Modernité de Flaubert.* Actes du Colloque polono-allemand organisé par l'Institut de Philologie Romane et le Centre interuniversitaire de Civilisation Française de l'Université de Varsovie dans le cadre de la coopération avec l'Université de la Sarre, sous la direction de Henryk Chudak et Uwe Dethloff (Varsovie, avril 1992).

Textes réunis et présentés par Joanna Zurowska. Varsovie, Centre de Civilisation française, 1994. 108p. (*Les Cahiers de Varsovie*, 23.) (Contains the following articles: Bray, Bernard: Le *Dictionnaire des idées reçues* entre tradition et modernité, 9–19; Parvi, Jerzy: La lettre, est-elle un genre littéraire? Quelques réflexions sur la *Correspondance* de Flaubert, 21–30; Linsen, Ehrhart: La pollution mentale et la fascination du vide dans l'œuvre de Flaubert, 31–8; Zurowska, Joanna: Proust et Flaubert, 41–7; Nallwajek, Zbigniew: *L'Éducation sentimentale*: entre George Sand et György Lucács, 49–57; Chudak, Henryk: La critique de la conscience face au problème du temps chez Flaubert, 59–66; Schwartz, Helmut: Flaubert précurseur? Lectures de Flaubert chez Alain Robbe-Grillet, Jean Ricardou et Nathalie Sarraute, 69–75; Dethloff, Uwe: Flaubert et Mario Vargas Llosa. La rencontre littéraire de deux modernes, 77–84; Lesbats, Claude: Michel Butor lecteur de Flaubert, 87–92; Walter, Klaus-Peter: Réalisme littéraire et réalisme cinématographique. *Madame Bovary* au cinéma. Renoir, Minnelli, Chabrol, 93–105.)

*L'Œuvre de l'œuvre. Études sur la "Correspondance" de Flaubert.* Textes réunis et présentés par Raymonde Debray-Genette et Jacques Neefs. Saint-Denis: Presses de l'Université de Vincennes, 1993. 188p. (Essais et savoirs.) (Contains the following articles on Jean Bruneau's edition of the *Correspondance* of Flaubert: Bruneau, Jean: Une édition en cours, 15–20; Pierrot, Roger: Éditer une correspondance, 21–8; Debray-Genette, Raymonde: Lettres à Jules Duplan; la pot-bouille et l'ensouple, 31–41; Gothot-Mersch, Claudine: La *Correspondance* de Flaubert. Une méthode au fil du temps, 43–57; Beizer, Janet: Les lettres de Flaubert à Louise Colet, une physiologie du style, 59–83; Mouchard, Claude: Flaubert critique, 87–160; Guidis, Odile: Bibliographie de la *Correspondance* de Flaubert, 163–88.)

*Salammbô.* Film de Pierre Marodon (France, 1926). Musique de Florent Schmitt.In: *L'Avant-Scène Opéra.* Numéro hors série (juillet 1991) 99p. (Contains the following articles: Tournier, Michel: *Salammbô* ou le rire de Flaubert, 4–5; Costantin, Catherine: Le roman de Flaubert: provocation, contradiction, révolution esthétique, 6–9; Michel, Claude: Florent Schmitt: Repères chronologiques, 10–11; Lorent, Catherine: Florent Schmitt et l'Orient, 12–7; Suhamy, Ariel: L'œuvre la plus musicale de Flaubert? 18–9; Kermabon, Jacques: Le film de Pierre Marodon, 20–1; Lorent, Catherine: La partition de Florent Schmitt, 22–3; Le Roy, Éric: Générique et synopsis du film, 24–5. The book also contains commentaries on the music and the film, and articles on Pierre Marodon and Florent Schmitt.)

**Monographs**

Addison, Claire: *Where Flaubert Lies. Chronology, Mythology and History.* Cambridge: Cambridge University Press, 1996. xv + 393p. (Cambridge Studies in French, 48.)

Adert, Laurent: *Les Mots des autres. Lieu commun et création romanesque dans les œuvres de Flaubert, Nathalie Sarraute et Robert Pinget.* Essai. Villeneuve-d'Ascq: Presses universitaires du Septentrion, 1996. 301p.

Alexis, Paul: *Les Romanciers au théâtre. Flaubert. 1887.* Édition de Jean de Palacio. Rheims: A l'Écart, 1991. 39p.

Amossy, Ruth: *Les Idées reçues. Sémiologie du stéréotype.* Paris: Nathan, 1991. 215p. (Le texte à l'œuvre.)

Aurégan, Pierre. *Flaubert. Grandes œuvres, commentaires, critiques, documents complémentaires.* Paris: Nathan, 1991. 126p. (Balises: Les écrivains, 1.)

Barillet, Pierre: *Gustave et Louise d'après les textes de Gustave Flaubert et Louise Colet.* Paris: Actes-Sud Papiers. 39p. (Dramatic production, 5 February 1991, Théâtre des Petits Mathurins.)

Bellemin-Noël, J.: *Le Quatrième Conte de Flaubert.* Paris: Presses universitaires de France, 1990. 127p.

Biasi, Pierre-Marc de: *Flaubert: les secrets de l'"homme-plume".* Paris: Hachette, 1995. 125p. (Coup double.)

Bienvenu, Jacques: *Maupassant, Flaubert et "Le Horla".* Marseille: B. Muntaner, 1992. 143p.

Borie, Jean: *Frédéric et les amis des hommes.* Présentation de *L'Éducation sentimentale.* Paris: Grasset, 1995. 276p.

Bourdieu, Pierre, *Les Règles de l'art. Genèse et structure du champ littéraire.* Paris: Seuil, 1992. 480p.

Breut, Michèle: *Le Haut et le bas. Essai sur le grotesque dans "Madame Bovary" de Flaubert.* Amsterdam & Atlanta: Rodopi, 1994. 256p. (Faux Titre, 78.)

Brochu, André: *Roman et énumération. De Flaubert à Perec.* Montréal: Université de Montréal, 1996. 142p. (Paragraphes.)

Butor, Michel: *Improvisations sur Flaubert.* Postface de René Adrienne. Paris: Presses Pocket, 1989. 227p. (Agora, 32.)

Cellard, Jacques: *Emma, Oh! Emma!* Paris: Balland, 1992. 425p.

Chessex, Jacques: *Flaubert ou le désert en abîme.* Paris: Grasset, 1991. 279p.

Chouard, Robert: *Promenade en Normandie avec "Madame Bovary" et Flaubert.* Préface de Jean Dutourd. Condé-sur-Noireau: Charles Corlet, 1991. 168p.

Colwell, David John: *Bibliographie des études sur Flaubert, 1857–1920*. Egham: Runnymede Books, 1989. 192p.

Colwell, David John: *Bibliographie des études sur Flaubert, 1983–1988*. Egham: Runnymede Books, 1990. 151p.

Curry, Corrada Biazzo: *Description and Meaning in Three Novels by Flaubert*. New York: Lang. 197p. (On *Madame Bovary, Salammbô* and *L'Éducation sentimentale*.)

Daunais, Isabelle: *Flaubert et la scénographie romanesque*. Paris: Nizet, 1993. 220p.

Donato, Eugenio: *The Script of Decadence. Essays on the Fiction of Flaubert and the Poetics of Romanticism*. New York; Oxford: Oxford University Press, 1993. 208p.

Du Camp, Maxime: *Souvenirs littéraires, 1822–1850*. Genève: Slatkine Reprints, 1993. 400p. (Published in the *Revue des deux mondes* (juillet 1881–octobre 1882) and in book form: Paris: Hachette, 1882–1883, 2 vols.)

Dufour, Philippe: *Flaubert et le pignouf. Essai sur la représentation romanesque du langage*. *Saint*-Denis: Presses universitaires de Vincennes, 1993. 192p. (L'Imaginaire du texte.)

Dufour, Philippe: *Flaubert ou la prose du silence*. Paris: Nathan, 1997. 192p. (Le Texte à l'œuvre.)

Duncan, Alastair B.: *Flaubert. "Madame Bovary"*. London: Longman, 1989. 71p. (York notes.)

Durey, Jill Felicity: *Realism and Narrative Modality. The Hero and the Heroine in Eliot, Tolstoy and Flaubert*. Tübingen: Narr, 1993. 225p. (Studies in English and Comparative Literature.)

Ferraro, Thierry: *Flaubert, œuvres majeures*. Alleur: Marabout, 1992. 345p. (Marabout service, 59.)

Finlay, John: *Flaubert in Egypt. Essays on the Gnostic Spirit in Modern Literature and Thought*. Edited by David Middleton. Santa Barbara: Fithian Press, 1994. 176p.

Frølich, Juliette: *Au parloir du roman de Balzac et de Flaubert*. Paris: Didier; Oslo: Solum Forlag, 1991. 531p.

Frølich, Juliette: *Des Hommes, des femmes et des choses. Langages de l'objet dans le roman de Balzac à Proust.* Saint-Denis: Presses universitaires de Vincennes, 1997. 122p. (Collection Essais et savoirs.)

Gagnebin, Bernard: *Flaubert et "Salammbô". Genèse d'un texte.* Paris: Presses universitaires de France, 1992. 373p. (Écrivains.)

Gallina, Bernard: *Eurydices fin de siècle. Emma Bovary et le roman naturaliste.* Udine: Aura Editrice, 1992. 238p.

Gans, Eric: *"Madame Bovary". The End of Romance.* Boston: G. K. Hall, 1989. xiii + 138p. (Twayne's Masterwork Studies, 23.)

Gendolla, Peter: *Phantasien des Askese.* Über die Entstehung innerer Bilder am Beispiel der "Versuchung des heiligen Antonius". Heidelberg: Winter, 1991. 231p.

Gengembre, Gérard: *Flaubert. "Madame Bovary".* Paris: Presses universitaires de France, 1990. 128p. (Études littéraires.)

Girard, Marc: *La Passion de Charles Bovary.* Paris: Imago, 1995. 176p.

Goldbaek, Henning: *Ein beduin vid namn Gustave. Tre essays om orientalismen; Baudelaires og Flauberts tidsalder.* København: Tuseulanums Forlag, 1993. 112p.

Heath, Stephen: *Flaubert. "Madame Bovary".* Cambridge: Cambridge University Press, 1992. xxi + 157p. (Landmarks of World Literature.)

Hermine, Micheline: *Destins de femme, désir d'absolu. Essai sur "Madame Bovary" et Thérèse de Lisieux.* Paris: Beauchesne, 1997. 292p. (Cultures et christianisme, 5.)

Hoffmann, Frank: *Flaubert und der Vergleich.* Frankfurt etc.: Lang, 1995. 239p. (Europäische Hochschulschriften, 13.)

Hohl, Anne Mullen: *Exoticism in "Salammbô". The Languages of Myth, Religion and War.* Birmingham, Alabama: Summa Publications, 1995. 177p.

Israel-Pelletier, Aimée: *Flaubert's Straight and Suspect Saints. The unity of "Trois contes".* Amsterdam; Philadelphia: Benjamins, 1991. 165p.

Kaplan, Louise J.: *Female Perversions. The Temptations of Emma Bovary.* New York: Doubleday, 1991. 580p.

Kempf, Roger: *Bouvard, Flaubert et Pécuchet.* Paris: Grasset, 1990. 289p.

Kim, Yong-Eun: *"La Tentation de saint Antoine", version de 1849. Genèse et structure.* Préface de Jean Bruneau. Kangweon, Korea: Kangweon University Press, 1990. 395p.

Lambros, Anna V.: *Culture and the Literary Text. The Case of Flaubert's "Madame Bovary"*. New York: Lang, 1996. 85p. (American University Studies, Series II. Romance Languages and Literatures, Vol. 162.)

Le Calvez, Éric: *"Bouvard et Pécuchet". Flaubert*. Paris: Nathan, 1994. 128p. (Balises.)

Le Calvez, Éric: *Flaubert topographe. "L'Éducation sentimentale". Essai de poétique génétique*. Amsterdam: Rodopi, 1997. 294p.

Leclerc, Yvan: *Crimes écrits. La Littérature en procès au XIX$^e$ siècle*. Paris: Plon, 1991. 447p. (On *Madame Bovary*.)

Leclerc, Yvan: *Gustave Flaubert. "L'Éducation sentimentale"*. Paris: PUF, 1997. 127p. (Collection Études littéraires.)

Leinen, Frank: *Flaubert und der Gemeinplatz. Erscheinungsformen der Stereotypie im Werk Flauberts*. Frankfurt etc.: Lang, 1990. xii + 279p.

Ley, Klaus: *Die Oper im Roman. Erzählkunst und Musik bei Stendhal, Balzac und Flaubert*. Heidelberg: Winter, 1995. 445p.

Lloyd, Rosemary: *Madame Bovary*. London: Unwin Hyman, 1989. 192p. (Unwin Critical Library.)

Lottman, Herbert: *Flaubert*. New York: Little, Brown and Co.; London: Methuen, 1989. x + 396p. (French edition: translated by Marianne Véron; Préface by Jean Bruneau. Paris: Fayard, 1989. 580p. German edition: translated by Joachim Schultz. Frankfurt; Leipzig: Insel Verlag, 1992, 515p. Spanish Edition: translated by Emma Catalyud. Barcelona: Tusquets, 1991. 514p.)

Lund, Hans Peter: *Flaubert. "Trois contes"*. Paris: Presses universitaires de France, 1994. 128p. (Études littéraires, 50)

Maraini, Dacia: *Cercendo Emma. Flaubert e la Signora Bovary. Indagini attorno a un romanzo*. Milano: Rizzoli, 1993. 180p.

Martinez, Michel: *"Madame Bovary". Flaubert*. Paris: Bertrand-Lacoste, 1991. 127p. (Parcours de lecture, 27.)

Masson, Bernard: *Lectures de l'imaginaire*. Paris: Presses universitaires de France, 1993. 221p. (Écriture.) (On Flaubert and Musset.)

Matsuzawa, Kazuhiro: *Introduction à l'étude critique et génétique des manuscrits de "L'Éducation sentimentale" de Flaubert*. 2 vols. Préface de Pierre-Marc de Biasi. Postface de Jacques Neefs. Tokyo: France Tosho, 1992. 574p.

Ozanam, Anne-Marie: *"Madame Bovary". Flaubert.* Résumé analytique, commentaire, documents complémentaires. Paris: Nathan, 1989. 118p. (Balises.)

Palermo di Stefano, Rosa Maria: *Il problema del testo di "Un Coeur simple".* Chieti: Vecchio Faggio Editore, 1989. 278p.

Pape, Klaus: *Sprachkunst und Kunstsprache bei Flaubert und Kafka.* St. Ingbert: Röhrig, 1996. 356p. (Mannheimer Studien zur Literatur- und Kulturwissenschaft, Band 10.)

Paulson, William R.: *"Sentimental Education". The Complexity of Disenchantment.* New York: Twayne; Toronto: Macmillan, 1992. xv + 149p. (Twayne's Masterwork Series, 45.)

Perfézou, Laurence: *"L'Éducation sentimentale". Flaubert.* Paris: Bordas, 1990. 95p. (L'œuvre en clair.)

Philippot, Didier: *Vérité des choses, mensonge de l'homme dans "Madame Bovary" de Flaubert.* De la Nature au Narcisse. Paris: Honoré Champion, 1997. 466p.

Pietromarchi, Luca: *L'illusione orientale. Flaubert e l'esotismo romantico (1836–1851).* Milano: Guerini, 1990. 169p.

Privat, Jean-Marie: *Bovary, Charivari. Essai d'ethno-critique.* Paris: CNRS, 1994. 314p. (CNRS-littérature.)

Privitera, Tiziana: *Didone mascherata; per il codice genetico di Emma Bovary.* Pisa: ETS, 1996. 83p.

Raitt, Alan W.: *Trois Contes.* London: Grant & Cutler, 1991, 86p. (Critical Guides to French Texts, 89.)

Redman, Harry, Jr.: *Le Côté homosexuel de Flaubert.* Rheims: A l'écart, 1991.

Reid, Martine: *Flaubert correspondant.* Paris: SEDES, 1995. 204p.

Rey, Pierre-Louis: *"Madame Bovary" de Flaubert.* Paris: Gallimard, 1996. 191p. (Foliotèche.)

Reynaud, Patricia: *Fiction et faillite. Économie et métaphores dans "Madame Bovary".* New York: Lang, 1994. 233p.

Roberts, James L.: *Flaubert's "Madame Bovary".* Notes. Lincoln, Nebraska & London: University of Nebraska Press, 1991. 76p.

Roe, David. *Flaubert.* London: Macmillan, 1989. 128p. (Macmillan Modern Novelists.)

Ronell, Avital: *Crack Wars. Literature, Addiction, Mania.* Lincoln, Nebraska & London: University of Nebraska Press, 1992. 175p. (On *Madame Bovary.*)

Schlossman, Beryl, *The Orient of Style. Modernist Allegories of Conversion.* Durham and London: Duke University Press, 1991. 294p.

Schulz-Buschhaus, Ulrich: *Flaubert. Die Rhetorik des Schweigens und die Poetik des Zitats.* Münster: 1995. 146p. (Ars Rhetorica, Band 6.)

Segal, Naomi: *The Adulteress's Child. Authorship and Desire in the Nineteenth-Century Novel.* Oxford & Cambridge, MA: Polity Press, 1992. (On *Madame Bovary* and *L'Éducation sentimentale*, see pp. 75–88.)

Séginger, Gisèle: *Naissance et métamorphoses d'un écrivain. Flaubert et les "Tentations de saint Antoine".* Paris: Honoré Champion, 1997. 448p.

Sutterman, Marie-Thérèse: *Dostoïevski et Flaubert. Écritures de l'épilepsie.* Paris: Presses universitaires de France, 1993. 268p. (Le Fil rouge.)

Tipper, Paul Andrew: *The Dream Machine. Avian Imagery in "Madame Bovary".* Durham: University of Durham, 1994. 31p. (Durham Modern Languages Series, FM13.)

Troyat, Henri: *Flaubert.* Paris: LGF, 1992. 416p. (Le Livre de Poche, 4380.)

Unwin, Timothy A.: *Art et infini. L'œuvre de jeunesse de Flaubert.* Amsterdam & Atlanta: Rodopi, 1991. 211p.

Valtat, Jean-Christophe: *Premières leçons sur "L'Éducation sentimentale", un roman d'apprentissage.* Paris: Presses universitaires de France, 1996. 116p.

VanderWolk, William: *Flaubert Remembers. Memory and the Creative Experience.* New York etc.: Lang, 1990. 204p.

Volpe, Sandro: *Il tornio di Binet. Flaubert, James e il punta di vista.* Roma: Bulzoni, 1991. 158p.

Wannicke, Rainer: *Sartres "Flaubert". Zur Misanthropie der Einbildungskraft.* Berlin: Reimer, 1990. 300p. (Reihe historische Anthropologie, 10.)

Westerwelle, Karin: *Ästhetisches Interesse und nervöse Krankheit. Balzac, Baudelaire, Flaubert.* Stuttgart; Weimar: Metzler, 1993. vii, 482p. (On *Madame Bovary.*)

Willemart, Philippe: *Dans la chambre noire de l'écriture: "Hérodias" de Flaubert.* Toronto: Éditions Paratexte, 1996. 125p.

Willenbrink, George A.: *"Un Cœur simple". Remarques sur l'avant-texte.* Amsterdam & Atlanta: Rodopi, 1989. 120p. (Faux Titre, 43.)

Williams, Jonathan: *Uncle Gus Flaubert rates the Jargon Society in one hundred one laconic présalé sage sentences.* Chapel Hill: University of North Carolina, 1989. 32p. (Hanes Lecture.)

Williams, Tony: *The Construction of Character in Fiction.* Hull: University of Hull Press, 1996. 26p. (On *Madame Bovary* and *L'Éducation sentimentale.*)

Zanelli Quarantini, Franca: *Stendhal, Flaubert, Maupassant. Tre percorsi della memoria.* Firenze: Olschki, 1990. iv + 124p.

Zenkine, Serge: *"Madame Bovary" et l'oppression réaliste.* Clermont-Ferrand: Association des Publications de la Faculté des Lettres de Clermont-Ferrand, 1996. 144p.

Zuylen, Marina Van: *Difficulty as an Aesthetic Principle. Realism and Unreadability in Stifter, Melville and Flaubert.* Tübingen: Narr, 1994. 176p. (Studies in English and Comparative literature, 7.)

## Part Two: Selected Articles and Chapters in Books

Adert, Laurent: Critique de Proust en lecteur de Flaubert. Remarques sur le style et la métaphore dans le texte flaubertien. In: *Saggi e ricerche di letterature francese*, XXIX (1990) 189–200.

Agulhon, Maurice: *Madame Bovary*, une lecture historique. In: *Études normandes*, XLI (1992) 7–19.

Aprile, Max: Dureau de la Malle's *Carthage*. A documentary source for Flaubert's *Salammbô*. In: *French Studies*, XLIII (1989) 305–15.

Baron, Anne-Marie: La bureaucratie flaubertienne, du Garçon aux deux cloportes. In: *L'Esprit créateur*, XXXIV, 1 (1994) 31–41.

Barral, Marcel: Flaubert et les caricaturistes de son temps. In: *Bulletin de l'Académie des sciences et lettres de Montpellier*, XXIV (1993) 109–21.

Beizer, Janet: Writing with a Vengeance. Writing *Madame Bovary*. In: Beizer, Janet, *Ventriloquized Bodies. Narratives of Hysteria in Nineteenth-Century France*. Ithaca & London, 1994, 132–66.

Beizer, Janet: The Physiology of Style. Sex, Text and the Gender of Writing. Flaubert's Letters to Louise Colet. In: Beizer, Janet, *Ventriloquized Bodies. Narratives of Hysteria in Nineteenth-Century France*. Ithaca & London, 1994, 77–98.

Beizer, Janet: Reading Women. The Novel in the Text of Hysteria. In: Beizer, Janet, *Ventriloquized Bodies. Narratives of Hysteria in Nineteenth-Century France*. Ithaca & London, 1994, 55–73.

Bem, Jeanne: L'Éduc'centime. In: Bem, J.: *Le Texte traversé*. Paris, 1991, 115-130. (First published in 1986.)

Bem, Jeanne: L'épistolaire dans les romans de Flaubert. In: *Bulletin Flaubert–Maupassant*, 1 (1993) 57–72.

Bem, Jeanne: Henry Bouvard et Jules Pécuchet. In: Bem, J.: *Le Texte traversé*. Paris, 1991, 105–14. (First published in 1981.)

Bem, Jeanne: L'Orient ironique de Flaubert. In: Bem, J.: *Le Texte traversé*. Paris, 1991, 131–41.

Berthier, Philippe: La Seine, le Nil et le voyage du rien. In: Berthier, Philippe: *Figures du Fantasme*. Un parcours dix-neuviémiste. Toulouse: Presses universitaires du Mirail, 1992, 137-154. (On *L'Éducation sentimentale*.)

Best, Janice: The chronotope and the generation of meaning in novels and painting. In: *Criticism*, XXXVI (1994) 291–316. (On *L'Éducation sentimentale* and Manet.)

Biasi, Pierre-Marc de: Les carnets de travail de Flaubert. Taxinomie d'un outillage littéraire. In: *Littérature*, 80 (1990) 42–55.

Biasi, Pierre-Marc de: Flaubert. *L'Éducation sentimentale*. In: P.-M. de Biasi, J. Body, F. Hincker: *L'Histoire. Un thème, trois œuvres*. Paris: Belin, 1989, 59–121.

Biasi, Pierre-Marc de: Flaubert. *L'Éducation sentimentale*, histoire d'un titre. In: *Magazine littéraire*, 331 (1995) 45–8.

Biasi, Pierre-Marc de: La notion de "carnet de travail". Le cas Flaubert. In: *Carnets d'écrivains*. Sous la direction de Louis Hay. Paris: CNRS, 1990, 23–56.

Biasi, Pierre-Marc de: La traversée de Paris de Flaubert. L'image de Paris dans les carnets de travail. In: *Écrire Paris*. Préface de Daniel Oster et Jean-Marie Goulemot. Paris: Fondation Singer-Polignac, 1990, 89–105.

Bishop, Lloyd: Ambivalent and uncertain irony in Flaubert's *Madame Bovary*. In: Bishop, L.: *Romantic Irony in French Literature from Diderot to Beckett*. Nashville, Tennessee: Vanderbilt University Press, 1989, 114–29.

Bizer, Marc: *Salammbô*, Polybe et la rhétorique de la violence. In: *Revue d'Histoire Littéraire de la France*, XCV (1995) 974–88.

Blaikner-Hohenwart, Gabriele: *Madame Bovary* et l'imparfait. In: *Moderne Sprachen*, XXXVIII (1994) 66-76.

Bonaccorso, Giovanni: La composition flaubertienne face au présent et face au passé. In: *Messana*, 14 (1993) 119–33.

Bonaccorso, Giovanni: Flaubert et le sacré. In: *Les Écrivains et le sacré. La vigne et le vin dans la littérature*. Actes du XIIe Congrès de l'Association Guillaume Budé (Bordeaux, août 1988). Paris: Les Belles Lettres, 1989, 417–418. Also in: *Messana*, 2 (1990) 111–23.

Bonaccorso, Giovanni: Sulla cronologia de *Corpus Flaubertianum I*. In: *Messana*, 5 (1990) 149–67.

Bonaccorso, Giovanni: Verso il vero Flaubert. In: *Igitur*, III, 2 (1991) 49–60.

Bowman, Frank Paul: Flaubert's *Temptation of St. Anthony*. In: Bowman, F. P.: *French Romanticism. Intertextual and interdisciplinary readings*. Baltimore; London: Johns Hopkins University Press, 1990, 182–200.

Brix, Michel: Portrait d'un jeune homme "entortillé par sa maman": le personnage de Frédéric Moreau dans *L'Éducation sentimentale*. In: *Les Lettres Romanes*, 44 (1990) 297–313.

Buchet Rogers, Nathalie: Adultère, arsenic ou crème à la vanillle?: Écrire le scandale dans *Madame Bovary*. In *Nineteenth-Century French Studies*, XXVI (1997) 104–18.

Busi, Frederick: Flaubert's use of Saints' names in *Madame Bovary*. In: *Nineteenth-Century French Studies*, XIX (1990–91) 95–109.

Busst, A. J. L.: On the structure of *Salammbô*. In: *French Studies*, XLIV (1990) 289–99.

Campario, Jean-François: Quelques précisions sur la relation littéraire Maupassant-Flaubert d'après l'étude de leur "collaboration" pour le chapitre III de *Bouvard et Pécuchet*. L'excursion à Étretat. In: *Bulletin Flaubert-Maupassant*, 1 (1993) 7–42.

Campion, Pierre: Le piège de l'ironie dans le système narratif de *Madame Bovary*. In: *Revue d'Histoire Littéraire de la France*, XCII (1992) 863–74.

Campion, Pierre: Roman et histoire dans *L'Éducation sentimentale*. In: *Poétique*, XXII (1991) 35–52.

Christiansen, Hope: Two Simple Hearts: Balzac's Eugénie Grandet and Flaubert's Félicité. In: *Romance Quarterly*, XLII (1995) 195–202.

Constable, E. L.: Critical Departures: *Salammbô*'s Orientalism. In: *Modern Language Notes*, French Issue, 111 (1996) 625–46.

Cormet, Valérie: L'imaginaire et le voyage en Orient. *Salammbô* de Flaubert. In: *Recherches sur l'imaginaire*, XXIII (1992) 117–30.

Cronk, Nicholas: Reading "Un Cœur simple". The pleasure of the intertext. In: *Nineteenth-Century French Studies*, XXIV (1995–6) 154–61.

Crouzet, Michel: "Ecce" Homais. In: *Revue d'histoire littéraire de la France*, LXXXIX (1989) 980–1014.

Curry, Kristina E. and Andrews, Larry R.: Emma Bovary's Lost Brother: a Study of Flaubert's Use of "Minor" Details in the Structure of *Madame Bovary*. In: *Nineteenth-Century French Studies*, XXV (1996–7) 92–9.

Czyba, Lucette: Flaubert et la peinture. In: *Litérales. Art et littérature*. Actes du Séminaire de littératures de Besançon. Textes réunis par Jacques Houriez. Paris: Les Belles Lettres, 1994, 127–47.

Czyba, Lucette: Roman familial, sadisme et sainteté dans "La Légende de Saint Julien l'Hospitalier". In: *Texte, lecture, interprétation*. Vol. II. Paris: Les Belles Lettres, 1994, 153–69.

Danahy, M.: *Madame Bovary*, a tongue of one's own. In: Danahy, M: *The Feminization of the novel*. Gainesville: University of Florida Press, 1991, 126–58; 218–22.

Daprini, Pierre B.: De l'imaginaire "oriental" de Flaubert dans ses œuvres de jeunesse. In: *New Zealand Journal of French Studies*, X, i (May 1989) 5–17.

Daunais, Isabelle: L'Ésthétique de la façade chez Flaubert. In: *Études littéraires*, XXV, 1-2 (été-automne 1992) 169–78.

Daunais, Isabelle: Flaubert et la résistance des objets. In: *Poétique*, XXIV (1993) 63–75.

Debray-Genette, Raymonde: Frontières de la critique génétique. Cris et chuchotements dans *Madame Bovary*. In: *Romanic Review*, LXXXVI (1995) 561–70.

Debray-Genette, Raymonde: Genèse d'une description. Les écuries d' "Hérodias". In: *Les manuscrits des écrivains*. Sous la direction de Louis Hay. Paris: CNRS-Hachette, 1990, 162–83.

Debray-Genette, Raymonde: Simplex et Simplicissima. De Nanon à Félicité. In: *Mimesis et Semiosis. Littérature et représentation*. Miscellanées offertes à Henri Mitterand. Sous la direction de Philippe Hamon et de Jean-Pierre Leduc-Adine. Paris: Nathan, 1992, 229–46.

Debray-Genette, Raymonde: *Madame Bovary*: une trilogie pensive. In *Poétique*, 110 (1997) 131–40.

Denommé, Robert T.: From innocence to experience. A retrospective view of Dussardier in *L'Éducation sentimentale*. In: *Nineteenth-Century French Studies*, XVIII (1989–1990) 424–36.

Dethloff, Uwe: "Liberté et égalité". Flaubert et les acquis de la Révolution. In: *Lendemains*, XIV, 55-56 (1989) 124–28.

Digeon, Claude: Flaubert et le scientisme, d'après Sartre. In: *Hommage à Claude Faisant*. Paris: Les Belles Lettres, 1991, 203–21.

Donaldson-Evans, Mary: A pox on love. Diagnosing *Madame Bovary*'s blind beggar. In: *Symposium*, XLIV (1990) 15–27.

Doyle, Nathalie: Flaubert's *L'Éducation sentimentale*. 1848 as parody. In: *Australian Journal of French Studies*, XXVIII (1991) 39–49.

Dufour, Philippe: Le chaudron et la lyre. In: *Poétique*, XXII (1991) 193–214.

Dufour, Philippe: Flaubert et la parole de l'autre. Citer dans la correspondance. In: *Romanic Review*, LXXXIII (1992) 323–38.

Dufour, Philippe: Le lecteur introuvable. In: *La lecture littéraire, revue de recherche sur la lecture des Textes Littéraires*, 1 (1996) 87–103.

Falconer, Graham: Le statut de l'histoire dans *L'Éducation sentimentale*. In: *Littérature et Révolutions en France*. Textes réunis par G. T. Harris et P. M. Wetherill. Amsterdam & Atlanta: Rodopi, 1991, 106–20.

Festa-Peyre, Diana: Aging by default. Frédéric Moreau and his times in Flaubert's *Sentimental Education*. In: *Symposium*, XLVII (1993-1994) 201–18.

Feyler, Patrick: L'invention technique dans *Bouvard et Pécuchet*. In: *Eidôlon*, 42 (mai 1994) 181–99.

Feyler, Patrick: Paris, Carthage. In: *Eidôlon*, 45 (décembre 1995) 173-200.

Feyler, Patrick: La Révolution française vue par Flaubert. In: *Écrire la liberté*. Actes du Colloque "Images littéraires de la Révolution" (Bordeaux, octobre 1989). Textes réunis par Bernard Cocula et Michel Hauser. Bordeaux: L'Horizon Chimérique, 1991, 141–51.

Fournier, Louis: Flaubert nihiliste: une idée reçue? In: *Lettres romanes*, LI (1997) 53–73.

Fournier, Louis: Trois lecteurs de *Bouvard et Pécuchet*. Maupassant, Thibaudet, Sabatier. In: *French Studies*, XLIX (1995) 29–48.

Frey, Hans-Jost: Flauberts Monotonie. In: Frey, H.-J.: *Der unendliche Text*. Frankfurt: Suhrkamp, 1990, 202–29.

Frølich, Juliette: L'homme kitsch ou le jeu des masques dans *L'Éducation sentimentale* de Flaubert. In: *Romantisme*, XXIII, 79 (1993) 39–52.

Gaillard, Françoise: L'agent simple. In: *Études françaises*, XXXIII (1997) 37–44. (On *L'Éducation sentimentale*.)

Gallagher, Edward J.: Undiscovered countries. The rôle of some minor characters in Flaubert's *Madame Bovary*. In: *French Studies Bulletin*, 65 (Winter 1997) 7–11.

Girard, Maurice: Regard sur la révolution ou révolution du regard. A propos de Flaubert. In: *Littérature et Révolutions en France*. Textes réunis par G. T. Harris et P. M. Wetherill. Amsterdam & Atlanta: Rodopi, 1991, 121–31.

Gleize, Joëlle: Deux romans de livres: *Bouvard et Pécuchet*, tombeau de livres. In: Gleize, J.: *Le double miroir. Le livre dans les livres, de Stendhal à Proust*. Paris: Hachette, 1992, 165–95.

Gleize, Joëlle: Le livre au risque de la représentation. In: Gleize, J.: *Le double miroir. Le livre dans les livres, de Stendhal à Proust*. Paris: Hachette, 1992, 135–64.

Gothot-Mersch, Claudine: Pour une édition du *Voyage en Orient* de Flaubert. In: *Bulletin de l'Académie Royale de Langue et de Littérature françaises*, LXIX (1991) 169–203.

Gothot-Mersch, Claudine: Quelques réflexions sur la conception et la genèse de la première *Éducation sentimentale*. In: *Équinoxe*, XIV (1997) 19–28.

Gothot-Mersch, Claudine: *Salammbô* et les procédés du réalisme flaubertien. In: *Parcours et rencontres*. Mélanges de langue, d'histoire et de littérature françaises offertes à Enea Balmas. Paris: Klincksieck, 1993, Tome II, 1119–1237.

Gothot-Mersch, Claudine: Sur le renouvellement des études de correspondances littéraires. L'exemple de Flaubert. In: *Romantisme*, XXI (1991) 5–29.

Granger, Gilles G.: Savoir scientifique et défaut du jugement dans *Bouvard et Pécuchet*. In: *Littérature*, 82 (1991) 86–95.

Green, Anne: La fin de *Salammbô*. In: *Ideology and Religion in French Literature*. Essays in honour of Brian Juden. Edited by Harry Cockerham & Esther Ehrman. Camberley: Porphyrogenitus, 1989, 165–72.

Green, Anne: Paris, elsewhere. In: *Romance Studies*, 22 (Autumn 1993) 7–15.

Green, Anne: Les spirales de Flaubert. In: *Création littéraire et traditions ésotériques ($XV^e - XX^e$ siècles)*. Actes du Colloque international à la Faculté des Lettres de Pau, 16–18 novembre 1989, recueillis et publiés par J. Dauphiné. Biarritz: J. D. Éditions, 1991, 119–29.

Green, Anne: Time and history in *Madame Bovary*. In: *French Studies*, XLIX (1995) 283–91.

Griffin, Robert: Flaubert : The transfiguration of matter. In: *French Studies*, XLIV (1990) 18–33.

Haig, Stirling: Parrot and parody. Flaubert. In: *The Shaping of the Text. Style, Imagery and Structure in French literature*. Essays in honor of John Porter Houston. Lewisburg: Bucknell University Press; London & Toronto: Associated University Press, 1993, 105–12.

Hamilton, James: The ideology of place. Flaubert's depiction of Yonville-l'Abbaye. In: *French Review*, LXV (1991–92) 206–15.

Heep, Hartmut: Degendering the Other. In: *Dalhousie French Studies*, XXXVI (1996) 69–77.

Hélein-Koss, Suzanne: Les avatars prosodiques du Martichoras dans *La Tentation de saint Antoine*. Du "risible" au "grotesque triste". In: *Romanic Review*, LXXXIII (1992) 193–206.

Hélein-Koss, Suzanne: Le risible dans *La Tentation de saint Antoine*. In: *Romantisme*, XXI, 74 (1991) 65–71.

Hélein-Koss, Suzanne: Le tracé ironique du "velours vert" dans *Madame Bovary*. In: *Nineteenth-Century French Studies*, XXI (1992-1993) 66–72.

Hendrycks, Anne-Sophie: Flaubert et le paysage oriental. In: *Revue d'Histoire Littéraire de la France*, XCIV (1994) 996–1010.

Herschberg-Pierrot, Anne: Les dossiers de *Bouvard et Pécuchet*. In: *Romanic Review*, LXXXVI (1995) 537–49.

Herschberg-Pierrot, Anne: Figures de la parodie chez Flaubert. In: *Dire la parodie*. Colloque de Cerisy. Edited by Clare Thomson & Alain Pagès. New York etc.: Lang, 1989, 213–30.

Herschberg-Pierrot, Anne: Flaubert journaliste. Présentation. In: *Littérature*, 88 (décembre 1992) 115–126.

Hilliard, Aouicha Elosmani: Le retour au préœdipien. *Salammbô* et le rejet du patriarcat. In: *Mosaic*, XXVI, 1 (1993) 35–52.

Ingram, Julia Simon: The aesthetics of fragmentation. *L'Éducation sentimentale*. In: *Nineteenth-Century French Studies*, XVIII (1989–90) 112–32.

Jurt, Joseph: *Madame Bovary*. Genetische Betrachtungsweise. In: *Französisch Heute*, XXIII (1992) 1–14.

Kairet, Jane E.: Sur la signification mytho-poétique du motif des "trois cercueils" de *Madame Bovary*. In: *French Review*, LXX (1997) 676–86.

Kanasaki, Haruyuti: Apollonius ou un rival de Jésus-Christ. In: *Équinoxe*, XIV (1997) 92–105.

Killick, Rachel: "The power and the story?" Discourses of authority and tricks of speech in *Trois contes*. In: *Modern Language Review*, LXXXVIII (1993) 307–20.

Kim, Yon Eun: Quête mystique et science du vivant chez le jeune Flaubert. In: *Équinoxe*, XIV (1997) 7–18.

Kinoshita Tadataka: Sur le statut narratif d'un passage de *Salammbô*. In: *Équinoxe*, XIV (1997), 71–91.

Knight, Diana: Object choices. Taste and fetishism in Flaubert's *L'Éducation sentimentale*. In: *French Literature, Thought and Culture in the Nineteenth century. A Material World*. Essays in honour of D.G. Charlton. Edited by Brian Rigby. London: Macmillan, 1993, 198–217.

Lacoste, Francis: *Bouvard et Pécuchet* ou *Quatre-vingt treize* "en farce". In: *Romantisme*, 95 (1997) 99–112.

Lalonde, Normand: *Bouvard et Pécuchet*, poème bucolique. In: *French Studies*, XLIX (1995) 155–63.

Leal, R. B.: La réception critique de *La Tentation de saint Antoine*. In: *Œuvres et critiques*, XVI (1991) 115–34.

Leal, R. B.: The unity of Flaubert's *Tentation de saint Antoine* (1874). In: *Modern Language Review*, LXXXV (1990) 330–40.

Le Calvez, Éric: La description modalisée. Un problème de poétique génétique. A propos de *L'Éducation sentimentale*. In: *Poétique*, XXV (1994) 339–68.

Le Calvez, Éric: Description et psychologie; génétique et poétique de l'indice dans *L'Éducation sentimentale*. In: *Narrative Voices in Modern French Fiction*. Edited by Michael Cardy, George Evans & Gabriel Jacobs. Cardiff: University of Wales Press, 1997, 113–42.

Le Calvez, Éric: Description, stéréotype, intertextualité. Une analyse génétique de *L'Éducation sentimentale*. In: *Romanic Review*, LXXXIV (1993) 27–42.

Le Calvez, Éric: La description testimoniale. *L'Éducation sentimentale* de Flaubert. In: *Les Lettres romanes*, XLVIII (1994) 27–41.

Le Calvez, Éric: A genetic approach to teaching "Madame Bovary". In: *Nineteenth-Century French Studies*, XXIII (1994-1995) 127-137.

Le Calvez, Éric: Génétique et hypotextes descriptifs. La Forêt de Fontainebleau dans *L'Éducation sentimentale.* In: *Neophilologus,* LXXVIII (1994) 219–32

Le Calvez, Éric: De la note documentaire à la description. (Quelques remarques génétiques à propos de *L'Éducation sentimentale.*) In: *Revue d'Histoire Littéraire de la France,* XCII (1992) 210–33.

Le Calvez, Éric: Notes de repérage et descriptions dans *L'Éducation sentimentale.* II. Genèse de la forêt de Fontainebleau. In: *Neuphilologische Mitteilungen,* XCIV (1993) 359–75; XCV (1994) 363–83.

Le Calvez, Éric: Structurer le topos et sa graphie. La description dans *L'Éducation sentimentale.* In: *Poétique,* XX (1989) 151–71.

Le Calvez, Éric: Visite guidée. Genèse du Château de Fontainebleau dans *L'Éducation sentimentale.* In: *Genesis,* 5 (1994) 99–116.

Leclerc, Yvan: Notes sur *Salammbô.* In: *Équinoxe,* XIV (1997) 60–70.

Leclerc, Yvan: Les œuvres de jeunesse de Flaubert. In: *Études normandes,* XLI, 1 (1992) 35-41.

Le Juez, Brigitte: "La femme au perroquet", un portrait de la femme au XIXe siècle? In: *French Studies Bulletin,* 47 (1993) 10–12. (On "Un Cœur simple" et Manet.)

MacNamara, Matthew: Detached adjectives and mimesis in the style of *Madame Bovary.* In: *Neophilologus,* LXXIX (1990) 520–6.

MacNamara, Matthew: La fabrication d'un paragraphe dans les brouillons de *Madame Bovary.* In: *Neuphilologische Mitteilungen,* XCI (1991) 145–57.

McEachern, Patricia A.: True Lies: Fasting for Force or Fashion in *Madame Bovary.* In: *Romance Notes,* XXXVII (1997) 289–98.

Madureira, Luis: Savages in the City. The Worker and the "End of History" in Flaubert's *L'Éducation sentimentale.* In: *Repression and Expression. Literary and Social Coding in Nineteenth-Century France.* Edited by Carol F. Coates. New York etc.: Lang, 1996, 65–72.

Magné, Bernard: Un "nous" à l'étude. In: *Conséquences,* 15–6 (1991) 3–20. (On *Madame Bovary.*)

Malgor, Didier: *Bouvard et Pécuchet,* ou la recherche du nom. In: *Poétique,* XXVI (1995) 319–30.

Malgor, Didier: Le coq, l'arbre et le forgeron. In: *Littérature*, 99 (octobre 1995) 112–25. (On *Bouvard et Pécuchet*.)

Martin-Berthet, Françoise: L'expression "éducation sentimentale". In: *Mutations et sclérose. La langue française 1789–1848*. Stuttgart: Steiner, 1993, 107–21.

Masson, Bernard: Dans la forêt profonde. L'épisode de Fontainebleau dans *L'Éducation sentimentale*. In: Masson, B.: *Lectures de l'imaginaire*. Paris: Presses Universitaires de France, 1993, 99–115.

Masson, Bernard: L'eau et les rêves dans *L'Éducation sentimentale*. In: Masson, B.: *Lectures de l'imaginaire*. Paris: Presses Universitaires de France, 1993, 182–206. (Article published in 1969.)

Masson, Bernard: Écrire le vitrail. La "Légende de Saint Julien l'Hospitalier". In: Masson, B.: *Lectures de l'imaginaire*. Paris: Presses Universitaires de France, 1993, 116–30.

Masson, Bernard: Flaubert, écrivain de l'impalpable. In: Masson, B.: *Lectures de l'imaginaire*. Paris: Presses Universitaires de France, 1993, 131–44. (Article published in 1988.)

Masson, Bernard: Le langage des signes dans *Madame Bovary*. In: *Équinoxe*, XIV (1997) 29–40.

Matsuzawa, Kazuhiro, Un Essai de commentaire génétique de l'épisode des Bertaux dans *Madame Bovary*. In: *Équinoxe*, XIV (1997) 41–59.

Matsuzawa, Kazuhiro: Une lecture génétique des manuscrits *de L'Éducation sentimentale*. Autour de la dernière visite de Mme Arnoux. In: *Études de langue et de littérature françaises*, 54 (mars 1989) 18–34.

Matthey, Cécile: Les langages de la servante silencieuse dans "Un Cœur simple". In: *Lendemains,* XX, 78–9 (1995) 195–206

Meyer, E. Nicole: Facts into fiction in Flaubert's *Bouvard et Pécuchet*. In: *Nottingham French Studies*, XXXIII, 2 (Autumn 1994) 37–46.

Meyer, E. Nicole: Flaubert's gymnastic prescription for *Bouvard et Pécuchet*. In: *Nineteenth-Century French Studies*, XXIII (1994–1995) 373–81.

Meyer, E. Nicole: Fragmentation and irony in Flaubert's *Dictionnaire des idées reçues*. In: *Discontinuity and Fragmentation*. Edited by Freeman G. Henry. Amsterdam; Atlanta: Rodopi, 1994, 91–100.

Moussa, Sarga: Signatures: ombre et lumière de l'écrivain dans la *Correspondance* de Flaubert. In: *Littérature*, 104 (1996) 74–88.

Moussaron, Jean-Pierre: Flaubert et le discours réversible. In: *Poétique*, XX (1989) 35–61.

Murphy, Ann L.: The order of speech in Flaubert's *Trois contes*. In: *French Review*, LXV (1991–1992) 402–14.

Neefs, Jacques: *Bouvard et Pécuchet*, the prose of knowledge. In: *Sub-Stance*, XXIII, 71–2 (1993) 154–64. (Translation by Roxanne Lapidus.)

Neefs, Jacques: Carnets de romanciers. Flaubert, Zola, James. In: *Littérature*, 80 (décembre 1990) 56–70.

Neefs, Jacques: Noter, classer, briser, montrer, les dossiers de "Bouvard et Pécuchet". In: *Penser, classer, écrire*. Études réunies et présentées par Béatrice Didier et Jacques Neefs. Saint-Denis: Presses universitaires de Vincennes, 1990, 69–90.

Neefs, Jacques: La projection du scénario. In: *Études françaises*, 28 (1992) 67–82.

Nelson, Brian: Flaubert and Semanalysis; rereading *L'Éducation sentimentale*. In: *Narrative Voices in Modern French Fiction*. Edited by Michael Cardy, George Evans & Gabriel Jacobs. Cardiff: University of Wales Press, 1997, 101–13.

Niang, P. M.: L'insertion de l'histoire dans *L'Éducation sentimentale*. In: *Littérature et révolutions en France*. Amsterdam: Rodopi, 1991, 77–105.

Okita, Yoshibo: Le Droit de propriété dans *L'Éducation sentimentale*. In: *Études de langue et de littérature françaises*, 68 (1996) 98–115.

Orr, Mary: Cloaks and copes; revelations of the veiled man in Flaubert's *Salammbô*. In: *Perversions*, 6 (Winter 1995–1996) 120–39.

Orr, Mary: Reading the other. Flaubert's *L'Éducation sentimentale* revisited. In: *French Studies*, XLVI (1992) 412–23.

Orr, Mary: Reflections on "bovarysme": the Bovarys at Vaubyessard. In: *French Studies Bulletin*, 61 (1996) 6–8.

Orr, Mary: Les *Trois contes* et leur identité intertextuelle: figures, figurations, transfigurations. In: *French Studies in Southern Africa*, 23 (1995) 76–83.

Palermo Di Stefano, Rosa Maria: Sul "testo definitivo" di "Un Cœur simple". In: *Messana*, 14 (1993) 135–56.

Patti, Graziella: "Un Cœur simple". Autobiografia e realismo? In: *Messana*, 5 (1990) 169–78.

Plante, Christine: Les Cendres et la goutte d'eau. In: *Poétique*, 111 (1996) 343–58. (On *Madame Bovary*.)

Porter, Dennis: The perverse traveler. Flaubert's *Voyage en Orient*. In: *L'Esprit créateur*, XXIX (1989) 24–36.

Porter, Laurence M.: Emma Bovary's Narcissism revisited. In *Kaleidoscope. Essays on Nineteenth-Century French Literature in Honor of Thomas H. Goetz*. Edited by Graham Falconer and Mary Donaldson-Evans. Toronto: Centre d'études romantiques Joseph Sablé, 1996, 85–97.

Porter, Laurence M.: The rhetoric of deconstruction. Donato and Flaubert. In: *Nineteenth-Century French Studies*, XX (1991–1992) 128–36.

Raitt, Alan W.: Le Balzac de Flaubert. In: *L'Année Balzacienne*, XII (1991) 335–61.

Raitt, Alan W.: The date of the projected epilogue of *Madame Bovary*. In: *French Studies Bulletin*, 62 (1997) 7–11.

Ramazani, Vaheed K.: Historical cliché. Irony and the sublime in *L'Éducation sentimentale*. In: *Publications of the Modern Language Association of America*, CVIII (1993) 121–35.

Rastier, François: Thématique et génétique. L'exemple d' "Hérodias". In: *Poétique*, XXIII (1992) 205–28.

Redfield, Marc: Aesthetics and History: *L'Éducation sentimentale*. In: Marc Redfield, *Phantom Formations*. Ithaca and London: Cornell University Press, 1996, 171–200.

Reynaud, Patricia: Economics and counter-productivity in Flaubert's *Madame Bovary*. In: *Literature and money*. Edited by Anthony Purdy. Amsterdam & Atlanta: Rodopi, 1993, 137–54.

Rifelj, Carol: "Ces tableaux du monde": Keepsakes in *Madame Bovary*. In *Nineteenth-Century French Studies*, XXV (1997), 360–85.

Roberts, Paula: L'espace dans *Madame Bovary*. In: *Chimères*, XXI, 2 (Fall 1994) 1–12.

Schlossman, Beryl: "(Pas) encore!" — Flaubert, Baudelaire and *Don Giovanni*. *Romanic Review*, LXXXII (1990) 350–67.

Schmid, Marion A.: Reading it Right: Transparency and Opacity in the *Avant-Texte* and the Published Text of *L'Éducation sentimentale* In: *Nineteenth-Century French Studies*, XXVI (1997–8) 119–32.

Schor, Naomi: Fetichism and its ironies. In: *Nineteenth-Century French Studies*, XVII (1988–1989) 89–97. (On "Mémoires d'un fou".)

Schor, Naomi: Il et elle. Nohant et Croisset. In: *George Sand. Une correspondance*. Textes réunis par Nicole Mozet. Saint-Cyr-sur-Loire: C. Pirot, 1994, 269–82.

Schweiger, Amélie: L'épistolaire flaubertien comme problématique voie d'accès au littéraire. In: *L'Épistolarité à travers les siècles*. Colloque de Cerisy. Stuttgart: Steiner, 1990, 87–91.

Segal, Naomi: "Voilà le poète hystérique". Flaubert, Frédéric and Emma. In: *Narrative Voices in Modern French Fiction*. Edited by Michael Cardy, George Evans & Gabriel Jacobs. Cardiff: University of Wales Press, 1997, 78–100.

Séginger, Gisèle: Poétique de l'invention et poétique de l'œuvre. Les scénarios des *Tentations de saint Antoine*. In: *Revue d'Histoire Littéraire de la France*, XCIII (1993) 879–902.

Stipa, Ingrid: Desire, repetition and the imaginary in Flaubert's "Un cœur simple". In: *Studies in Short Fiction*, XXXI (1994) 617–26.

Tipper, Paul Andrew: Flower imagery in *L'Éducation sentimentale*. In: *Nineteenth-Century French Studies*, XX (1991–1992) 158–76.

Tipper, Paul Andrew: *Madame Bovary* and the bitter-sweet taste of romance. In: *Orbis Litterarum*, L (1995) 207–13.

Tondeur, Claire-Lise: Flaubert. Le désir, la fluidité et la dissolution. In: *Neophilologus*, LXIII (1989) 512–21.

Tooke, Adrianne: Flaubert on painting. The Italian Notes (1851). In: *French Studies*, XLVIII (1994) 155–73.

Unwin, Timothy A.: Louis Bouilhet, friend of Flaubert. A case of literary conscience. In: *Australian Journal of French Studies*, XXX (1993) 207–13.

VanderWolk, William C.: Writing the masculine. Gender and creativity in *Madame Bovary*. In: *Romance Quarterly*, 77 (1990) 147–56.

Wallen, Jeffrey: *Salammbô* and the resistance of the aesthetic. In: *Romance Notes*, XXX (1989–1990) 237–45.

Wetherill, P. M.: "C'était le jeudi". L'émergence de la ville dans *Madame Bovary*. In: *Rhétorique*. Edited by Marcel Muller. *Michigan Romance Studies*, XIII (1993) 43–66.

Wetherill, P. M.: L'éclosion de Paris dans les manuscrits de *L'Éducation sentimentale*. In: *Neuphilologische Mitteilungen*, XCVIII (1997) 15–31.

Wetherill, P. M.: L'élaboration des chambres d' "Hérodias". In: *Orbis Litterarum*, XLVIII (1993) 245–68.

Wetherill, P. M.: Flaubert and Revolution. In: *Literature and Revolution*. Edited by David Bevan. Amsterdam: Rodopi, 1989, 19–33.

Wetherill, P. M.: Flaubert, l'homme et l'œuvre. In: *Zeitschrift für französische Sprache und Literatur*, XCIC (1989) 36–46.

Wetherill, P. M.: Masculine and feminine voices in conflict. In: *New Comparison*, 15 (Spring 1993) 120–36. (On *Madame Bovary*; Maupassant; Proust.)

Williams, John R.: Emma Bovary and the Bride of Lammermoor. In: *Nineteenth-Century French Studies*, XX (1991–1992) 352–60.

Williams, Tony: Champfleury, Flaubert and the novel of adultery. In: *Nineteenth-Century French Studies*, XX (1991–1992) 145–57.

Williams, Tony: Une chanson de Rétif et sa réécriture par Flaubert. In: *Revue d'Histoire Littéraire de la France*, XCI (1991) 239–42.

Williams, Tony: From document to text. The "terrasse au bord de l'eau" episode in *L'Éducation sentimentale*. In: *French Studies*, XLVII (1993) 156–71.

Williams, Tony: Gender stereotypes in *Madame Bovary*. In: *Forum for Modern Language Studies*, XXVIII (1992) 130–39.

Williams, Tony: A missing section of a scenario for *L'Éducation sentimentale*. In: *French Studies Bulletin*, 56 (Autumn 1995) 12–5.

Williams, Tony: La structuration du récit dans les scénarios de *L'Éducation sentimentale*. In: *Sur la génétique textuelle*. Études réunies par D. J. Bevan et P. M. Wetherill. Amsterdam & Atlanta: Rodopi, 1990, 77–89.

Wing, Nathaniel: Reading simplicity. Flaubert's "Un cœur simple". In: *Nineteenth-Century French Studies*, XXI (1992–1993) 88–101.

Zagona, Helen G.: The Flaubert manuscripts at the Pierpont Morgan Library. In: *French Review*, LXIII (1989–1990) 524–8.

Zuylen, Marina Van: From "horror vacui" to the reader's boredom. *Bouvard et Pécuchet* and the art of difficulty. In: *Nineteenth-Century French Studies*, XXII (1993–1994) 112–22.

# A REPORT ON FLAUBERT AND THE NEW TECHNOLOGIES
## Timothy Unwin

### I. Preamble

Like most authors, Flaubert is now appearing on World Wide Web sites, CD-ROMs and other databases, though disappointingly he has yet to become the subject of a major computing project. Flaubert texts are now to be found online (in varying formats and varying quality of edition, but many of them accurate textual reproductions) and it is likely that over the next few years more of them will become available, together with increasingly sophisticated options for online searches.

On a general note, it is clear that, whereas some information technology resources simply make available what can be found elsewhere, others challenge us to engage with the corpus and the subject in innovative ways. But in many cases, the dividing line between "teaching" and "research" cannot easily be drawn, and we should be aware that, whatever category resources may fall into, the widespread use of them is likely to impact on the ways in which we perceive the subject or develop our ideas. Indeed, one of the commonest misconceptions about the application of computers to Humanities-based disciplines is that they are simply a tool which enables us to do the same jobs more efficiently than before — find a quotation, search a text or corpus, copy and paste extracts, incorporate pictures, statistical files, bibliographical information and so on. Certainly this is the case, but the use of IT (even for quite low-grade operations) is about far more than merely speeding up conventional scholarship or making it more efficient or accurate. Although improvements in practice can and should occur, the concomitant effect of this new medium is that the very nature of our scholarship is going to change in the process.

These are early days, and the shock of the new has barely yet been felt in Flaubert Studies. The shape of things in five, ten or fifteen years is therefore quite unpredictable from our present perspective. The following selective and provisional list of resources can therefore barely be more than a curtain-raiser, leading the way into what is to come and perhaps also suggesting the need for a collective effort at an early stage.

## II. Resources

The resources divide into two main categories: CD-ROMs and WWW sites (discography and webliography). Of the WWW sites, four sub-categories might be suggested at this stage:

1) Online texts and editions;

2) Sites relating specifically to Flaubert and his work;

3) Online details of film and TV adaptations (filmography);

4) General and related sites.

Given the medium, it should be stressed that links often become obsolete, as WWW pages are changed, taken to different addresses, taken over by other individuals or institutions etc. Similarly, more sites and resources will no doubt have been developed by the time these words, written in March 1998, reach print stage. A regular update of the information given here will be available on the World Wide Web at the University of Liverpool site, *Dix-Neuf*, listing nineteenth-century French and Francophone resources at the following address:

**http://www.liv.ac.uk/french/dix-neuf/**

### A. CD-ROMs

The *Bibliorom 98* catalogue (available through CPEDERF and other outlets) provides the best single inventory of CD-ROMs. The following are currently available for Flaubert:

Gustave Flaubert, *L'Œuvre romanesque*, texte intégral (Paris: Égide, 1997, Collection "Catalogue des Lettres"). One of a growing series of CD-ROMs on nineteenth-century novelists (others are available in the same series for Balzac, Stendhal, Zola and the frères Goncourt). Designed principally to enable advanced search functions through the texts. Price 349 FF.

Gustave Flaubert, *Madame Bovary* (Paris: Ubi Soft, 1997, Collection "L'Autre Plume"). Contains the text of the novel, extracts from the correspondence, sound and graphics, biographical and background information. Price 249 FF.

### B. WORLD WIDE WEB SITES

#### 1. Online texts and editions

This section lists the main online libraries or catalogues which point to Flaubert texts currently available (in some cases, several versions of texts are indicated). Where appropriate, brief explanatory comments are added.

- *ABU (Association des Bibliophiles Universelle)*:
  http://cedric.cnam.fr/ABU/
  Lists *Madame Bovary, Un Cœur simple, Bouvard et Pécuchet*.

- *Athena, textes français*:
  http://un2sg4.unige.ch/athena/html/francaut.html/
  Lists *Madame Bovary, Un Cœur simple, La Légende de Saint Julien l'hospitalier, Bouvard et Pécuchet*.

- *Bibliothèque électronique de Lisieux*:
  http://ourworld.compuserve.com/homepages/bib_lisieux/
  Currently gives a selection from the first letters to Louise Colet (August 1846). More texts are likely to be added to the many gems which dix-neuvièmistes will find in this excellent online library.

- *ClicNet, littérature francophone virtuelle du XIX<sup>e</sup> siècle*:
  http://www.swarthmore.edu/Humanities/clicnet/litterature/sujets/XIX.html/
  The ClicNet site is the largest single listing of online texts in nineteenth-century French and Francophone Studies, and is regularly updated. ClicNet gives links to the following Flaubert texts (WWW site, where given, follows in brackets in the listing), and we can assume that this effectively represents the totality of what is currently available:

    *Smarh* (1839) (Gallica)

    *Premières lettres à Louise Colet* (août 1846) (Bibliothèque de Lisieux)

    *Écrits de jeunesse: Par les champs et par les grèves: "Les alignements de Carnac"* (1847)

    *Madame Bovary* (1857) (ABU)

    *L'Éducation sentimentale* (1869) (Alexandrie)

    *La Tentation de Saint Antoine* (1874) (Gallica)

    *La Légende de Saint Julien l'Hospitalier* (1877) (ClicNet)

    *Un Cœur simple* (1877) (ABU)

    *Bouvard et Pécuchet* (1880) (ABU)

  (It should be noted that at the time of going to press the Alexandrie site — the only source for an online version of *L'Éducation sentimentale* — is impossible to locate. It is to be hoped that this is a temporary problem since the version of the text proposed at the site is reliable and well presented.)

- *Gallica (Bibliothèque nationale de France)*:

http://gallica.bnf.fr/

*Gallica* is an experimental server at the BnF, and has been online since 9 October 1997. The eventual aim is to put online as large a proportion of the holdings of the BnF as possible. Texts are available either in text format (i.e. they can be integrated into word-processing programmes) or in image format (meaning that they can only be viewed or printed, but not recognised and manipulated by word-processing software). *Gallica* contains exclusively nineteenth-century holdings. For Flaubert, the following texts are listed:

(In image mode): *Madame Bovary* (Paris: Charpentier, 1877); *Salammbô* (Paris: Charpentier, 1879)

(In text mode): *La Tentation de saint Antoine* (1849, 1856 and 1874 versions); *Smarh* (the texts reproduced in each case are those of the 1910 Conard edition)

Currently there are also listings for Louis Bouilhet and Maxime Du Camp, though none yet for Louise Colet. The *Gallica* project is likely to become one of the most important IT resources for nineteenth-century scholars, and it will certainly be worth following its development.

- *University of Liverpool, Critical Editions of French Texts*:
Finally, it should be mentioned that there are currently plans to establish a site of online critical editions at the University of Liverpool WWW site, where an edition of *Mémoires d'un fou* is scheduled to appear. For further updates, please consult The University of Liverpool French Department home page at:
http://www.liv.ac.uk/French/

## 2. Sites relating to or including Flaubert

There is currently no major scholarly site devoted to Flaubert, a gap that is all the more astonishing since many other nineteenth-century authors — inter alia, Balzac, Stendhal, Verne, Zola, Maupassant — are already the subjects of major online computing projects (see section 4, General sites or sites of related interest, for further details). There is certainly room for a team project here, e.g. for the construction of an interactive resources archive with searchable hypertext, iconographical documentation, bibliographies, online critical editions and articles, etc. (see the concluding remarks in this article). Although a search on the WWW will currently reveal some two to three thousand sites where the name of Flaubert is mentioned, this is not an accurate guide since the mentions are in almost all cases marginal or of no scholarly interest. At present, only the following two listed sites can be considered relevant:

*Gustave Flaubert (1821–1880)*:
http://www.scopus.ch/users/torrent_j/Flaubert.html/

*Le Pavillon Flaubert (site de la Fondation Napoléon)*:
http://www.napoleon.fr/scripts/napoleon-bin/guide-detail.idc?num=106

### 3. Filmography

The Internet Movie Database is one of the best known and most comprehensive sites on the WWW. It sets extremely high standards of presentation and accuracy, and offers a user-friendly, searchable database at the following site:

http://us.imdb.com/

Full details of directors and actors, as well as plot summary and details of how to purchase or consult films are available at the site. A search for "Flaubert" provides a list of films and TV adaptations of *Madame Bovary* (nothing on *L'Éducation sentimentale* though) and a further page of biography for Flaubert. The following films are listed, with links to further details:

*Unholy Love* (USA, 1932, directed by Albert Ray)

*Madame Bovary* (France, 1934, directed by Jean Renoir)

*Madame Bovary* (Germany, 1937, directed by Gerhard Lamprecht)
*Madame Bovary* (USA, 1949, directed by Vincente Minnelli)
*Madame Bovary* (France, 1991, directed by Claude Chabrol).

The following TV adaptations of *Madame Bovary* (again with full details) are listed:
West Germany, 1968 (directed by Hans-Dieter Schwarze); UK, 1975 (directed by Rodney Bennett).

### 4. General sites or sites of related interest

*Centre d'Études sur le Naturalisme* (University of Toronto):
http://www.chass.utoronto.ca:8080/french/zola/

*Centre d'Études Romantiques J. Sablé* (University of Toronto):
http://www.chass.utoronto.ca:8080/french/sable/

*Dix-Neuf, sites et ressources sur le dix-neuvième siècle* (University of Liverpool):
http://www.liv.ac.uk/www/french/dix-neuf/

*La France et les Français du dix-neuvième siècle* (University of West Virginia):
http://www.as.wvu.edu:80/~mlasting/19.htm/

*Guy de Maupassant, localisation des textes électroniques*:
http://lib.univ-fcomte.fr/PEOPLE/selva/Maupassant.html/

*Recherche hypertextuelle dans la Comédie Humaine* (Université de Nice)
http://lolita.unice.fr/~brunet/BALZAC/balzac.htm/

*Stendhal*:
http://www.alpes-net.fr/~reysset/

*The Jules Verne Collection*:
http://www.math.technion.ac.il/~rl/JulesVerne/

*Webmuseum: Revolution and restoration (1740–1860)*:
http://www.southern.net:80/wm/paint/theme/revolution.france.html/

*Webmuseum, Paris: Impressionism (1860–1900)*:
http://www.southern.net:80/wm/paint/theme/impressionnisme.html/

*Zola and Naturalism Archive* (University of Toronto):
http://www.chass.utoronto.ca:8080/french/zola/table.htm/

## III.   Conclusion

The obvious remark which emerges from the foregoing list is that Flaubert Studies appear to be falling behind studies of other major nineteenth-century authors when it comes to the provision of IT resources. Clearly, it is essential that the international community of Flaubert scholars see their way to filling this gap. But why?

What needs to be stated unambiguously is that this is absolutely not about "keeping up with the Zolas" (or the Balzacs, or the Vernes). What is at stake here is something far more important either than some pecking order of nineteenth-century novelists, or their popularisation through the medium of the new technologies. Effectively deployed and developed, the new technologies will offer: 1) the possibility of radically new insights into and perceptions of the author's writings; 2) the enhancement of scholarly exchange and co-operation; 3) a thoroughgoing revision of what constitutes "Flaubert Studies" and of what they they represent; 4) an enhanced recognition of the ways in which the medium of our knowledge and scholarship shapes our most fundamental beliefs about the subject.

It should also be stressed that "putting Flaubert on the web" — if it is to be done effectively — should ideally not be left to the devices of a single enthusiast. It should be a collective enterprise with a collective strategy, which groups together different skills and different interests. Alongside the task of developing a searchable and reliably edited database of texts (including, most importantly, the *Correspondance*), there needs also to be an archive of critical material, online articles, graphical documentation, regularly updated lists of bibliographical and other resources, and a forum for online discussion and announcements. Given the importance of manuscript studies in current Flaubert scholarship, the technology will also lend itself effectively to the viewing and editing of manuscripts by widely scattered groups of scholars in a virtual environment. Hypertext markup of manuscript transcriptions offers far greater flexibility than does print for the presentation and viewing of different states of the text. Of course, it will be possible to develop both WWW and CD-ROM versions of manuscript material, the two media being entirely complementary and compatible.

These suggestions are merely a framework, and the real developments will take place when a sufficient critical mass of Flaubert scholars have the resources to undertake the many tasks involved in computerisation. There is much uncharted territory ahead, but the application of information technology resources to Flaubert Studies — "HÉNAURME" though it doubtless seems — is full of challenge and promise.

## STUDIES IN FRENCH LITERATURE

1. Gerald Groves (trans.), **Germain Nouveau's Symbolist Poetry 1851-1920: Valentines**
2. Anne-Marie Brinsmead, **Strategies of Resistance in** *Les Liaisons Dangereuses*: **Heroines in Search of "Author-ity"**
3. Jean-Jacques Thomas (compiler), **Concordance de** *Poemes* **by Yves Bonnefoy**
4. René Daumal, **René Daumal's** *Mugle* **and** *The Silk*, translated with an Introduction by Phil Powrie
5. Leonora Timm (trans. & ed.), **A Modern Breton Political Poet -- Anjela Duval: A Biography and An Anthology**
6. Sharon Harwood-Gordon, **The Poetic Style of Corneille's Tragedies: An Aesthetic Interpretation**
7. David Bryant, **The Rhetoric of Pessimism and Strategies of Containment in the Short Stories of Guy de Maupassant**
8. Pierre Nguyen-Van-Huy, **Le devenir et la conscience cosmique chez Saint-Expupéry**
9. Roxanne Hanney, **The Invisible Middle Term in Proust's** *A La Recherche Du Temps Perdu*
10. Michael G. Paulson, **A Critical Analysis of de La Fayette's** *La Princesse de Clèves* **as a Royal Exemplary Novel: Kings, Queens, and Splendor**
11. Jeri Debois King, **Paratextuality in Balzac's** *La Peau de Chagrin*: **The Wild Ass's Skin**
12. Emil Zola, **My Hatreds/Mes Haines**, translated and with an introduction by Palomba Paves-Yashinsky and Jack Yashinsky
13. Larry W. Riggs, **Resistance to Culture in Moliére, Laclos, Flaubert, and Camus, A Post-Modernist Approach**
14. Alphonse de Lamarine, *Poetical Meditations/Méditations Poétiques*, translated and with an introduction by Gervase Hittle
15. Jehan de Paris, *The Romance of Jehan de Paris/Le Romant de Jehan de Paris*, Guy R. Mermier (trans.)
16. Gerald Macklin, **A Study of Theatrical Vision in Arthur Rimbaud's** *Illuminations*
17. Maxwell Adereth, **Elsa Triolet and Louis Aragon, An Introduction to Their Interwoven Lives and Works**

18. Christopher Todd, **A Century of French Best-Seller (1890-1990)**

19. Anne Judge and Solange Lamothe, **Stylistic Developments in Literary and Non-Literaty French Prose**

20. Thomas J. McCormick, **A Partial Edition of** *Les Fais Des Rommains* **with a Study of Its Style and Syntax: A Medieval Roman History**

21. Andrée Chedid, **Selected Poems of Andée Chedid**, translated and edited by Judy Cochran

22. Edmund J. Campion, **Montaigne, Robelais, and Marot as Readers of Erasmus**

23. Honoré de Blazac, *The Last Fay*, translated and with an introduction by Eric du Plessis

24. David Bryant, **Short Fiction and the Press in France, 1829-1841: Followed by a Selection of Short Fiction from the Periodical and Daily Press**

25. Emily Zants, **Chaos, Theory, Complexity, Cinema, and the Evolution of the French Novel**

26. Katharine G. MacCornack, **Mental Representation Theory in Old French Allegory From the Twelfth and Thirteenth Centuries**

27. Pierre L. Horn, **Modern Jewish Writers of France**

28. Peter Broome, **André Frénaud,** *Dans la Crique***: du lieu du poème à l'univers**

29. **A Critical Edition of** *La Route De Thèbes* **by Alexandre Dumas** *fils,* Edited with an introduction by H..D. Lewis

30. Michael G. Lerner, **Pierre Loti's Dramatic Works**

31. Noel Heather, **DuBartas, French Huguenot Poet and His Humorous Ambivalence**

32. J.H. Mazaheri, **Myth and Guilt-Consciousness in Balzac's** *La Femme de trente ans*

33. Edward Ford, **Alain-Fournier and** *Le Grand Meaulnes (The Wanderer)*

34. Tony Williams and Mary Orr (eds.), **New Approaches in Flaubert Studies**